Praise for the First Edition

"This publication is a majo[r] understanding of the proc[ess] from each other in helping our future built environments. It brings together experience that exists in Britain with international experience from across the globe. The layout brings a new standard of design excellence to the art of communication in this field. I highly recommend it as a practical tool for communities and their activists. It has a truly international perspective."

Michael Parkes, Expert on Urban Policy to the European Commission, Directorate General Development, Brussels, Belgium

"The clear and concise copy as well as the very appealing graphic formatting of the material make this an excellent handbook which will be useful to so many different users in so many ways."

Tony Costello, Professor of Architecture, Ball State University, USA

"Community planning is set to become part of the mainstream planning process. Whether you are a developer, a planning professional or an active member of your community, The Community Planning Handbook will be an invaluable guide in helping you choose and plan the participatory events and structures to meet your needs."

John Thompson, architect and community planner

"I like it and I like the format. It should be a useful tool in the toolbox."

Simon Croxton, International Institute for Environment and Development

"An excellent book and well worth while."

Rod Hackney, community architect

"Comprehensive and useful."

Sonia Khan, Freeform Arts Trust

"A really useful document – I like the approach, layout and methodology."

Babar Mumtaz, Development Planning Unit, London

THE
COMMUNITY
PLANNING
HANDBOOK

Second edition

*"If you want to know how the shoe fits, ask the
person who is wearing it, not the one who made it."*

THE
COMMUNITY
PLANNING
HANDBOOK

How people can shape their cities, towns and villages in any part of the world

Second edition

Compiled and edited by
Nick Wates

Designed by
Jeremy Brook

Published in association with
The Urban Design Group
The Prince's Foundation
South Bank University, London

With the generous support of
Department of the Environment, Transport
and the Regions, England
Department for International Development, UK
European Commission Humanitarian Office
John Thompson & Partners
Urban Regeneration Office, Taipei City and
The Urbanists Collaborative, Taipei

Routledge
Taylor & Francis Group

LONDON AND NEW YORK

from Routledge

The Community Planning Handbook
How people can shape their cities, towns and villages in any part of the world.

Compiler and Editor: Nick Wates.
Design and production: Jeremy Brook, Graphic Ideas

Advisory Group 2000: Roger Bellers, John Billingham, Roger Evans, Nick Hall, Birgit Laue, Arnold Linden, Jenneth Parker, David Lunts, Michael Mutter, Renate Ruether-Greaves, Jon Rowland, Ros Tennyson, John Thompson, John F C Turner.

Advisory Group 2014: Charles Campion, Jane Freund, Mike Gibson, Keith Gillies, Malgorzata Hanzl, Ollie Pendered, Debbie Radcliffe, Wendy Sarkissian.

First edition published 2000 by Earthscan

This edition published 2014 by Routledge,
2 Park Square, Milton Park, Abingdon, Oxon,
OX14 4RN
Simultaneously published in the USA and Canada
by Routledge, 711 Third Avenue, New York,
NY 10017

© 2014 Nick Wates

Published in association with:
The Urban Design Group;
The Prince's Foundation;
South Bank University, London.

With the generous support for the first edition of:
Department of the Environment, Transport and the Regions, England; Department for International Development, UK; European Commission Humanitarian Office.

And for the second edition of: John Thompson & Partners; Urban Regeneration Office, Taipei City; The Urbanists Collaborative, Taipei.

British Library Cataloguing in Publication Data

A catalogue record for this book is available from the British Library

Library of Congress Cataloging-in-Publication Data

Wates, Nick.
The community planning handbook : how people can shape their cities, towns & villages in any part of the world / Nick Wates. -- Second edition.
pages cm
Includes bibliographical references and index.
1. Community development--Planning--Handbooks, manuals, etc. 2. Planning--Citizen participation--Handbooks, manuals, etc. I. Title.
HN49.C6W38 2014
307.1'4--dc23
2013040897

ISBN13: 978-1-84407-490-7 (pbk)
ISBN13: 978-1-315-84871-6 (ebk)

See www.communityplanning.net for updates

This document is an output from a project partially funded by the UK Department for International Development (DFID) for the benefit of developing countries. The views expressed are not necessarily those of the DFID or any of the other supporting organisations.

Freestanding quotations are from interviews by the editor unless otherwise indicated.

Cover photographs:
Lanice Park reconnaissance trip, Zvolen, Slovakia; 2009; Charlotte site visit, Vermont, USA, 2003; Housing Renewal Area workshop, St Leonards on Sea, UK, 2003; Fishbowl workshop, Taipei, Taiwan, 2013; Neighbourhood plan housing site allocation consultation, Ringmer, UK, 2013.

Frontispiece:
Design workshops at a planning weekend in Liverpool, UK, 1997.

Typeset in Frutiger by Graphic Ideas

Printed and bound by Ashford Colour Press Ltd

"I know of no safe depository of the ultimate powers of society, but the people themselves; and if we think them not enlightened enough to exercise their control with a wholesome discretion, the remedy is not take it from them, but to inform their discretion."

Thomas Jefferson, Architect and President of the United States, 1820
Letter to William Charles Jarvis

"When dwellers control the major decisions and are free to make their own contribution to the design, construction or management of their housing, both the process and the environment produced stimulate individual and social well-being."

John F C Turner, *Freedom to Build*, 1972

"Public participation should be an indispensable element in human settlements, especially in planning strategies and in their formulation, implementation and management; it should influence all levels of government in the decision making process to further the political and economic growth of human settlements."

Delegate communiqué, United Nations Habitat 1 conference, Vancouver, 1976

"The professionals need to consult the users of their buildings more closely. The inhabitants have the local knowledge: they must not be despised. People are not there to be planned for; they are to be worked with… There must be one golden rule – we all need to be involved together – planning and architecture are much too important to be left to the professionals."

HRH The Prince of Wales, *A Vision of Britain*, 1989

"Community designers draw out of people their heroic insights and find ways to implement them."

Richard Meier, Architect, *Community Design Primer*, 1990

"When people feel they 'belong' to a neighbourhood which is theirs through their own efforts, then it will become a place which is worth struggling to retain and develop. People will safeguard what they have helped to create."

Lord Scarman and Tony Gibson, *The Guardian*, 11 December 1991

"Environmental issues are best handled with the participation of all concerned citizens, at the relevant level. At the national level, each individual shall have appropriate access to information… and the opportunity to participate in decision making processes. States shall facilitate and encourage public awareness and participation by making information widely available."

United Nations Rio Declaration, Principle 10, 1992

"Community planning is a vehicle through which we can hope to re-engage people with their community and with society."

Charmian Marshall, Campaign Director, Urban Villages Forum, 1993

"Community involvement has been shown to make a positive contribution to planning and development processes. At its best, community involvement can enable: processes to be speeded up; resources to be used more effectively; product quality and feelings of local ownership to improve; added value to emerge; confidence and skills to increase – for all; conflicts to be more readily resolved."

Department of the Environment England, Summary of planning research programme, 1994

"Design participation is the best education a community can get. The people here have been involved down to the last nail and screw. People round here know more about architecture than anywhere else in the country! It's helped us to get what we want and to get it right."

Tony McGann, Chair, Eldonian Community-based Housing Association, Liverpool, *Building Homes People Want*, 1994

"Putting cities back on the political agenda is now fundamental. What's needed is greater emphasis on citizens' participation in city design and planning. We must put communal objectives centre-stage."

Sir Richard Rogers, Architect, Reith Lecture, 1995

"This is a good time to be alive as a development professional. For we seem to be in the middle of a quiet but hugely exciting revolution in learning and action."

Robert Chambers, *Whose Reality Counts?*, 1997

"Experience shows that success depends on communities themselves having the power and taking the responsibility to make things better. A new approach is long overdue. It has to be comprehensive, long-term and founded on what works."

Tony Blair, Prime Minister, *Bringing Britain Together; a national strategy for Neighbourhood Renewal*, 1998

"Community planning gave us the opportunity to work alongside the powers that be, have our say and feel, for the first time, that we were really being listened to. Residents now feel much more connected with decision making and things are really beginning to improve around here."

Sydney Massop, Resident, South Acton Estate, Ealing, UK, 1999

"Community participation lies right at the heart of sustainable development. Sustainable communities will take different forms from place to place, but one thing that none of them will be able to do without is a broad and deep level of participation."

Action Towards Local Sustainability, website introduction, 1999

"We're giving local people more power over what happens in their neighbourhoods – so communities can come together to keep pubs open, stop post offices from closing, run parks and take control over the look and feel of new developments in their area."

David Cameron, Prime Minister, Sun Newspaper, 8 October 2010

"Working with local communities comes as second nature [to us]. We understand that if we are to deliver houses that not only meet the aspirations of those who seek to live in them but also enhance the existing neighbourhood, then we need to talk to and engage with local people – residents, businesses and their elected representatives."

Linden Homes (housebuilders), promotion leaflet, 2012

Contents

Introduction

All over the world there is increasing demand from all sides for more local involvement in the planning and management of the environment.

It is widely recognised that this is the only way that people will get the surroundings they want. And it is now seen as the best way of ensuring that communities become safer, stronger, wealthier and more sustainable.

But how should it be done? How can local people – wherever they live – best involve themselves in the complexities of architecture, planning and urban design? How can professionals best build on local knowledge and resources?

Over the past few decades, a wide range of methods has been pioneered in different countries. They include new ways of people interacting, new types of event, new types of organisation, new services and new support frameworks.

This handbook provides an overview of these new methods of community planning for the first time in one volume. It is written for everyone concerned with the built environment. Jargon is avoided and material is presented in a universally applicable, how-to-do-it style. Whether you are a resident wanting to improve the place where you live, a policymaker interested in improving general practice, or a development professional working on a specific project, you should quickly be able to find what you need.

The methods described here can each be effective in their own right. But it is when they are combined together creatively that community planning becomes a truly powerful force for positive and sustainable change. Just a few of the many possibilities are featured in the scenarios section later in the book.

In years to come it is possible to imagine that every human settlement will have its own architecture centre and neighbourhood planning offices; that all development professionals will be equipped to organise ideas competitions and planning weekends; that everyone will have access to planning aid and feasibility funds; that all architecture schools will have urban design studios helping surrounding communities; and that everyone will be familiar with design workshops, mapping, participatory editing, interactive displays and other methods described in this book.

When that happens, there will be more chance of being able to create and maintain built environments that satisfy both individual and community needs, and that are enjoyable to live and work in.

In the meantime the art of community planning is evolving rapidly. Methods continue to be refined and new ones invented. There is a growing network of experienced practitioners. This handbook will hopefully help with the evolution of community planning by allowing people to benefit from the experience gained so far and by facilitating international exchange of good practice.

Update 2014

Much has happened since this book was first published in the year 2000.

Probably the most important change has been the maturing of the Internet which has affected the way we all do everything. The potential of the Internet and social media for community planning is covered in this edition. And the book itself has been integrated with its online version, communityplanning.net. While you can find all the key generic aspects of community planning in this revised edition, information that is continually changing, like contact details and publications, is signposted here and exists in full only on the website.

A second important development has been the adoption of community planning by charities and governments to achieve certain of their own goals and the setting up of programmes to implement this. For instance, the introduction of neighbourhood planning in England which is an ambitious experiment in attempting to use community based planning approaches to create statutory development plans. We also feature in this revised edition the distinctive Heart & Soul Community Planning programme in the United States offered by the Orton Family Foundation and Taipei City Council's ambitious urban regeneration programme.

There have also been attempts all over the world by communities to get involved in planning for climate change. Both to protect themselves against it. And to reduce the likelihood of it

happening by planning for Low Carbon
Communities. Some ways of helping with this are
included in this edition and we hope to cover
more on the website over the coming years.

But the biggest change since the first edition has
been that community planning has moved from
the preserve of a few enthusiasts to something
that a great many people come into contact with
at some stage in their lives. And that an
increasing number of organisations are actively
involved with. Whatever aspect of placemaking
you are involved with – whether it be siting new
housing or introducing a new traffic management
scheme – you are unlikely to get far unless you
engage effectively with the community.

The Community Planning Handbook and
communityplanning.net have played a part in the
evolution of community planning to date, and
will continue to do so. We hope you enjoy using
them and welcome any and all feedback.

info@nickwates.co.uk

2014

Why get involved?

When people are involved in shaping their local surroundings, the benefits can include:

1 Additional resources
Governments rarely have sufficient means to solve all the problems in an area. Local people can bring additional resources which are often essential if their needs are to be met and dreams fulfilled.

2 Better decisions
Local people are invariably the best source of knowledge and wisdom about their surroundings. Better decision making results if this is harnessed.

3 Building community
The process of working together and achieving things together creates a sense of community.

4 Compliance with legislation
Community involvement is often, and increasingly, a statutory requirement.

5 Democratic credibility
Community involvement in planning accords with people's right to participate in decisions that affect their lives. It is an important part of the trend towards democratisation of all aspects of society.

6 Easier access to funding
Many grant-making organisations prefer, or even require, community involvement to have occurred before handing out financial assistance.

7 Empowerment
Involvement builds local people's confidence, capabilities, skills and ability to co-operate. This enables them to tackle other challenges, both individually and collectively.

8 More appropriate results

Design solutions are more likely to be in tune with what is needed and wanted. Involvement allows proposals to be tested and refined before adoption, resulting in better use of resources.

9 Professional education

Working closely with local people helps professionals gain a greater insight into the communities they seek to serve. So they work more effectively and produce better results.

10 Responsive environment

The environment can more easily be constantly tuned and refined to cater for people's changing requirements.

11 Satisfying public demand

People want to be involved in shaping their environment and mostly seem to enjoy it.

12 Speedier development

People gain a better understanding of the options realistically available and are likely to start thinking positively rather than negatively. Time-wasting conflicts can often be avoided.

13 Sustainability

People feel more attached to an environment they have helped create. They will therefore manage and maintain it better, reducing the likelihood of vandalism, neglect and subsequent need for costly replacement.

Getting started

How do you get started with community planning? How do you decide which methods to use, and when? How do you design an overall strategy geared to your own circumstances?

The approach adopted will be different for every community. There is rarely a quick fix or blueprint. Each place needs to carefully devise its own community planning strategy to suit local conditions and needs.

But there are principles, methods and scenarios which appear to be universally relevant, and can be drawn on for inspiration and guidance. These are set out in this handbook. They are based on pioneering projects and experience from many countries over the past few decades.

It is unlikely that you will be able to draw up a complete strategy at the outset. Flexibility is important, in any case, to be able to respond to new circumstances and opportunities. But planning a *provisional* overall strategy is a useful discipline so that everyone understands the context in which the chosen methods are being used and the purpose of each stage.

First, define the goal or purpose. Then devise a strategy to achieve it. Try doing some or all of the following:

- Look through the General principles A–Z (pp13–25) to understand the basic philosophy of community planning;

- Skim through the Methods A–Z (pp27–149) to get a feel for the range of options available;

- Scan the Scenarios A–Z (pp151–199) to see if there are any which relate to your own context or provide inspiration;

- Sketch out a scenario for your own situation (similar to those in the Scenarios A–Z);

- Complete your own strategy planner (p224), community planning event planner (p219) or progress monitor (p223);

- Think through who might be involved (see checklist, p234) and discuss with your local planning authority;

- Produce an itemised budget, cost out in-kind support and allocate responsibilities;

- Organise a Process Planning Session similar to that in the Methods A–Z (p126).

Once you have done this you should be in a position to assess the options available and resources required. You may be working to a fixed budget with known contributors, in which case your options are limited. More likely, securing financial and other support will be part of the process. Raising funding may not be easy, but organisations of all kinds are increasingly prepared to contribute as they begin to see how community planning activity can benefit the communities they are located in, or are responsible for. And there is a great deal that can be achieved by obtaining 'support in kind'; help and assistance in non-financial terms.

And so the adventure begins…

Book format

On the next few pages some **General principles** are set out. These are mostly universal and apply to any community planning activity. As with most material in the book they are listed in alphabetical order for easy reference.

The **Methods A–Z** covers a selection of methods for helping people get involved in physical planning and design. Each is summarised on a double-page spread in enough detail for you to understand how it works and decide whether to pursue it further. Information provided is shown on the right. A list of methods covered is on page 27.

The **Scenarios A–Z** shows how a number of methods can be combined in an overall strategy. A range of scenarios cover some common development situations. The format used is shown top right. A list of scenarios covered is on page 151.

Programmes covers some government and agency initatives to harness community planning. **Case studies** provides a few real examples.

In the appendices, the **Glossary A–Z** explains common terms in simple language.

Sources of further information are in the **Publications A–Z**, **Contacts A–Z and Websites A–Z. Useful formats** and **Useful checklists** contain documents which may save you time.

Finally, the **Feedback section** makes it easy for you to tell us how to make future editions of this book better.

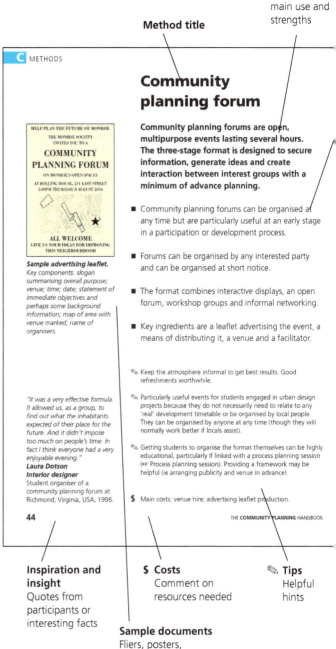

Purpose
The method's main use and strengths

Method title

Community planning forum

Community planning forums are open, multipurpose events lasting several hours. The three-stage format is designed to secure information, generate ideas and create interaction between interest groups with a minimum of advance planning.

HELP PLAN THE FUTURE OF MONROE
THE MONROE SOCIETY
INVITES YOU TO A
COMMUNITY PLANNING FORUM
ON MONROE'S OPEN SPACES
AT ROLLING HOUSE, 211 EAST STREET
5.00PM THURSDAY 8 AUGUST 2016

ALL WELCOME
GIVE US YOUR IDEAS FOR IMPROVING
THIS NEIGHBOURHOOD

Sample advertising leaflet.
Key components: slogan summarising overall purpose; venue; time; date; statement of immediate objectives and perhaps some background information; map of area with venue marked; name of organisers.

- Community planning forums can be organised at any time but are particularly useful at an early stage in a participation or development process.

- Forums can be organised by any interested party and can be organised at short notice.

- The format combines interactive displays, an open forum, workshop groups and informal networking.

- Key ingredients are a leaflet advertising the event, a means of distributing it, a venue and a facilitator.

"It was a very effective formula. It allowed us, as a group, to find out what the inhabitants expected of their place for the future. And it didn't impose too much on people's time. In fact I think everyone had a very enjoyable evening."
Laura Dotson
Interior designer
Student organiser of a community planning forum at Richmond, Virginia, USA, 1996.

✎ Keep the atmosphere informal to get best results. Good refreshments worthwhile.

✎ Particularly useful events for students engaged in urban design projects because they do not necessarily need to relate to any 'real' development timetable or be organised by local people. They can be organised by anyone at any time (though they will normally work better if locals assist).

✎ Getting students to organise the format themselves can be highly educational, particularly if linked with a process planning session (☞ Process planning session). Providing a framework may be helpful (ie arranging publicity and venue in advance).

$ Main costs: venue hire; advertising leaflet production.

44

THE **COMMUNITY PLANNING** HANDBOOK

Inspiration and insight
Quotes from participants or interesting facts

$ Costs
Comment on resources needed

✎ Tips
Helpful hints

Sample documents
Fliers, posters, newspaper cuttings

Features
The method's main characteristics

Sample formats
Timetables, procedures, forms, other detailed information

Layouts
Room layouts, physical arrangements

Timescale
Rough timing of activities

Activities
Sequence and brief description

METHODS C

Sample Community Planning Forum format

1 Interactive displays
As people arrive they are guided towards a variety of interactive displays where they are encouraged to make comments using Post-its, marker pens or stickers (☞ Interactive display). General mingling and discussion. Refreshments. (45 mins)

2 Open forum
People are seated in a horseshoe shape, perhaps with model, plan or drawing on a table in the centre. Introductions by organisers. Feed back on interactive displays by pre-warned rapporteurs. Open debate chaired by organiser. (45 mins)

3 Workshop groups
People are divided into groups and work around tables on various topics/areas, either pre-selected or agreed during the open forum. (45 mins)

4 Networking
Informal mingling and discussion. Refreshments. (45 mins)

5 Feedback (optional)
Reports from workshop groups to plenary. (Or separate presentation session later.)

Total running time: 3 hours minimum
Ideal numbers 30 – 150

Ideal layout in a large hall

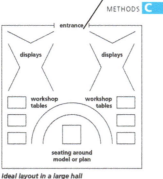

Open forum
Debate in a horseshoe arrangement following a warm-up interactive display and before dividing up into workshop groups.

Key roles at a planning forum
☐ Chairperson for open forum
☐ Facilitator/stage manager
☐ Hosts as people arrive
☐ Photographer
☐ Reporters for each interactive display
☐ Workshop and forum recorders
☐ Workshop facilitators

FURTHER INFORMATION

☞ Methods: *Elevation montage. Interactive display. Table scheme display. Task force.*
   Scenarios: *Community centre. Village revival.*

☆ Richard John

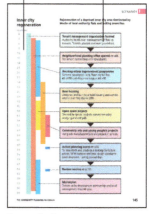

Scenario layout
Possible strategy for a particular development situation

Images
Explanatory photos from case studies. Locations are identified on page 286

Where to find more details

☞ *Method* or *Scenario* pages with related information

@ *Publication title.*
Refer to pages 260–265 (or the website) for details

✉ *Contact organisation.*
Refer to pages 266–273 for further details

▤ *Websites.*
Refer to pages 274–283 for further details

☆ Contributors to this page. Special thanks

Checklists
Roles, equipment lists, things to remember

Project stages

		Initiate ▶	Plan ▶	Implement ▶	Maintain
Self Help Community control		Community initiates action alone	Community plans alone	Community implements alone	Community maintains alone
Partnership Shared working and decision making		Authorities & community jointly initiate action	**Authorities & community jointly plan and design**	Authorities & community jointly implement	Authorities & community jointly maintain
Consultation Authorities ask community for opinions		Authorities initiate action after consulting community	Authorities plan after consulting community	Authorities implement with community consultation	Authorities maintain with community consultation
Information One way flow of information Public relations		Authorities initiate action	Authorities plan and design alone	Authorities implement alone	Authorities maintain alone

Level of community involvement

Participation matrix
A simple illustration of how different levels of participation are appropriate at different stages of a project. Most community planning operates in the shaded areas. Any party may initiate action but the crucial ingredient is joint planning and design, shown in the dark square. Implementation and maintenance will either be carried out jointly or by the authorities after consulting the community. (☞ 'Ladder of Participation' in the Glossary.)

General principles A–Z

Whatever community planning approach you choose, there are general principles which apply to most situations. This section summarises some of the most important. Adopt and adapt as appropriate. Also at:

www.communityplanning.net/principles/principles.php

Accept different agendas

People will want to be involved for a variety of reasons, for instance: academic enquiry, altruism, curiosity, fear of change, financial gain, neighbourliness, professional duty, protection of interests, socialising. This need not be a problem but it helps to be aware of people's different agendas.

Accept limitations

No community planning activity can solve all the world's problems. But that is not a reason for holding back. Limited practical improvements will almost always result, and community planning activity can often act as a catalyst for more fundamental change.

Accept varied commitment

Far too much energy is wasted complaining that certain people do not participate when the opportunity is provided. All of us could spend our lives many times over working to improve the local environment. Everyone has their own priorities in life and these should be respected. If people do not participate it is likely to be because they are happy to let others get on with it, they are busy with things which are more important to them or the process has not been made sufficiently interesting or relevant.

Agree rules and boundaries

There should be a common understanding by all main interest groups of the approach adopted. Particularly in communities where there is fear – for instance that others may be trying to gain territorial advantage – it is vital that the rules and boundaries are clearly understood and agreed.

Avoid jargon

Use plain language. Jargon prevents people from engaging and is usually a smokescreen to hide incompetence, ignorance or arrogance.

Be creative

The best community engagement is often innovative and imaginative. Use toolkits such as this but don't be afraid to think outside the box.

Be honest

Be open and straightforward about the nature of any activity. Be clear about the parameters. Avoid raising unrealistic expectations. People will participate more enthusiastically if they know that something can be achieved through their participation (e.g. if there is a budget for a capital project). But they may be happy to participate 'at risk' providing they know the odds. If there is only a small chance of change as a result of people participating, say so. Avoid hidden agendas.

Be transparent

The objectives and people's roles should be clear and transparent at events. For instance, it may seem trivial but the importance of name badges to prevent events being the preserve of the 'in-crowd' can never be stressed enough.

Be visionary yet realistic

Nothing much is likely to be achieved without raising expectations. Yet dwelling entirely on the utopian can be frustrating. Strike a balance between setting visionary utopian goals and being realistic about the practical options available.

Be visionary yet realistic
As the proverb says: 'Where there is no vision, the people perish'. (Proverbs 29:18)

Build local capacity
*Employing residents to
organise community planning
activity is invariably worthwhile.*

Communicate
*Let people know what you are
doing and how they can get
involved.*

Build local capacity

Long-term community sustainability depends on developing human and social capital. Take every opportunity to develop local skills and capacity. Involve local people in surveying their own situation, running their own programmes and managing local assets. Help people to understand how planning processes work and how they can be influenced. Communications and cultural activities are particularly effective at building capacity.

Communicate

Use all available media to let people know what you are doing and how they can get involved. Community newspapers and, increasingly, websites are invaluable. Information provision is a vital element of all participatory activities.

Consider disabilities

Consider people with disabilities when designing activities. Make sure that people with visual and hearing disabilities, as well as physical disabilities, are not prevented from participating.

Encourage collaboration

Create partnerships wherever possible between the various interest groups involved and with potential contributors such as financial institutions.

Flexibility

Be prepared to modify processes as circumstances dictate. Avoid inflexible methods and strategies.

Focus on attitudes

Behaviour and attitude are just as, if not more, important than methods. Encourage self-critical awareness, handing over control, personal responsibility and sharing.

Focus on existing interests

Start participatory working with a focus on the existing interests and motivations of local people. They will then see the relevance of being involved.

Follow up

Lack of follow-up is the most common failing, usually due to a failure to plan and budget for it. Make sure you set aside time and resources for documenting, publicising and acting on the results of any community planning initiative.

Go at the right pace

Rushing can lead to problems. On the other hand, without deadlines things can drift. Using experienced external consultants may speed up the process but often at the expense of developing local capacity. Get the balance right.

Go for it

This is the phrase used most by people who have experienced community planning when asked what their advice would be to others. You are bound to have doubts, it is usually a leap in the dark. But you are unlikely to regret taking the plunge.

Have fun
Planning your environment can be enjoyable. Community planning in the Philippines (top) and in the UK (bottom).

Go to the people

Go to where people are rather than expecting them to come to you.

Have fun

Being involved in creating and managing the environment should not be a chore. It can be a great opportunity to meet people and have fun. The most interesting and sustainable environments have been produced where people have enjoyed creating them. Community planning requires humour. Respect local culture, but use cartoons, jokes and games whenever possible.

Involve all sections of the community
Non-literate women draw a systems diagram, Pakistan (top). Children present ideas for the future of their community, UK (bottom).

Human scale

Work in communities of a manageable scale. This is usually where people at least recognise each other. Where possible, break up larger areas into a series of smaller ones and translate regional issues to a local scale. Working on regional planning issues requires a high level of coordination between community and interest groups and the use of specific methods.

Integrate with decision making

Community planning activity needs to be integrated with government decision making processes. Participatory processes are undermined if there is no clear link to decision making.

Involve all those affected

Community planning works best if all parties are committed to it. Involve all the main interested parties as early as possible, preferably in the planning of the process. Activities in which key players (such as landowners or planners) sit on the sidelines are all too common and rarely achieve their objectives completely. Time spent winning over cynics before you start is well worthwhile. If there are people or groups who cannot be convinced at the outset, keep them informed and give them the option of joining in later on.

Involve all sections of the community

People of different ages, gender, backgrounds, faiths and cultures almost invariably have different perspectives. Ensure that a full spectrum of the community is involved. This is usually far more important than involving large numbers.

Learn from others
There is no need to re-invent the wheel. One of the
best sources of information is people who have done it
before. Don't think you know it all. No one does. Be
open to new approaches. Get in touch with people
from elsewhere who have relevant experience. Go and
visit them and see their projects; seeing is believing.
Do not be afraid of experienced 'consultants' but
choose and brief them carefully.

Local ownership of the process
The community planning process should be 'owned'
by local people. Even though consultants or national
organisations may be providing advice and taking
responsibility for certain activities, the local community
should take responsibility for the overall process.

Maintain momentum
Regularly monitor progress to ensure that initiatives are
built on and objectives achieved. Development
processes are invariably lengthy, the participation
process needs to stay the course. If there has to be a
break, start again from where you left off, not from
the beginning. Periodic review sessions can be very
valuable to maintain momentum and community
involvement.

Make a difference
Make it clear at the outset how people's contributions
will make a difference and, later on, make it clear how
people's contributions *have* made a difference.

Learn from others
*Seeing is believing. Group of
farmers visit a farm where
innovation is taking place,
Honduras (top). Group of
residents visit a housing
scheme before designing their
own new homes, UK (bottom).*

Mixture of methods
Use a variety of involvement methods as different people will want to take part in different ways. For instance, some will be happy to write letters, others will prefer to make comments at an exhibition or take part in workshop sessions.

Now is the right time
The best time to start involving people is at the beginning of any programme. The earlier the better. But if programmes have already begun, participation should be introduced as soon as possible. Start now.

Ongoing involvement
Community involvement in planning issues needs to be an ongoing and continuous activity and be supported accordingly. One-off consultations with tight deadlines have only limited value.

Personal initiative
Virtually all community planning initiatives have happened only because an individual has taken the initiative. Don't wait for others. That individual could be you!

Plan your own process carefully
Careful planning of the process is vital. Avoid rushing into any one approach. Look at alternatives. Design a process to suit the circumstances. This may well involve combining a range of methods or devising new ones.

Plan for the local context
Develop unique strategies for each neighbourhood. Understand local characteristics and vernacular traditions and use them as a starting point for planning. Encourage regional and local diversity.

Prepare properly

The most successful activities are invariably those on which sufficient time and effort have been given to preliminary organisation and engaging those who may be interested.

Process as important as product

The way that things are done is often as important as the end result. But remember that the aim is implementation. Participation is important but is not an end in itself.

Professional enablers

Professionals and administrators should see themselves as enablers, helping local people achieve their goals, rather than as providers of services and solutions.

Quality not quantity

There is no such thing as a perfect participation process. The search for one is healthy only if this fact is accepted. Generally, the maximum participation by the maximum number of people is worth aiming at. But any participation is better than none and the quality of participation is more important than the numbers involved. A well organised event for a small number of people can often be more fruitful than a less well organised event for larger numbers.

Reach all sectors

Use methods to reach all sectors of the community – for example young people, minority ethnic communities, small businesses, the 'silent majority', the 'hard to reach'. But take care to avoid further alienation of disadvantaged groups by creating separate processes.

Prepare properly
Set up events so they are self explanatory and will work even if the key organisers fail to show up for any reason.

Process as important as product
A closed ballot box is probably unnecessary but it demonstrates transparency.

Attendance:
Exhibition of plans
Monday 27 May 2000

Name	Organisation (if any)	Contact details	Comments

Record and document
So easily forgotten.

Record and document

Make sure participation activities are properly recorded and documented so that it can be clearly seen who has been involved and how. Easily forgotten, such records can be invaluable at a later stage.

Respect cultural context

Make sure that your approach is suitable for the cultural context in which you are working. Consider local attitudes to gender, informal livelihoods, social groupings, speaking out in public and so on.

Respect local knowledge

All people, whether literate or not, whether rich or poor, whether children, women or men, have a remarkable understanding of their surroundings and are capable of analysing and assessing their situation, often better than trained professionals. Respect local perceptions, choices and abilities and involve local people in setting goals and strategies.

Shared control

The extent of public participation in any activity can vary from very little to a great deal. Different levels are appropriate at different stages of the planning process but shared control at the planning and design stage is the crucial ingredient (☞ participation matrix, page 12).

Special interest groups

Groups representing different special interests have a vital role to play in shaping the environment because of its complexity. Decision-makers need to consider evidence which represents best the variety of interests of current and future communities, including taking into account views of specific interest groups with particular knowledge.

Spend money

Effective participation processes take time and energy. There are methods to suit a range of budgets and much can be achieved using only people's time and energy. But over-tight budgets usually lead to cutting corners and poor results. Remember that community planning is an important activity, the success or failure of which may have dramatic implications for future generations as well as your own resources. The costs of building the wrong thing in the wrong place can be astronomical and make the cost of proper community planning pale into insignificance. Budget generously.

Tea and cake

There is nothing like good food and drink to entice people to spend time engaging. And in most cultures it seems to be an acceptable level of bribery!

Think on your feet

Once the basic principles and language of participatory planning are understood, experienced practitioners will find it easy to improvise. Avoid feeling constrained by rules or guidance (such as this handbook)!

Train

Training is invaluable at all levels. Encourage visits to other projects and attendance on courses. Build in training to all your activities.

Translate where necessary

Ensure people can understand each other and make sure key nuances are not lost in translation.

Trust in others' honesty

Start from a position of trusting others and generally this will be reciprocated. Lack of trust is usually due to lack of information.

Spend money
Demolition of perfectly sound buildings because people do not want them; an all too frequent occurrence. The cost of failing to involve people properly in planning and design can be astronomical.

Tea and cake
Free sandwiches and tea on the pavement outside an exhibition aiming to engage people with planning the future of the area.

Visualise
Venn diagram of village institutions, Sri Lanka (above). Before and after of proposed changes to a public square, Czech Republic (below).

Use experts appropriately

The best results emerge when local people work closely and intensively with experts from all the necessary disciplines. Creating and managing the environment is very complicated and requires a variety of expertise and experience to do it well. Do not be afraid of expertise, embrace it. But avoid dependency on, or hijacking by, professionals. Keep control local. Use experts 'little and often' to allow local participants time to develop capability, even if it means they sometimes make mistakes.

Use facilitators

Orchestrating group activities is a real skill. Without good facilitation the most articulate and powerful may dominate. Particularly if large numbers of people are involved, ensure that the person (or people) directing events has good facilitation skills. If not, hire someone who has.

Use local talent

Make use of local skills and professionalism within the community before supplementing them with outside assistance. This will help develop capability within the community and help achieve long-term sustainability.

Use outsiders, but carefully

A central principle of community planning is that local people know best. But outsiders, if well briefed, can provide a fresh perspective which can be invigorating. Getting the right balance between locals and outsiders is important; avoid locals feeling swamped or intimidated by 'foreigners'.

Visualise

People can participate far more effectively if information is presented visually rather than in words, A great deal of poor development, and hostility to good development, is due to people not understanding what it will look like. Use graphics, maps, illustrations, cartoons, drawings, photomontages and models wherever possible. And make the process itself visible by using flipcharts, Post-it notes, coloured dots and banners.

Walk before you run

Developing a participatory culture takes time. Start by using simple participation methods and work up to using more complex ones as experience and confidence grow.

Work on location

Wherever possible, base community planning activities physically in the area being planned. This makes it much easier for everyone to bridge the gap from concept to reality.

Work on location
Village improvement consultations, Kenya (top). Community garden design workshop, UK (bottom).

People's wall at a design fest,
Hong Kong, 1998

Methods A–Z

A selection of the most effective methods for helping people to get involved in physical planning and design. For latest see:

www.communityplanning.net/methods/methods_a-z.php?tab=1

Activity week

Activity weeks are a way of focusing energy and attention on the local environment and initiatives to improve it. They are particularly effective if they become an annual event and even more so if part of a national programme.

Public focus
Local newspaper promotes an 'Environment Week' programme. Other common themes are 'Architecture Week', 'Urban Design Week', 'Preservation Week'.

- A programme of events and activities is produced on a suitable theme. One week is a good length for making an impact but it can be longer or shorter.

- Organisations and individuals are invited to organise activities and events during the week and have them advertised in the programme.

- The programme is promoted by a coordinating body which may be a partnership, preferably including local media.

✎ Organising a first activity week will take a lot of effort. Once established as an annual event, they become relatively easy to organise as participating organisations know what is expected of them. The main coordinating task then involves compiling the programme.

✎ Make sure the programme is produced well in advance and widely publicised. Get it printed in the local paper in full, preferably as a pull-out.

✎ It helps if national organisations can provide an overall framework and get local organisations to co-ordinate local programmes.

✎ If you have an event longer than a week (one month, one year), make sure you have the stamina to maintain the momentum.

Fact: Over half a million pieces of publicity were printed by the Civic Trust for 'Environment Week 1991' which included 350,000 leaflets, 50,000 ideas for action booklets, 250,000 badges, 40,000 window stickers, 65,000 posters, 500 balloons and 100 banners. Over 3,000 events were held throughout the UK. Interviews were screened on 13 national TV programmes and at least 2,200 items published in newspapers.

$ Core costs: printing programme, co-ordination (several person weeks), launch event. Costs of individual activities should be covered by participating organisations. Plenty of scope for securing sponsorship.

Activity week activities

☐ **Award ceremony**
For most imaginative local project, group or individual.

☐ **Competition**
For best kept gardens or shopfronts, best improvement ideas, best kids' drawings, etc.

☐ **Exhibition**
Exhibitions on week theme by local businesses, voluntary groups, artists, etc.

☐ **Guided tour**
Around area of interest. Or for birdwatching, looking at wild flowers, etc.

☐ **Launch reception**
Pre-week gathering for organisers, exhibitors, sponsors, the media, etc.

☐ **Lecture or film show**
On subject of interest.

☐ **Litter-pick**
Help clear up an eyesore. Bags provided.

☐ **Open day**
For projects, organisations, etc.

☐ **Open building or garden**
See round fine local buildings or gardens.

☐ **Opening ceremony**
Formal event for press, dignatories, etc.

☐ **Party**
End of week celebration for organisers, etc.

☐ **Project opening or launch**
Unveil a plaque for a recently completed project or launch a new initiative.

☐ **Public meeting**
On a theme of current interest, inaugural meeting of new group, new initiative, etc.

☐ **Reception or 'coffee morning'**
Refreshments with a relevant theme.

☐ **Self build project**
Create a garden, build a play structure, dig a ditch, paint a mural, clear a pond, etc.

☐ **Street party**
Clear out the cars for an evening.

☐ **Workshop, Forum, Symposium, Debate**
On relevant subjects.

☐ ....

Plus normal festival activities: facepainting, music, dancing, juggling, theatre, poetry readings, sculptures, races and lots more.

ANYTOWN URBAN DESIGN WEEK
5 to 12 April 2014
Making places work better

Co-ordinated by Anytown Urban Forum
Sponsored by Viz Inc and The Herald

Day	Time	Event details	Organiser
Mon	2.30	Town Centre Walk. See the latest plans with the City Planner. Meet in Town Square.	Planning Dept.
	All day	Exhibition. Competition entries for Broadway. At Space Gallery.	Old Town Trust
	18.00	Prize giving and party. For Broadway competition. At Space Gallery	*The Herald*
Tues	10.00	Rubbish clearance. Downs Park. Sacks and refreshments provided.	Down residents
	12.00	etc etc	

ON ALL WEEK

Open House   See how the Duke Street project office works, 7 Duke Street. 10.00 to 17.00

Gardening   Help Love Lane residents create a community garden on the derelict sidings land. Tools provided. 11.00 to 18.00 daily.

Further information: 446488

Sample programme format
Key ingredients: theme; dates; timetable of activities; map with location of activities; credits; further info contact. A way of suggesting ideas for next year's programme could also be added.

FURTHER INFORMATION

☞ Scenario: *Urban conservation.*

✉ Royal Institute of British Architects (Architecture Week). Urban Design Group (Urban Design Week).

Architecture centre

Architecture centres are places set up to help people understand, and engage in, the design of local buildings and the built environment. They can become focal points for local environmental initiatives and a shop window and meeting place for all those involved in shaping the future of their surroundings.

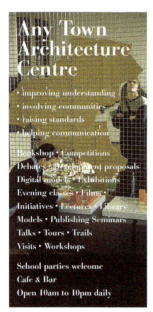

Sample promotional poster

"You just want to reach out and touch and play with all the displays. I never knew buildings could be so exciting."
Janet Ullman, resident, London, on Hackney Building Exploratory, London, 1998.

"The number of visitors we've had in our first two years – 30,000 – shows there is a real public demand for what we have to offer."
Sasha Lubetkin, Director, Bristol Architecture Centre, 1998.

"These organisations are the key to greater public participation and access to the wider debates on architecture and related social and political issues."
Marjorie Allthorpe-Guyton Director of Visual Arts, Arts Council of England, Report, 1999.

■ A suitable building is found with space for exhibitions, seminars and social activities. It will normally be a building of architectural or historic interest.

■ Permanent and temporary exhibits are mounted relating to the local built environment.

■ A programme of activities is organised designed to stimulate interest, start initiatives and provide educational experiences for young people.

✎ Lots of space is needed in order to be able to house models and exhibits.

✎ Centres need time to generate momentum. At least a three-year set up timetable is advisable.

✎ Centres can be themed depending on the needs of the locality. A historic area might be better off calling it a 'Conservation Centre' or 'Heritage Centre' and focusing the exhibits and activities accordingly. A rundown area might have a 'Regeneration Centre'. Where the emphasis is entirely on education, it might be called an 'Urban Studies Centre'.

✎ Centres can be set up by local authorities, education institutes or local amenity societies. They are likely to work best if they are independent, perhaps starting off as a partnership venture.

$ Main costs: building and running costs, staff, exhibits. Scope for sponsorship from the building industry and educational grants.

Architecture centre exhibit ideas

- ☐ **Aerial photo.** Of local area (people love aerial photos of where they live).
- ☐ **Building date maps.** Showing what was built when.
- ☐ **Building models and plans.** For typical or interesting local buildings.
- ☐ **Conservation map.** Showing location of historic buildings and landscapes.
- ☐ **Construction models.** Models of vernacular building methods, brick bonds, window details, etc.
- ☐ **Development proposals and ideas.** Drawings and models of proposed new construction in the local area with comment facilities.
- ☐ **Electronic or digital map.** Computer terminal (☞ p 64).
- ☐ **Geological model.** Showing rock strata. 'What is beneath your home?'
- ☐ **Historical maps.** Showing development of the area, war damage, etc.
- ☐ **House-type photos.** 'Put a sticker on the house you would most like to live in' (distinguish between adults, children, visitors).
- ☐ **Local area map.** 'Stick in a pin to show where you live.'
- ☐ **Local area model.** Accurate and detailed or conceptual (see photo right).
- ☐ **Neighbourhood jigsaw.** Lift up pieces based on district boundaries to reveal street plans, transport links, sewage systems, etc.
- ☐ **Site models.** Block models of a range of different styles of development in the area. 'Guess which is which?'
- ☐ **Space photo.** The view from a satellite. Good crowd puller.
- ☐ **Technical services.** Displays showing how things work; plumbing, insulation, electrics.
- ☐ **Tracing paper ideas.** 'Sketch your ideas on overlays of maps or drawings'.
- ☐ **World map.** Stick in pins to show where your parents come from.
- ☐ ....
....

Bringing the built environment alive
Discussion takes place around a model of the local area built from recycled materials over 6 months by 350 school children.

FURTHER INFORMATION

- ☞ Methods: *Community design centre. Environment shop.* Scenarios: *New neighbourhood. Regeneration infrastructure. Urban conservation.*
- 🖳 Architecture Centres Network.
- ☆ Polly Hudson. Barry Shaw.

Art workshop

Art workshops allow local people to help design and construct artworks to improve their environment. This can be an end in itself or part of a wider regeneration effort. Community arts projects are particularly useful for helping people express their creativity and develop skills, a sense of identity and community pride.

Community art
Street lights designed by local residents with community artists.

- Ideas are generated by local people working closely with community artists and sculptors in studio workshop sessions. People of all ages, backgrounds and abilities can be involved.

- Architects, landscape designers and other technical experts ensure that the designs are buildable.

- The community chooses which of the design options generated should be built, usually through some form of voting at an exhibition.

- The artworks are manufactured and installed, often with the assistance of local residents.

- A celebration is held to mark completion.

✎ Good way of involving people in development who might not be attracted by more conventional consultation methods. Can break down social barriers and help communities form a common vision.

✎ Finding artists willing and able to work with community groups is essential. Providing leadership without dominating is a vital skill.

"Community arts was a way of communicating more easily and excitingly and to get real ideas from people."
Waheed Saleem, Chair, Caldmore-Palfrey Youth Forum, Walsall, UK
Free Form Update, 1998.

$ Can be relatively expensive in professional input and project costs. Needs to be seen as a cultural and educational initiative as well as a way of achieving environmental improvements. In this way costs can be partially covered by education or other budgets. Using recycled or scrap materials can reduce costs.

Designing
School children work with artists in studio workshops developing designs for a pavement mosaic using poster paints, cardboard and scissors.

Making
The mosaic is made by local people with no previous experience under the supervision of artists and architects.

Celebrating
Local people celebrate an attractive improvement to the street scene which has been designed and made with their help. In contrast to much corporate artworks, such initiatives provide a visible sign of local communities' participation in the environment and can help create places which are successful, safe and respected.

Community arts opportunities

☐ Bicycle paths
☐ Bridge decoration
☐ Community gardens and parks
☐ Fountains
☐ Murals
☐ Paving
☐ Play areas
☐ Railings and gateways
☐ School buildings
☐ Sculptures and statues
☐ Street lighting
☐ ....

FURTHER INFORMATION

☞ Scenarios: *Derelict site re-use. Environmental art project. Inner city regeneration.*

☆ Sonia Kahn.

Award scheme

Award schemes provide a way to stimulate activity and spread good practice at a local, national or even international level. They can be set up by any organisation from a local community group to an international agency.

- The organisers establish the purpose of the scheme and assemble partners and sponsors.

- An entry form is drafted setting out the themes, categories (if any), entry criteria, judging procedure and prizes and the scheme is widely publicised to attract entries.

- Entries are judged and an award ceremony is held to focus publicity on the winning entry and the themes behind the awards.

- Procedures are refined and the awards held on a regular, often annual, basis.

✎ Financial incentives are not usually necessary. People will enter for the prestige. But a good plaque or framed certificate which can be publicly displayed will be highly valued.

✎ High profile patrons are very helpful in attracting entries and getting publicity, eg royalty or local mayor.

✎ Use schemes to develop a catalogue of case studies for information exchange.

✎ Judging can be highly educational. Have as many judges as possible and get them to visit short-listed schemes. Such visits can be valuable for both the judges and local projects.

$ Local schemes: few costs involved. National schemes can be complex and involve considerable administration. The more successful they become, the more administration is required to ensure fairness and impartiality. Great scope for sponsorship.

Do you know of a community planning project worthy of an award?

Entry forms from:
Community Planning Awards
PO Box 7, Anytown

Organised by Environment Agency
Sponsored by Glass Ltd, Big Land and Grassroots Foundation

Closing date for entries:
7 May 2014

"The awards are an uplifting experience. They raise the spirits of those of us who are fortunate enough to be short-listed. They raise the horizons of those who miss out this time but look on and think 'we could do that' and have a crack next time. And they raise the profile of our kind of work amongst a much wider audience than we might ever otherwise hope to address."
David Robinson, Director, Community Links, London
Acceptance speech, 1.3.1994.

"All over the country there are remarkable groups of people working incredibly hard to make a real difference to their communities. The whole object of these awards is to reward and recognise all these unsung heroes."
HRH The Prince of Wales, Chairman, UK Community Enterprise Awards, 1995.

Anytown Shopfront award

presented to

....

by

....

dated

....

An annual award for the best shopfront improvements in Anytown.

Sponsored by the Anytown Trust and Anytown Chamber of Commerce

Local award certificate

National community enterprise award

Category **Community buildings**

presented to _____

by _____

dated _____

An annual award for the most enterprising and sustainable community projects in Anycountry.

Patrons: Princess Mary, Sir John Knevitt. Organised by the Housing Institute and Planners Network. Sponsored by Glass Ltd, Big Land and Grassroots Foundation.

National award certificate

Sample judging criteria

For community projects

☐ **Need or value**
The project's value to the community for which it is designed.

☐ **Community involvement**
The quality of community involvement in the project's initiation and development.

☐ **Design**
The appropriateness of the design solution adopted.

☐ **Sustainability**
The ability for the project to be maintained over time.

Spreading the word

Securing an award, or even just being considered for an award, can generate publicity for a project which can help with funding and other support.

FURTHER INFORMATION

☞ Scenarios: *Regeneration infrastructure. Urban conservation.*

✉ Business in the Community.

Briefing workshop

Briefing workshops, also known as 'topic' workshops, are simple, easy-to-organise working sessions held to establish a project agenda or brief. Simultaneously they can:
- **introduce people to the project;**
- **help establish the key issues;**
- **get people involved and motivated;**
- **identify useful talent and experience;**
- **identify the next steps needed.**

They are useful at the start of a project or community planning event.

■ Potential users of the project are invited to attend a workshop, usually lasting around 1.5 hours. Similar workshops may be held with different interest groups (eg: staff, leaders, young people, etc) or on different topics (eg: housing, jobs, open space, etc).

■ The workshop is facilitated by one or more individuals who will have planned a format to suit the context (☞ example, right).

■ A record is kept of those who attend, the points made and key issues identified.

■ People's contributions are unattributable unless agreed otherwise.

✎ If people find it hard to get started, say "Just write down the first thing that comes into your head, however big or small."

✎ The record should ideally include typing up all Post-it notes and flip-chart sheets as well as key points from all debate.

✎ Follow up by circulating a summary to all participants.

$ Core costs: facilitator's fees; venue hire; typing up workshop notes (allow one person day per workshop).

Main steps
1 Individual brainstorm on Post-it notes or cards;
2 Categorising in small groups sitting round a table or on the floor;
3 Presenting the results;
4 General discussion and planning the next steps.

Briefing workshop format
Sample covering most contexts.
Participants are divided into groups of
8–10, seated around tables.

1 Introduction
Purpose of event explained by facilitator.
Everyone introduces themselves and
explains briefly their interest. Notetaker
and flipchart identified for each group.
(15 mins)

2 Individual brainstorm
Everyone is given Post-it notes or cards of
3 different colours and asked to write
down their responses, in relation to any
given topic, to 3 questions:

What is wrong?	What is your dream?	How can it happen?

Or 'Dislikes', 'Likes' and 'Ideas for
Improvement'. Each Post-it note should
contain only one response. A limit can be
set for the number of responses per person
to make the total manageable. Symbols
can be used if people are illiterate. (15 mins)

3 Categorising
Groups categorise Post-its of each colour
by arranging them on large sheets of
paper and making headings. Graphics can
be added if helpful. (20 mins)

4 Presenting
Each group explains its findings to all
participants. (20 mins)

5 Discussion
On the results and next stage in the
process. Strategic recommendations and
immediate action identified. (20 mins)

Running time: 1.5 hours.
Ideal numbers: **9–24**. With larger numbers,
split up into more subgroups for
categorising **or** have a facilitating team
doing the categorising (see right).

Facilitated categorising
A team of facilitators (who may be volunteers)
read out responses one by one and place them in
categories on wall sheets. An alternative to the
procedure outlined left, useful when there are
large numbers.

Briefing workshop props
☐ Attendance sheets
☐ Banners with workshop title
☐ Display material, eg maps, photos, plans
☐ Flip-chart (or paper on wall)
☐ Felt-tip markers (or chalk)
☐ Pens or pencils
☐ Post-it notes (or small pieces of paper or
   card) in three colours
☐ Tape (or drawing pins or Blu-tack)

FURTHER INFORMATION

☞ Method: *Design workshop.*
   Scenarios: *Community centre. Housing
   development.*

Choice catalogue

A choice catalogue provides a way to make design choices within a predetermined structure. It is particularly useful for helping people understand the range of options available and providing a way for making choices where large numbers of people are involved.

Fixtures and fittings options
Catalogues used by future occupants of a large housing development. Standard choices can be made which have no real cost effect. Residents can choose up to 400 points-worth of other items.

- Choice catalogues can be used to make design choices at a range of levels; from housing layouts to sanitary fittings.

- Options available are worked out by the experts in consultation with a small group of residents.

- The options are presented in the form of a simple menu made as visual as possible, using photographs or simple sketches. Choices can be costed using a simple points system if necessary.

- People make choices based on the catalogue. This may be done individually or in groups using workshop procedures.

✎ Makes it possible to give residents of large housing developments individual choice, particularly using computers to log people's selections.

✎ Can be used as a way of generally finding out people's attitudes to design issues as well as for making specific selections.

$ Dependant on scale of consultation. Main costs: graphics; printing; distribution. If well managed and planned at an early stage, providing choice on large housing schemes need not add to overall capital costs. Indeed savings can be made by avoiding the provision of items that some people do not want.

What would you like your housing to look like?

Instructions
1 Select the images you like most and least.
2 Discuss your selection in a group.
3 Make a group decision on the group's most and least liked images.

House image options
Choice menu format for use by future residents of a housing scheme in a group. Useful for briefing an architect. Images are selected which reflect locally available options.

Uses for choice menus

☐ Bathroom fittings
☐ Front entrance
☐ House image
☐ House type
☐ Light fittings
☐ Room layout
☐ Security equipment

What room arrangement do you want?

Instructions
1 Select the options you prefer.
2 Fill in the points score and add up.
3 Revise until the total score is less than 41
  OR
3 The cost of your home will be roughly the number of points multiplied by $..,......

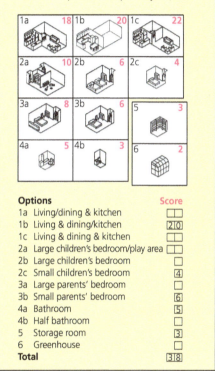

Options		Score
1a	Living/dining & kitchen	☐☐
1b	Living & dining/kitchen	2 0
1c	Living & dining & kitchen	☐☐
2a	Large children's bedroom/play area	☐☐
2b	Large children's bedroom	☐
2c	Small children's bedroom	4
3a	Large parents' bedroom	☐
3b	Small parents' bedroom	6
4a	Bathroom	5
4b	Half bathroom	☐
5	Storage room	3
6	Greenhouse	☐
Total		3 8

Room layout options
Choice menu for selecting alternative room layouts.

FURTHER INFORMATION

☞ Scenario: *Housing development.*

⟲ *Building Homes People Want. Participatory Design.*

✉ North Carolina State University. Halsall Lloyd Partnership.

☆ Bill Halsall. Henry Sanoff.

Community design centre

Community design centres are places where communities can get affordable technical help to plan and manage their environment. They are the environmental equivalent of health centres and are invaluable for helping local people design and implement environmental projects, particularly in poor communities.

■ Community design centres are staffed by people with a range of the technical skills needed for environmental management. They are also known as 'community *technical aid* centres'.

■ Centres provide services to local voluntary groups – and sometimes individuals – covering all aspects of environmental management. Services will normally be free unless groups are able to afford to pay for them or fees can be built into capital project bids.

■ Centres will normally be independent charitable agencies funded by governments, local authorities, universities, charities or private sponsors. Sometimes they are controlled by the groups to whom they provide services. Independent consultants may also provide the same service, subsidised by other work.

✎ Securing funding is a constant headache. Centres are most likely to be sustainable if they carry out fee earning work as well as providing free services.

$ Dependent on the number of paid staff and cost of premises. For instance a well equipped centre with 5 full-time technical staff could cost US$200,000 per annum. A centre run by volunteers or secondees using free accommodation could cost very little.

Are you
• a community organisation?
• a tenants' association?
• a residents' association?
• an ethnic organisation?
• a women's group?

Do you want to
• Clear up an eyesore?
• Build a community hall?
• Build a women's refuge?
• Develop a play area?
• Landscape a derelict site?

We can provide
• Architects
• Planners
• Surveyors
• Ecologists
• Project management
• Help with fundraising and constitutions
• Publications and videos

Contact
Anytown Community Technical Aid Centre
01234 666444

A free service to community groups funded by Anytown City Council, Ministry for Environment and Jet plc

"What makes the community architect different from the traditional architect is that he's available, he's there – seven days a week, twenty-four hours a day to feel the vibration and pulse of the community. The architect's presence on site is essential. That very presence is wealth – not just for the architect but for the whole community."
Rod Hackney, Community architect
Architects Journal, 20.2.1985.

Community design centre services

Customise to satisfy local needs.

- ☐ Art and graphics
- ☐ Community arts
- ☐ Community planning
- ☐ Competition management
- ☐ Construction work supervision
- ☐ Design of buildings and landscape
- ☐ Employment generation
- ☐ Feasibility studies; buildings and landscape
- ☐ Fundraising
- ☐ Maintenance of buildings and landscape
- ☐ Organisation formation and development
- ☐ Planning advice and advocacy
- ☐ Plant nursery development and maintenance
- ☐ Property management and development
- ☐ Rectifying building defects
- ☐ Strategic planning
- ☐ Training in environmental management and design
- ☐ ....

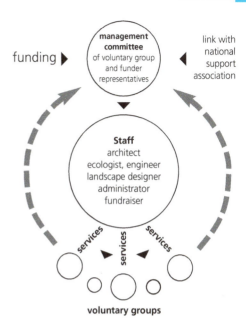

Organisation chart for a community design centre managed by a committee of representatives of groups that use it and funders.

Technical expertise
A community-based nerve centre providing skills and experience on environmental management.

FURTHER INFORMATION

☞ Methods: *Environment shop. Neighbourhood planning office. Urban design studio.* Scenarios: *Derelict site re-use. Regeneration infrastructure. Shanty settlement upgrading. Urban conservation.*

✉ Association for Community Design.

🖥 Architecture Centres Network

Community planning event

You are invited to a:

CHARRETTE

Community Planning Forum

DESIGN FEST

Design Workshop

FUTURE SEARCH CONFERENCE

Microplanning Workshop

OPEN SPACE WORKSHOP

Planning for Real Session

PLANNING WEEKEND

Community planning events allow people to produce plans of action at carefully structured sessions at which all those affected work creatively together. They can be used at any stage of the development process and provide an alternative to reliance on bureaucratic planning. There are several common models.

- The nature of the community planning event is decided on and agreed by the main parties involved. There are many common types and the scope for inventing new formats is unlimited. Events may last for an afternoon, a weekend, a week or a month.

- Preparation takes place including arranging timetables, venues, publicity, equipment, technical support, background information.

- The event is held, often assisted by a facilitator or team of facilitators from elsewhere. Proposals for action result.

- The event is followed up to ensure that proposals are put into action.

✎ Careful planning and preparation are essential. Try and get some documented research and preliminary consultation input from key interested parties prior to an event. The creative burst is always part of – albeit a key part of – a longer process.

✎ Imaginative timetabling is crucial. Try linking up with other activities such as local festivals, anniversaries, conferences, etc.

$ Costs vary immensely from virtually nothing to tens of thousands of dollars. There is usually an event suited to most budgets, and scope for securing support in kind from interested parties.

Community planning event timetable structure

Common for many events, regardless of length.

1 Introduction
Tours, briefings, icebreakers, launch.

2 Problems/Issues
Workshops, plenaries, individual and group working.

3 Solutions/Options
Workshops, plenaries, design sessions, individual and group working.

4 Synthesis/Analysis
Individual and group working.

5 Production
Report writing, photo selection, drawing, model-making.

6 Presentation
Slide show, film, public meeting, symposium.

Working together
Local residents, business people, professionals, officials and politicians all work creatively together for an intensive period. Conventional boundaries tend to break down, releasing spirit, humour, imagination, positive thinking and collective creativity. Photos such as this are often taken to celebrate this energy.

FURTHER INFORMATION

☞ Methods: *Community planning forum. Design fest. Design workshop. Future search conference. Microplanning workshop. Open Space workshop. Planning day. Planning for Real. Planning weekend. Roadshow. Task force.*

Scenarios: *Inner city regeneration. Local neighbourhood initiative.*

✐ *The Charrette Handbook. The Community Planning Event Manual.*

Community planning forum

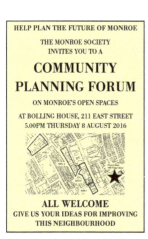

Sample advertising leaflet.
Key components: slogan summarising overall purpose; venue; time; date; statement of immediate objectives and perhaps some background information; map of area with venue marked; name of organisers.

Community planning forums are open, multipurpose events lasting several hours. The three-stage format is designed to secure information, generate ideas and create interaction between interest groups with a minimum of advance planning.

- Community planning forums can be organised at any time but are particularly useful at an early stage in a participation or development process.

- Forums can be organised by any interested party and can be organised at short notice.

- The format combines interactive displays, an open forum, workshop groups and informal networking.

- Key ingredients are a leaflet advertising the event, a means of distributing it, a venue and a facilitator.

✎ Keep the atmosphere informal to get best results. Good refreshments worthwhile.

✎ Particularly useful events for students engaged in urban design projects because they do not necessarily need to relate to any 'real' development timetable or be organised by local people. They can be organised by anyone at any time (though they will normally work better if locals assist).

✎ Getting students to organise the format themselves can be highly educational, particularly if linked with a process planning session (☞ Process planning session). Providing a framework may be helpful (ie arranging publicity and venue in advance).

"It was a very effective formula. It allowed us, as a group, to find out what the inhabitants expected of their place for the future. And it didn't impose too much on people's time. In fact I think everyone had a very enjoyable evening."
Laura Dotson
Interior designer
Student organiser of a community planning forum at Richmond, Virginia, USA, 1996.

$ Main costs: venue hire; advertising leaflet production.

Sample Community Planning Forum format

1 Interactive displays
As people arrive they are guided towards a variety of interactive displays where they are encouraged to make comments using Post-its, marker pens or stickers (☞ Interactive display). General mingling and discussion. Refreshments. (45 mins)

2 Open forum
People are seated in a horseshoe shape, perhaps with model, plan or drawing on a table in the centre. Introductions by organisers. Feed back on interactive displays by pre-warned rapporteurs. Open debate chaired by organiser. (45 mins)

3 Workshop groups
People are divided into groups and work around tables on various topics/areas, either pre-selected or agreed during the open forum. (45 mins)

4 Networking
Informal mingling and discussion. Refreshments. (45 mins)

5 Feedback (optional)
Reports from workshop groups to plenary. (Or separate presentation session later.)

Total running time: 3 hours minimum
Ideal numbers 30 – 150

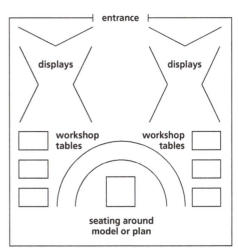

Ideal layout in a large hall

Open forum
Debate in a horseshoe arrangement following a warm-up interactive display and before dividing up into workshop groups.

Key roles at a planning forum

☐ Chairperson for open forum

☐ Facilitator/stage manager

☐ Hosts as people arrive

☐ Photographer

☐ Reporters for each interactive display

☐ Workshop and forum recorders

☐ Workshop facilitators

FURTHER INFORMATION

☞ Methods: *Elevation montage. Interactive display. Table scheme display. Task force.*

Scenarios: *Community centre. Village revival.*

☆ Richard John

Community profiling

Community profiling involves building up a picture of the nature, needs and resources of a community with the active participation of that community. It is a useful first stage in any community planning process to establish a context which is widely agreed.

Taking stock
Government officials analysing information gained from the community analysing itself using a variety of profiling methods.

- A range of methods are used to enable the community to develop an understanding of itself.

- The methods combine group working and group interaction techniques with data collection and presentation techniques.

- The focus is on methods which are visual in order to generate interest and make the process accessible to people who are illiterate and those unused to verbal communication.

- The results are in the public realm. Reports include as many of the words, writings and pictures of local people as possible.

✎ Good facilitation is particularly important to avoid manipulated or simply poor results. A strategy is often needed to prevent domination by the more powerful or aggressive. Facilitators should listen and learn at all times. Even when relaxing, insights into local dynamics can be gained.

✎ Closer attention and differing sessions may be needed to obtain the views of women and any under-represented groups.

✎ Informal observation is a powerful source of information on local dynamics.

"The benefit of using this method is the diverse number of people who can work together and still achieve an outcome which involves everyone."
Pat Jefferson, Carlisle City Council
Tidelines newsletter, Solway Firth Partnership, 1997.

$ Cost effective compared with conventional analysis by outside consultants. Main cost: facilitators' fees.

Community profiling methods

☐ **Activity chart.** Plotting people's activities each day, or each week. Useful for understanding divisions of labour, roles and responsibilities in a community.

☐ **Assets survey.** Recording physical and social assets in the community.

☐ **Building survey.** Recording the state of repair of buildings.

☐ **External relationship profiling.** Examining the roles and impact of external organisations.

☐ **Gender workshop.** Separate sessions for women (or sometimes men) to analyse their situation, needs and priorities.

☐ **Historical profile.** Identifying and listing key events, beliefs and trends in a community's past and their importance for the present.

☐ **Household livelihood analysis.** Comparing sources of income and support with expenditure patterns and looking at coping strategies for times of hardship.

☐ **Informal walk.** Walking in a group without a definite route, stopping to chat and discuss issues as they arise. (☞ *Reconnaissance trip*)

☐ **Mapping.** Making maps showing various characteristics, eg resources. (☞ *Mapping*)

☐ **Organisation review.** Review of existing groups and organisations to assess their roles, membership, plans and potential.

☐ **Personal history.** Recording detailed oral accounts of individuals' lives, perhaps asking them to emphasise specific issues.

☐ **Photo survey.** Taking and discussing photos of the locality. (☞ *Photo survey*)

☐ **Problem tree.** Analysing the inter-relationships among community issues and problems using a graphic based on a tree. (☞ *Glossary,* and illustration, below)

☐ **Role play.** Adopting the role of others and acting out scenarios. (☞ *Gaming*)

☐ **Seasonal calendar.** Exploring changes taking place throughout the year, eg in work patterns, production. (☞ *Diagrams*)

☐ **Semi-structured interview.** Conversational open discussion using a checklist of questions as a flexible guide instead of a formal questionnaire. Different types include; individual, group, focus group, and key informant. (☞ *Glossary*)

☐ **Simulation.** Acting out a real event or activity to understand its effect. (☞ *Simulation*)

☐ **Skills survey.** Assessing skills and talent in a community. (☞ *Glossary*, and p233)

☐ **Transect walk.** Systematic walk through an area to observe and record key features, for instance land use zones. (See also *Reconnaissance trip*)

☐ **Well-being or wealth ranking.** Assessing levels of well-being of different households using pile sorting. (☞ *Glossary*)

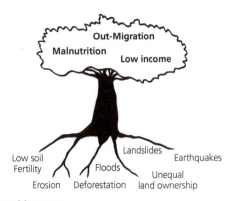

Problem tree
Simple graphic used to analyse complex issues.

FURTHER INFORMATION
☞ Methods: *Diagrams. Gaming. Mapping. Photo survey. Reconnaissance trip. Simulation.* Scenarios: *Community centre. Village revival.*
⟲ *Participatory Learning & Action.*
☆ Roger Bellers. Nick Hall.

Design assistance team

Team members' luggage

- ☐ Camera.
- ☐ Clothes with lots of pockets for camera, notebook, pens, etc.
- ☐ Favourite creative tools, eg drawing pens.
- ☐ Material for special presentation if required.
- ☐ Pocket notebook.
- ☐ Useful general facts and figures or illustrative material likely to be relevant.
- ☐ ....

Independent expertise
Team members discuss options with a local landowner.

"We owe thanks to all our 'outsiders'. They were so friendly from the start. It was like one big happy family."
Local resident, Ore Valley Action Planning Weekend, 1997.

Assistance teams comprise a number of specialists from a variety of relevant disciplines who visit an area and take part in a participation process (for instance, a planning weekend). They are particularly useful for providing a fresh and independent viewpoint.

■ Assistance teams are invited in by local people or agencies and provided with a brief. This may be simply to listen and advise, or to act as facilitators.

■ Teams will normally be multidisciplinary and be led by a team chairperson.

■ Team members are often paid expenses only, to ensure independence. If they are paid a fee, this needs to be made clear.

■ The team will usually prepare a report with their recommendations before leaving.

✎ Good briefing beforehand is essential; on both content and process.

✎ Strong leadership is vital to keep events moving forward. Give team members roles (see box, right) to focus people's energy.

✎ Get each team member to supply quotes (soundbites) and recommendations to standard bullet point format, in 3 categories: background; issues; recommendations (to make sure they listen and provide evidence of their contribution).

✎ Ensure that team members commit themselves to attending for the whole event.

$ Main costs for team: travel; accommodation; meals; film; equipment and supplies.

Assistance team roles

For large community planning events where the team is facilitating and preparing a report. Several compatible roles may be taken by one individual. Not all roles will be needed in every event. Customise.

- ☐ **Contacts person.** Keep names and phone numbers of useful resource people.
- ☐ **Diplomats.** Liaise between different workshops to create linkages.
- ☐ **Follow-up co-ordinator.** Ensure follow-up takes place and publicise.
- ☐ **Photographer.** Ensure key events are photographed.
- ☐ **Report editor.** Commission, gather and edit copy and illustrations.
- ☐ **Report subeditor.** Subedit copy. Assist editor.
- ☐ **Report production manager.** Liaise with printer and photo lab.
- ☐ **Slide show editor.** Select images for presentations.
- ☐ **Sound recorder.** Record key sessions and index recordings.
- ☐ **Stage manager.** Co-ordinate pool of people, usually volunteers, for errands etc.
- ☐ **Team chairperson.** Provide leadership, orchestrate event, take responsibility.
- ☐ **Team facilitator.** Keep roving eye on group dynamics, reporting back to team chairperson.
- ☐ **Workshop facilitators.** Steer workshop sessions (one per workshop).
- ☐ **Workshop note-takers.** Prepare notes of workshops in format for final report.
- ☐ ....

Team synthesis process

Sample process for drawing up proposals after public workshops or planning day.

1 **Roles and responsibilities meeting**
Team only. Determine tasks, report structure and division of roles.

2 **Individual team working**
All workshops analysed to standard format summarising points made and key themes. Proposals drawn up to standard format (heading plus summary paragraph).

3 **Team participatory editing**
Text and graphics displayed on wall for comment (using pens and Post-its).

4 **General participatory editing**
Non team members return (eg local enthusiasts) to make comments.

5 **Review session**
Open workshop session to discuss any major omissions or controversial issues.

6 **Final editing and production**
Team only.

Total running time: 1 day

FURTHER INFORMATION

☞ Methods: *Participatory editing. Planning day. Planning weekend.* Scenarios: *Industrial heritage re-use. Local neighbourhood initiative.*

✐ *The Charrette Handbook. The Community Planning Event Manual. Creating a Design Assistance Team for Your Community.*

Expertise needed on design assistance team

Checklist of skills and professional backgrounds likely to be useful. Customise for each event.

- ☐ Architecture
- ☐ Community development
- ☐ Ecology
- ☐ Economics and finance
- ☐ Energy
- ☐ Journalism
- ☐ Landscape design
- ☐ Law
- ☐ Management
- ☐ Planning
- ☐ Property development
- ☐ Sociology
- ☐ Urban design
- ☐ ....
- ☐ ....

It helps if people are also good at writing, drawing, internet research, analysing and team working.

Design fest

Design fests produce creative concepts for the future of an area by getting multidisciplinary design teams to develop and present their ideas in public. They are a good way to stimulate debate and develop imaginative solutions, particularly on controversial issues.

- Organisers decide on a theme that needs exploring and determine a brief. A specific, challenging site will normally be selected to focus creativity towards practical solutions.

- Multidisciplinary design teams are selected and briefed. The teams are likely to comprise architecture or planning students as well as practising professionals from a range of disciplines.

- The teams hold an intensive design workshop (or 'charrette') in public, coinciding with a public exhibition on the theme. The public are encouraged to respond to the theme and the team's ideas as they emerge and to develop their own.

- A high profile public symposium is held immediately after the workshops when the ideas generated are presented and debated by a prominent panel.

- The results are published and widely distributed.

✎ Ideally suited to being organised by university architecture and planning schools. Students learn a lot by taking part in teams, organising exhibition material, doing surveys of the public and helping the public to engage in design issues.

$ A well-organised, high profile design fest could cost US$40,000. But there is a great deal of scope for securing sponsorship.

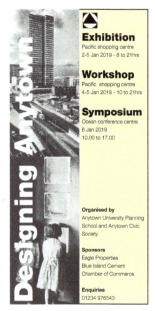

Sample poster
Key ingredients: theme; logo; visual image; details of activities; organisers, sponsors; further information.

"As the Saturday night deadline drew near, the pace was frenzied. Some drawings were coloured by up to six people at a time, models were being glued together, slides being taken for presentation at the Sunday symposium."
Designing Hong Kong report poster, 1998.

Designing in public

Multidisciplinary design teams develop ideas in three small cubicles erected inside a large shopping centre. Members of the public view the teams at work from the balconies above, explore exhibition material and interactive displays pinned to the outside of the screens, are interviewed by team members and develop and pin up their own ideas in a fourth cubicle (shown left above). The teams also have the use of a private resource room (not shown) with photocopying and other facilities. They are told to produce simple, straightforward and graphic presentation material to capture the attention of the viewing public on the balcony. The workshop may last for one or several days. Then, slides are made of the drawings and all the ideas emerging are presented and debated at a public symposium.

FURTHER INFORMATION

☞ Methods: *Design workshop. Interactive display.*

✉ Chinese University of Hong Kong (Department of Architecture)

☆ Jack Sidener

Design game

Design games are like jigsaw puzzles. They are a highly visual way of allowing people to explore physical design options for a site or internal space. They are particularly useful for designing parks and room layouts and can also be used for land-use planning. They can be used in isolation or as part of a broader participation process.

Movable pieces
Residents move pieces around until they are happy with their design.

- A base map of a site or room is prepared.

- Cut-out pieces representing items that could be incorporated are made to the same scale. Materials for making pieces are kept at hand to allow new items to be made as desired.

- Individuals or groups move pieces around until they are happy with the design, which is then photographed.

- Layouts produced by different individuals or groups are discussed and analysed as a basis for drawing up sketch designs and costings.

✎ Cut-outs are normally simple two-dimensional, hand-drawn illustrations, using coloured felt-tip on cardboard. Three-dimensional cut-outs are even better but take more time.

✎ Putting capital and revenue costings on pieces can make the design process more realistic.

✎ Make sure the pieces are visually explanatory so that photographs of the designs will make sense. Exhibiting or publishing photos of the designs of different groups can be a useful next step.

"The most vital aspect of our approach was the design game: it was intended to be, and was, fun; this made it less threatening, and thus more accessible.... Playing the game illustrated far better than words spoken by either side ever could, both the urban design principles discussed and residents' own preferences for the site."
Robert Brown, Architect
Urban Design Quarterly,
January 1998.

$ Depends on standard of design. Can be done very simply.

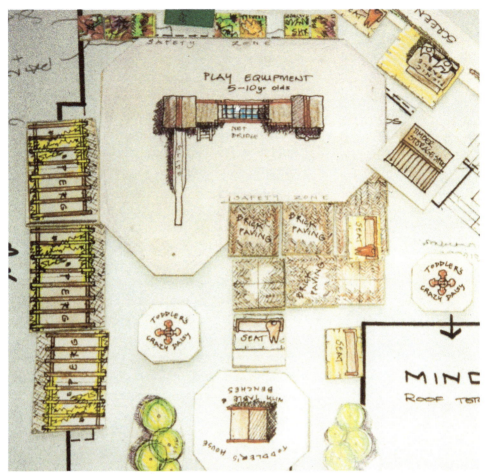

Park design
One resident group's design for a park showing layout of fencing, children's play facilities and planting.

Comparing options
Discussion of layouts prepared by different groups.

FURTHER INFORMATION

☞ Method: *Planning for Real.*

  Scenario: *Inner city regeneration.*

✆ *Good Practice Guide to Community Planning and Development. Participatory Design.*

☆ Alexandra Rook. Dee Stamp. Michael Parkes. Henry Sanoff.

Design workshop

Design workshops are hands-on sessions allowing small groups of professionals and non-professionals to work creatively together developing planning and design ideas. Often known as 'charrettes'. They will normally be held as part of a planning day or other community planning event.

Hands-on
Residents and architects devise improvements to a housing estate together.

Report back
Participant explains design workshop outcome to a plenary session.

"Brief intensive brainstorming workshops can be enormously productive – people of mixed backgrounds, grouped together for the first time, with clear challenges, find that they can focus their minds and tap hidden reservoirs of creativity."
Jack Sidener, Professor of Architecture, Chinese University of Hong Kong workshop brief, 1998.

■ People work in groups around a table with plans or a flexible model. Different groups can deal with different areas or the same area at different scales. Groups can be allocated a topic such as transport, open spaces or housing. Groups can vary in size (8–10 is a good average to aim at).

■ Everyone is encouraged to develop their ideas by drawing or making adjustments to the model. Each group usually needs a facilitator, a note-taker and a mapper (who marks points on a map or plan).

■ A structured workshop procedure is often followed, especially if people have not worked together before (☞ sample format opposite).

✎ Using plans is often more suitable than models because little preparation is needed. People generally find it surprisingly easy to read plans once they have started working with them. It helps though if the facilitator has previous experience of design workshops and urban design expertise.

✎ Design workshops often work best if people have done a briefing workshop first (☞ *Briefing workshop*).

✎ Get people going by telling them that "no idea is too big, no idea too small". At the end everyone should sign drawings and it is often useful to draw up a tidy version for presentation.

$ Main costs: planning and preparation; facilitator's fees; supplies (see box, right).

Creative working
Participants use tracing paper over a plan, mini Post-it notes and felt-tip pens to explore options for an inner city neighbourhood. Most have no previous design experience.

Design workshop format
Sample to suit most contexts.

1 Arrangements
People choose a workshop group and sit round tables with plan or model. (5 mins)

2 Introductions
People briefly introduce themselves. (10 mins)

3 Getting started
Facilitator asks people to write ideas on mini Post-it notes or cards and place them on the plan. Responses to questions such as:
• Where are the problems?
• Where are the opportunities?
• Where do you want things to happen?
(15 mins)

4 Design ideas
People use coloured pens to sketch ideas, discussing things as they do so. Different options can be drawn on separate sheets of tracing paper. (50 mins)

5 Prepare summary
Summary drawings prepared of main suggestions. (10 mins)

Running time: 90 mins.
Ideal numbers: 8–10 per workshop.

Design workshop supplies

On table
☐ Base plan of area.
☐ Tracing paper overlays (large sheets and A4 pads) taped with masking tape.
☐ Felt-tip coloured pens. Different colours.
☐ Mini Post-it notes or small cards.
☐ Ball point pens or pencils (one per person).
☐ Lined A4 writing pads (2 per group).

To one side
☐ Flipchart and marker pens.
☐ Pin-up space (Blu-tack or pins needed).
☐ Attendance sheets.
☐ Site photographs.

If using model
☐ Base model with movable parts.
☐ Spare cardboard or polystyrene.
☐ Scissors.
☐ Post-it notes and cocktail sticks.

FURTHER INFORMATION

☞ Methods: *Community planning event. Briefing workshop. Planning day. Planning weekend. Planning for Real.*

Development trust

Sample promotion leaflet
Key components: name of organisation; what it can do; how people can get involved; slogan summarising aim.

"The strength of development trusts is that they can demonstrate the creativity and added competence that comes from bringing together expertise and enthusiasm from public, private, voluntary and community sectors."
David Wilcox
The Guide to Development Trusts and Partnerships, 1998.

Development trusts and community land trusts provide a mechanism for communities to undertake regeneration and development projects themselves. They make it possible to achieve the long-term sustained effort that is needed to evolve a community's own plans and put them into action.

■ Development trusts are community-based organisations working for the regeneration of their areas. They may undertake a specific project or, more likely, a range of economic, environmental, cultural or social initiatives.

■ Development trusts are independent bodies with management structures ensuring accountability to local people. They are not-for-profit bodies, often with charitable status, making it possible to attract resources from public, private and charitable sectors.

■ Administrative structures are designed to allow development trusts to own and manage property, employ staff and develop efficient project management capability.

✎ Funding is easiest to secure at the outset in the form of grants from government and local authority regeneration budgets. The challenge is to build up a secure asset base, some committed sponsors and income generating capacity before grants expire. Having a linked trading company is often useful to make it possible to earn income without losing charity status.

✎ Having a clear focus, based on local priorities, is important to attract support. Select a name, slogan and style to reflect this.

$ Essential core costs: manager's wages, premises, office running. Desirable to have several staff and a project seed fund. Aim at $150,000 per annum but be prepared to start with volunteers.

Typical development trust activities

- ☐ Administering grant schemes
- ☐ Building and managing affordable housing
- ☐ Building and managing workspace
- ☐ Developing community plans
- ☐ Environmental education programmes
- ☐ Facilitating community planning activity
- ☐ Holding training programmes
- ☐ Organising competitions
- ☐ Organising events
- ☐ Preserving historic buildings
- ☐ Promoting community development
- ☐ Providing sports and recreational facilities
- ☐ Running childcare centres
- ☐ Running award schemes
- ☐ Running resource centres
- ☐ Setting up and managing arts facilities
- ☐ Setting up community enterprises
- ☐ Supporting community groups
- ☐ Supporting small businesses

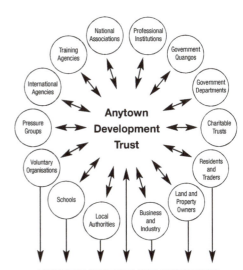

ACTION FOR IMPROVING THE ENVIRONMENT

Concept
Bringing together national, regional and local agencies – in the public, private and voluntary sectors – to promote action by local people to improve the environment.

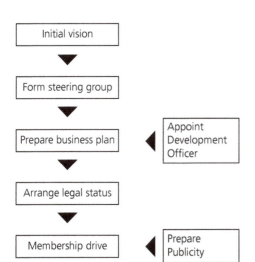

Setting up
The main steps. Likely to take at least one year.

Typical democratic management structure
Elected local members have a majority on the Board to ensure local accountability. Elections are usually held annually with members serving two years each.

FURTHER INFORMATION

☞ Scenarios: *Inner city regeneration. Local neighbourhood initiative. Urban conservation*

✉ Locality.

🖳 Community Land Trust Network.

📀 *The Guide to Development Trusts and Partnerships.*

Diagrams

Diagrams and charts are a highly effective visual way to collect, discuss and display information at all stages of the planning process.

Venn diagram
Showing relationships between village institutions.

Mind map
Showing perceptions of trends and linkages.

- Individuals or groups use the construction of diagrams as a basis for gathering and analysing information. Fairly complex issues or processes can be represented simply if the right type of diagram is chosen.

- The diagrams provide a focus for discussing issues – by both literate and non-literate people – and help stimulate creative thinking.

- The diagrams are used for ordering and presenting information, prioritising issues, decision making and monitoring.

- Making diagrams can form part of a workshop or be undertaken as an activity in its own right. A group diagramming process is similar to a group mapping process (☞ Mapping).

✎ If diagrams are made on the ground, photograph or draw them to keep a record.

✎ Involve people who are particularly knowledgeable, and involve as many others as possible. Facilitators should sit back and watch, not interfere too much.

✎ Minimise text. Use colour coding, symbols and local materials wherever possible.

$ Few expenses necessary. Main cost: facilitators' fees. May be worth spending money on materials to improve presentation.

Calendar
Showing seasonal changes in work patterns by plotting people's activities on a monthly basis.

Matrix
Assessing the value of different tree species by placing stones to score various attributes.

Network diagram
Identifying institutional changes needed by plotting flows and links between villages.

Common diagram types and their uses

- **Calendar.** For understanding seasonal patterns, eg planting, tourism or rainfall.

- **Flow diagram.** Showing the components of any activity and the linkages between them. For understanding the impact of an initiative.

- **Matrix.** Grid allowing comparison of two variables. Used for assessing options and prioritising.

- **Mind map.** Showing people's perceptions of trends and linkages. Used for collective brainstorming to develop a common outlook.

- **Network diagram.** Showing flows and linkages between people, organisations or places. Used for highlighting strengths and weaknesses in institutional relationships.

- **Organisation chart.** Showing who is responsible for what. Used for understanding how organisations work.

- **Pie chart.** Dividing a circle into different sized segments. For showing population structure, distances to work and so on.

- **Time-line.** List of events over time. For understanding historical trends.

- **Timetable.** For analysing regular routines, street activity and so on.

- **Venn diagram.** Using circles of different sizes to indicate roles of different organisations and the relationships between them.

FURTHER INFORMATION

☞ Methods: *Community profiling. Mapping.*

ⓐ *Participatory Learning & Action.*

Door knocking

Door knocking is a basic, and often overlooked, way for beginning to build up a picture of the property, activities and people in an area prior to developing an engagement strategy for a planning initiative. Particularly useful for consultants or developers unfamiliar with the area.

Direct engagement
Semi-structured interview being conducted with a local businessman.

Dear resident,

We are considering how to make best use of land our company owns in Anyplace and would like to get your views.

The land we own is shown on the attached plan.

Any proposals will need to be commercially viable and comply with Anyplace Local Plan. As a first step we are inviting you to have a discussion with our Community Planning Team or complete and return the attached questionnaire. The Team will be knocking on doors in your area from anydate to alaterdate and will also be contactable by phone or email.

When we have a clearer understanding of local views our architects will sketch out draft proposals and organise an event where there will be an opportunity for you to discuss them and provide further feedback.

We must stress that making comments at this stage will not affect your right to make formal representations to the planning authority in due course.

If you have any queries or would like to arrange a time for a discussion, please telephone 44448888 or email any@communityplanner.any

Yours sincerely

Director
Any Development Company

- A simple questionnaire is produced together with an introductory letter explaining who you are and why you are conducting the exercise.

- Doors to be knocked on are identified on a map. This may be all properties within a certain boundary or a sample selection of properties.

- Door knocking team members knock on doors and conduct semi-structured interviews with occupants if convenient. If not, or if nobody answers the door, the introductory letter is left together with a copy of the questionnaire.

- A report on the results is produced to decide on the next stage which might be a more rigorous survey or a community planning event of some kind.

✎ Let local politicians, community engagement officers and the police know what you are doing in advance to reassure them that it is legitimate and prevent them jumping to the wrong conclusions.

✎ Get anyone who is likely to be working on the project in the future to assist as it will be an invaluable experience for them.

Sample doorknocking letter
From a land owner or developer to local residents.
A similar version could be drafted for local businesses

✎ If you want to use the results as statistical evidence of local views, comprehensive coverage or a carefully defined sample is essential. Otherwise attempt to cover a range of property types and locations and do not attempt to claim that the results have statistical significance.

✎ You may need public liability insurance (not expensive) and Criminal Record Bureau (CRB) clearance if going into schools. Check requirements locally.

$ Can be very time consuming both doing door knocking and analysing the results. Largely proportional to numbers of people spoken with.

FURTHER INFORMATION

☞ Methods: *Community profiling.*

Glossary: *Semi-structured interview.*

☆ Jane Freund, Roland Karthaus, Ian Pankhurst, Pat Willoughby.

Questionnaire – The Future of Anyplace

This questionnaire has been produced on behalf of Any Development Company to seek local views before producing development proposals for land which the company owns. Please respond to the questions below or let us have any other thoughts. Use additional sheets or send a letter or email if you prefer. An electronic version of this questionnaire can be supplied if requested.

GENERAL

1 What do you **like** about Anyplace?

2 What do you **dislike** about Anyplace?

3 What would **improve** Anyplace?

ANY SITE (see map showing boundary)

4 What could be provided on Anysite that would make Anyplace better?

5 What concerns would you have about any development taking place on Anysite?

6 Please rate the following uses for Anysite

	Strongly Preferred	Preferred	No Opinion	Undesirable	Very Undesirable
Housing	☐	☐	☐	☐	☐
Offices	☐	☐	☐	☐	☐
Recreation	☐	☐	☐	☐	☐
Wildlife	☐	☐	☐	☐	☐
Etc	☐	☐	☐	☐	☐

7 Please rate the following possible locations for development on Anysite.

	Strongly Preferred	Preferred	No Opinion	Undesirable	Very Undesirable
Near the main road	☐	☐	☐	☐	☐
By the river	☐	☐	☐	☐	☐
Near to Anybuilding	☐	☐	☐	☐	☐
Spread out over the site	☐	☐	☐	☐	☐

8 Any other comments and information.

ABOUT YOU (optional - but please complete if you want to be kept informed directly)

How long have you lived or worked in Anyplace? ___ years
Your age group (please circle) 0-19 20-34 35-49 50-64 65+

Name _____

Address _____

Email _____ Tel _____

Many thanks for your time. Please return completed forms and direct any queries to: The community planning team, etc

Sample doorknocking questionnaire

Record Sheet				
Date	Time	Address	Action	Notes
			I = interview L= left pack	eg return visit arranged, name(s)

Sample doorknocking record sheet

Draft plan consultation

Consulting on draft plans and proposals is an important step to test whether they have public support and to engage people in finalising them. It can help focus the design process and be an ideal opportunity to generate good ideas. The method can be used for building design, landscaping or producing plans at all scales.

- Draft plans are presented as clearly as possible using text and graphics.

- Suitable communication mediums are selected; this will often be a wall mounted exhibition, a printed brochure and a webpage equivalent.

- Feedback mechanisms are established; this will often be asking for responses to specific questions and an opportunity for open ended responses.

- A report is produced setting out the consultation results and the proposals are amended accordingly.

- Feedback is provided to those consulted with on how their input has affected the amended scheme.

✎ Invest in high quality graphic design and editing. Communicating proposals clearly and concisely is vital if people are to be able to engage effectively.

✎ Avoid too much text. Background details and technical material can be made available separately at events and on the internet.

✎ Avoid keys on maps. Bubbles with pointers are generally much easier to follow.

Week 1
Consultation strategy meeting
Plan deemed ready to be consulted on by Steering Group / Neighbourhood Forum / local authority / developer. Agree concept of events and publicity methods.

Weeks 2–4
Consultation materials
Events plan and brochure design produced by engagement team. Draft Plan fine tuned by design team.

Week 5
Production
Brochure printing, website construction

Week 7
Brochure distribution
To all households, businesses, key stakeholders and media

Weeks 11–13
Events
Exhibition /open house /open days / workshop

Week 14
Interviews
Sample face to face interviews with a carefully selected sample of the public to test validity of self-completion questionnaire results.

Weeks 15–18
Response analysis
Analyse feedback from questionnaires

Weeks 19–23
Amend plan

Week 26
Circulate revised plan
With explanation of how consultation has influenced it. Full report on consultation results made available for those interested.

Note: Timing will depend on complexity of plan and efficiency of design team.

Sample timetable
for consultation on a draft plan

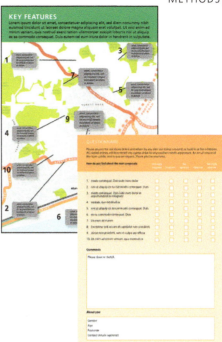

Anywhere

DRAFT PLAN

Your views wanted

WHAT
A new town centre plaza above the tracks at the train station.

WHY
To link the two sides of the town and increase passenger capacity.

WHEN
Within 5 years.

EXHIBITION
9.00 to 18.00
10 to 14 March, Shopping centre.

OPEN DAY – ALL WELCOME
11.00 to 16.00
Saturday 15 March
Shopping centre atrium.
Meet the design team. Have your questions answered.

MORE INFORMATION
Email: enquiry@anyconsultation.any
Web: www.anyconsultation.any
Tel: 0444 778899

A ANYWHERE COUNCIL | Anywhere Development Agency | Anywhere Community Forum | *any* consultants

---

Sample consultation brochure
Illustrating the key components of a 4 page A4 document with tear off questionnaire. 6 page A4 can also work well and provides more space for explaining the proposals.

Page 1 - *What the consultation is about, why it is interesting, who is conducting it, how people can get involved, further information sources.*

Page 2 - *Draft plan details and main issues summarised.*

Page 3 - *Questionnaire with tick box questions relating to main issues, space for open ended comment and collection of personal data for analysis purposes.*

Page 4 *(not shown)* - *Freepost address details.*

✎ Allow plenty of time for producing consultation materials; the process of producing them is likely to lead to design team members fine-tuning their ideas.

✎ Acrobat PDF editing is a useful tool for allowing production team members to be involved in developing consultation materials.

$ The brochure is used as a focus for the consultation process and serves many functions simultaneously. Despite the cost of printing (preferably in colour) it can often be cost effective.

$ Savings can be made by using the same images and design elements for an exhibition, and by using the same software to analyse the questionnaire and face to face interviews.

$ Main costs: brochure design; brochure printing; brochure distribution; questionnaire analysis; face to face interviews

FURTHER INFORMATION

☞ Scenario: *Neighbourhood development plan.*

☆ Jeremy Brook, Mike Ebbs, Keith Gillies, Clive Jacotine.

Electronic map

Electronic maps allow people to explore an area and make comments from computer terminals or mobile devices. They have immense potential for helping people to visualise proposals and make their views known.

Digital age participation
Finding out what is going on in your neighbourhood and making your views known at a computer terminal.

"Mapping for change provides mapping, geographical analysis and community engagement services for all types of projects and entities. We transform an organisation through the power of the map."
Mapping for Change,
website home page, 2013.

"Participatory Avenues acts as focal point for sharing lessons learned and innovation in practicing ethically-conscious community mapping and participatory GIS as means to add value and authority to people's spatial knowledge and improve bottom up communication."
Participatory Avenues,
website home page, 2013.

- Electronic maps are created as software which can be run on desk-top computers, touch screen monitors or on a website.

- Aerial photography, maps, video clips, sounds, photos and 3-dimensional visualisations can all be incorporated to build up a series of images of an area from a variety of perspectives.

- People can explore the map at computer terminals in libraries, cafes and cultural centres and add their own comments.

- The maps can be continually adapted to provide an ongoing information service and consultation process.

✎ Great potential for linking up with maps in different areas and for accessing via the Internet.

✎ Gathering the content for maps is itself a part of the exploration and participation process.

$ Developing software from scratch could cost as much as US$80,000. But it is now possible to purchase software under license for a few hundred dollars. So cost is reduced to gathering the raw material for your map. This could cost around US$15,000 or much less if you use material already available.

Exploring an early electronic map: a step by step example

1 Bird's eye view. Start with an aerial photo on screen. Use cursor keys to move about and to zoom in to the place you are interested in.

2 Map layers. Superimpose maps on the aerial photo or view them separately. Maps might include: regeneration initiatives (as shown), cultural facilities, proposed new buildings.

3 Street level walkabout. Click on a place you want to view and it fills the screen. It may be a photograph, drawing, photomontage or model of how it could be. Click arrows to move about.

4 Video clips. See live action through video clips. This might include presentations, art works, interviews with people (as shown), street scenes, performances.

5 Comment. See and hear what other people think. Add your own comment by typing or speaking.

FURTHER INFORMATION

☞ Method: *Mapping. The Internet.*
    Scenario: *New neighbourhood.*

☆ Example based on a map of Hackney, London by Muf Architects and ShoeVegas for Hackney Council in 1999.

Elevation montage

Elevation montages show the facade of a street by assembling photos of individual buildings. They can be useful for helping people gain an understanding of the building fabric and devise improvements.

- An elevation of a street is created by assembling a series of individual photographs. Both sides of a street can be done and pasted either side of a plan.

- Simple instructions ask people to make comments on Post-it notes or cards and place them underneath the relevant section (what they like/don't like/would like to see).

- The build up of Post-it notes or cards generates a dialogue amongst participants and useful data for later discussion and analysis.

Wall-mounted
Residents pasting Post-it notes on a wall-mounted montage.

Detail of above with comment.

- Table-mounted displays make it possible to have both sides of a street opposite each other on a plan. Wall mounted displays only work if it does not matter treating both sides separately.

- Useful debates can take place around the exhibit. Keep a notepad or tape recorder handy.

- Very useful as an ice-breaker at the beginning of a workshop, and as a visual prompt for all participants during a workshop. Also useful as part of an open house event.

$ Main costs: printing photographs. Preparation time (2 person days).

Advantages of elevation montages

- Good icebreaker at the beginning of workshop sessions

- Helps participants and design professionals gain a visual understanding of the environment they are dealing with.

- Secures the views of people lacking the confidence to speak in group discussions.

- Can be left as part of an unmanned exhibition over a period of time.

Disadvantages

- Can be costly to prepare and may not be cost-effective compared with other methods.

Tips on montage making

✎ Stand the same distance from the building line when taking all photos unless there are setbacks in the buildings, when you should move closer.

✎ If relating to a plan, then it is best to mount the montage on a long table. If on a wall, then one elevation will be upside down.

✎ Digital mapping which can be re-scaled is useful for adjusting the plan to fit the elevation.

✎ The plan is more understandable if photos are placed directly on the building line.

✎ Elevations are more understandable if photos are stuck together so that shop signs are readable even if there is some mismatch at roof level.

Table-mounted
Photomontages as part of a workshop aimed at generating urban design proposals.

FURTHER INFORMATION

☞ Methods: *Interactive display. Open house event. Photo survey.*

☆ Julie Withers, Kathryn Anderson, Roger Evans Associates.

Energy fair

Energy fairs help members of the general public find out about saving and generating energy. They provide a way for people to engage with installers and suppliers of the necessary equipment and to find out about funding mechanisms. A similar process can be useful for many complex technical issues where every individual's circumstances are slightly different.

- People are invited to attend a drop-in event where the possibilities for saving and generating energy are presented as clearly and simply as possible and where they will have the opportunity to discuss their personal options with experts and specialists.

- Specialist suppliers and technical experts take stalls where they display their wares and hold discussions with participants.

- Participants may be provided with the option of signing up for funding and installation schemes.

✎ If large numbers of participants are required hold the event in a supermarket lobby or town centre plaza. But often the value will be in providing quality time for people to communicate in a space in which they feel comfortable; eg a local hall.

✎ 'Energy cafe' or 'energy breakfast' may also be useful alternative terms to attract people to attend.

$ Energy suppliers and installers will usually be prepared to participate free of charge so costs are: venue rental; display material; refreshments; marketing.

Come to our

Energy Fair

Friday 8 May &
Saturday 9 May 2015
13.00 to 17.00

Any Hall, Anyplace

Drop in when you can
Refreshments
Short presentation 14.30

Find out more about:
- Home insulation
- Community energy projects
- New energy generation and heating systems
- Your local energy plan

Meet local installers and suppliers:
Anywhere Energy
Solar PV
Heat pumps R us
Bio energy solutions

Organisers:
Anywhere Energy CIC

Sample advertising leaflet.
Key components: venue; time; date; questions that will be answered; who will be there; name/s of organisers.

"Community engagement in the energy sector will be vital to our vision of the development of energy in the UK in the coming decades."
Greg Barker, Minister of State for Energy and Climate Change, *Community Energy Online, January 2013.*

Energy fair activities

For small scale event in local neighbourhood hall or similar. Customise.

☐ **Community buildings audit.** Reduce the energy use of schools, community halls, etc.

☐ **Draught proofing workshop.** Encourage residents to work together to draught proof their homes.

☐ **Energy monitors.** Buy one to share with neighbours.

☐ **Energy suppliers.** What are the options?

☐ **Feedback.** What do people think about this event? What else would be useful?

☐ **Funding scheme info.** Grants and loans available, simply explained.

☐ **Further information sources.** Local, national, websites.

☐ **Home energy efficiency measures.** How much energy and money is saved by: changing boiler; changing fuel; changing lighting; insulating; draught-proofing; composting; etc.

☐ **Installers displays.** biogas; heat pumps; solar panels; wood stoves; wind turbines.

☐ **LED lighting demonstration.** Benefits of changing to Light-Emitting Diode fittings.

☐ **Jargon buster.** Technical terms explained.

☐ **Local energy plan draft.** Short, medium and long-term plans for saving and generating energy. Interactive displays.

☐ **Property survey form.** To find out about your energy use and potential for savings.

☐ **Refreshments.** Constant supply. Table and chairs if space.

☐ **Renewable energy generation.** Options available with explanatory illustrations and models.

☐ **Sign up desk.** For property survey, more info on funding, be on mailing list.

☐ ....

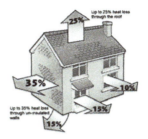

Simple explanatory diagrams
How our houses lose heat...

Supplier stall
Demonstrating the range of heat pumps available to a local resident at an 'energy cafe' in a village hall.

FURTHER INFORMATION

☞ Scenario: *Energy saving and generation.*

🖥 Website: Energy Saving Trust.

☆ Ollie Pendered, Communities Matter. Richard Watson, Energise Sussex Coast. Jane Freund.

E-voting

E-voting makes it possible to get instant and accurate feedback on people's views during a meeting or workshop event, or from dispersed locations. It can be useful at many stages in the planning process, particularly when statistical evidence is required of people's preferences. Emerging technologies make e-voting (including 'instant polling' or 'audience response systems') easier and more affordable than ever before.

- E-voting can be used at events with any number of participants or with a virtual audience.

- Participants are asked to respond to questions, where simple choices are required, using a handheld device. This can be a purpose made keypad, a tablet or smart phone, or even a simple mobile phone as long as it has texting capability.

- Specially designed and readily available software analyses the results and makes them available instantly to the organisers and participants.

- The results are used to inform the next stages in the process, for instance providing the basis for discussion in small or large groups.

✎ Use professional consultants or technically competent volunteers to run e-voting during an event.

✎ Start with a few fun questions to get people used to voting. Older and less tech-savvy participants may need help learning to use the technology, so be patient and allow time for this.

Fingers on buzzers
Meeting participants vote and can see how everyone else has voted moments later.

Supplies
Handheld polling devices and resource information, but also pads and pens in case of technical breakdown.

✎ Always have a back-up plan. Even if you test the system, technology can fail. Be prepared to entertain the group while someone troubleshoots, or to abandon the technology altogether and use a different method.

✎ The quality of the results will depend on the quality of the questions. Write and revise questions carefully and be sure to try them out with a test group before a live event.

✎ Choose an e-voting system that best fits your needs or mix and match them to reach a wider audience.

$ Main costs: administration; consultants; equipment and software. Keypad polling can be expensive and purchasing a system is not an option for most organisations. Renting or loaning may be possible. Cell phone voting is significantly cheaper.

FURTHER INFORMATION

💻 Websites: *Planning Tool Exchange (see Keypad Polling and Mobile Polling).*

☆ Rebecca Sanborn Stone, The Orton Family Foundation

How long have you lived in Anycounty?

1. Less than 1 year — 1. 7%
2. 1 to 5 years — 2. 18%
3. 5 to 10 years — 3. 17%
4. 11 to 20 years — 4. 26%
5. 21 to 40 years — 5. 22%
6. 41 to 60 years — 6. 9%
7. More than 60 years — 7. 1%

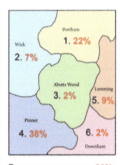

In which parish do you work or go to school?

(if you are retired or not employed vote 7)

1. 22%
2. 7%
3. 2%
4. 38%
5. 9%
6. 2%
7. retired or not employed 20%

Polling results
Sample Powerpoint slides which illustrate how users can gather and present information on demographics, location, opinions and many other topics.

Environment shop

Local environment shops provide a permanent way to disseminate information and create dialogue. They can be independent outfits or part of a local regeneration agency or community centre.

■ Ideally, a shop premises in a prominent location with a large window area is chosen, perhaps with offices behind or above. Alternatively, an open air stall or spare space in a building is used.

■ The shop combines the sale of useful material on environmental improvement with displays and information on local initiatives and projects.

■ The shop provides a first port of call for local people on how they can improve their environment, and perhaps a public face and reception area for a local regeneration agency or community centre as well.

✎ Setting up can take time and be complicated but, once established, shops can easily be manned by volunteers. Start with a small range of stock and build up slowly.

✎ Once up and running, shop material can easily be taken out to local festivals, markets and conferences.

✎ If 'Environment shop' is not the right name for your area try 'Regeneration shop', 'Conservation shop', etc.

$ Main need is for capital to purchase stock and display fittings. 'Sale or return' terms can be arranged for many items but requires more administration. Don't expect environment shops to make large profits although they can bring in useful income. Their value is as a local resource and in helping an agency get its act together (by putting it on show). If well organised they can ultimately relieve pressure on agency staff by allowing people to help themselves.

Visit our
Environment Shop

For information and advice on how to improve your environment

*Books • T-shirts
Leaflets • Posters • Gifts
Noticeboards • Postcards
Guides • Window stickers
Resource packs • Videos
Education packs*

**20 High Street, Anytown
Open Mon to Sat, 10am to 5pm**

Mobile shop
*We can arrange a stall at your local event.
Call for details.*

Sample promotion leaflet

Shop interior
Bird's eye view photo of neighbourhood; display boards on local projects; publications for loan or sale; somewhere to sit. (Not all shops need to be as smart and tidy as this one.)

Environment shop stock

Books, pamphlets, videos, manuals, postcards, models, T-shirts relating to:
- [ ] **Building** – how-to-do-it information on local vernacular building and architecture.
- [ ] **General merchandise** – to attract people in (eg environmental T-shirts, local crafts).
- [ ] **Local interest** – items on past, present and future of local environment.
- [ ] **Regeneration generally** – how-to-do-it material on community regeneration.
- [ ] **Visitor information** – items specifically for visitors to the area.
- [ ] ....

Benefits of shops

- Addition to local trading environment.
- Helps agencies to become user friendly by displaying what they can offer.
- Helps people to help themself rather than be dependent on development workers.
- Provides outlet for local publishers.
- Raises profile of local environmental issues and projects.
- Source of revenue for community development organisations (long-term).

Environment shop features

- [ ] **Bird's-eye view photograph** of local area (very useful for discussing issues and always a popular attraction, especially if lit up at night and visible from the street).
- [ ] **Community noticeboard** for job ads, competitions, events.
- [ ] **Magazine rack** for periodicals.
- [ ] **Model** of local area and developments.
- [ ] **Project information board** for info on local regeneration projects.
- [ ] **Reception desk** for info, access to project, purchasing items.
- [ ] **Reference library** for items not for sale.
- [ ] **Seating area** for reading and chatting.
- [ ] **Window display** promoting merchandise.
- [ ] **Window noticeboard** with constantly changing posters on local activities.
- [ ] ....

FURTHER INFORMATION

☞ Methods. *Architecture centre. Community design centre. Neighbourhood planning office.* Scenario: *Urban conservation.*

☆ Photo: Edinburgh World Heritage Trust.

Feasibility fund

Feasibility funds provide money to community organisations for paying experts to undertake feasibility studies on possible projects. They are a highly effective way of kick-starting local initiatives, by getting projects to a stage where they can attract capital funding and support.

- A Fund is established by a professional institute or other suitable local, regional or national organisation. Sponsors might include companies, local authorities, government departments or charities.

- The scheme is advertised and community groups are invited to apply for funding.

- Grants are awarded and feasibility studies undertaken. The study will establish whether the ideas are workable, the best options and the costs.

- If projects succeed in attracting capital funding, the grant money is repaid to the organising body.

✎ Grants need not be large to be effective. Depending on the nature of the project, US$1,500–5,000 is usually enough to enable a group to produce a highly professional study. The Fund can offer the total amount or a proportion.

✎ Money is not the only benefit. The award of a grant can also be a tremendous boost to community organisations, providing confidence and credibility.

✎ Award schemes are a good way of generating case study material for exchanging good practice.

$ An initial tranche of funding is required to establish the fund and operate it for a few years. Once up and running, quite a high proportion may eventually be paid back.

If you need professional advice to get started on a community project

BUT

Can't afford the fees

THEN CONTACT

The Community Projects Fund
Institute of Architects
High Street, Anytown
000 111 22222

"A helping hand at the initial stage has been to us what the first steps are to a child, and today we are walking tall."
Celeste Nre, Wandsworth Black Elderly Project, UK
RIBA Report, 1995.

"The Fund satisfies a growing demand for communities to get involved and have a say in generating something for themselves."
Ian Finlay, Chair, RIBA Community Projects Fund
Report 1986.

Fact: A feasibility fund run by the Royal Institute of British Architects triggered US$160 million for 150 projects over 12 years from an outlay of less than $2.4 million.

Feasibility fund
Types of projects funded

- ☐ **Community centres.** New build, or improvements. In urban and rural areas.
- ☐ **Community plans.** Plans for a site or neighbourhood, perhaps as alternatives to those existing.
- ☐ **Education facilities.** Schools, creches, heritage centres, art centres.
- ☐ **Employment initiatives.** Creating workspace or improved facilities.
- ☐ **Housing.** Renovations or improvements on estates, self build schemes, new housing for rent.
- ☐ **Landscaping.** Improvements to public areas: play areas, parks, streetscape, city farms, artworks.
- ☐ **Leisure facilities.** Sports halls, youth clubs, cultural centres.

Feasibility study
A Cultural Centre for Anytown

Prepared for the Anytown Forum
by Hope Architects and Planners

Contents
Summary
Background history
The proposal
Site conditions
Design options
Legal and planning
Organisation
Timetable of activity
Costings
Funding sources
Appendices
  Press cuttings
  Survey results

Study supported by the National Feasibility Fund for Community Projects

Sample cover
Good feasibility studies are one of the most effective ingredients for getting projects to happen.

Application form

Please read the Fund Guidelines before completing.

Name of organisation _____

Legal status (community group, charity, etc)

_____

Contact details _____

_____

Do you have a constitution? (if so attach copy)

_____

Brief description of organisation and activities

_____

How is the community involved in the organisation _____

How many people are involved? Employed ☐
Management committee ☐   Voluntary ☐
Other (specify)_____

Project title _____

Description of project _____

Why do you want to undertake the project?

_____

Who will benefit from the project?_____

What will the feasibility study cover?

_____

How much will the study cost? $ _____

Who will do it? (name and contact details)

_____

Other possible sources of income for the study

_____

Please submit a photo of the building or site and a copy of your latest annual report and accounts.

FURTHER INFORMATION

☞ Scenarios: *Community centre, Regeneration infrastructure.*

Field workshop

Field workshops are a way for local communities to draw up plans of action where there is little data available to start with. They are particularly suited to disaster prevention work in developing countries.

■ Field workshops involve a team of technical experts working closely with a handful of local facilitators, local officials and many local residents of all ages, backgrounds and interests.

■ A programme of activities lasting several days or even weeks is prepared in advance involving community profiling, risk assessment and plan making methods. The programme is agreed in advance by all parties but may be varied at any point to allow for results to be built on and developed.

■ The aim is to develop a common understanding of the nature of the community, the issues faced and possible solutions.

■ The technical team presents its recommendations to the whole community a few days after the main activity sessions and then lodges them with local policy makers.

✎ Technical team members need to be sensitive to local cultures. Ask permission before taking photos or taping interviews and liaise closely with local policymakers.

Evolving a common view
Group working. Informal walk. Model making. Mapping.

$ Planning a field workshop carefully in advance is essential if money is to be spent effectively. Materials need not cost much. The main costs will be people's time and accommodation and travel for the team.

Sample field workshop format
Example: Village suffering from typhoons.

DAY 1

08.00–08.10	**Ice breaker.** Music. Dance.
08.10–10.00	**Introductions.** Participants introduce themselves. Aims and process explained.
10.00–12.00	**Personal history.** A few participants tell their history.
12.00–13.00	**Historical profile.** Key events listed in date order.
14.00–16.00	**Map drawing.** Large map of village drawn on paper.
16.00–17.00	**Photo game.** Photos of all buildings (taken previously) located on map. Discussion.
18.30–21.00	**Social.** Music and dinner.
21.00–23.00	**Review session.** Day's activities reviewed. Plans revised if necessary.

DAY 2

07.00–08.00	**Review** of Day 1.
09.30–12.00	**Interviews.** Key public figures explain their roles and are questioned.
09.00–13.00 Group A	**Model making.** Model made of village showing hills, rivers, valleys and other main features.
09.00–13.00 Group B	**Map making.** Map made showing different house types (eg concrete, bamboo, mud, timber).
14.00–16.00	**Simulation exercise.** Disaster simulated to understand people's reactions. (eg to typhoon)
16.30–17.30	**Damage classification.** Models and maps used to classify extent of damage (total destruction, damage to roof, partial damage, etc)
19.00–21.00	**Review and planning.** Review of activities and process. Schedule revised.

DAY 3

08.30–12.00	**Reconnaissance.** Of buildings and sites identified in previous day's review.
09.00–12.00	**Interviews.** With key officials and politicians (by some).
13.00–16.00	**Review session.** For research team and facilitators. Information gathered so far structured using a matrix. Process reviewed.
13.00–20.00	**Construction workshop.** Scale models of houses built by local carpenters to identify structural problems. Queries by research team. Discussion.
15.00–19.00	**Gender workshop.** Participants divide into male and female groups. Analysis of different roles and responsibilities.
19.00–19.30	**Informal walk.** For research team and facilitators.

DAY 4

09.00–13.00	**Interviews.** Further questions to key figures.
09.00–13.00	**Construction workshop.** Continued.
09.00–13.00	**Gender workshop.** (cont.)
14.30–16.00	**Summary session.** Review of activities by research team.
14.30–16.00	**Next steps.** Workshop groups prepare list of recommendations.
19.00–24.00	**Social.** Dinner and music.

DAYS 5–9

All day	**Research and analysis.** Research team prepares report and presentation.

DAY 10

20.00–22.00	**Presentation.** Research team presents proposals to open community meeting.
	Ideal numbers: research team 4; facilitators 2; locals 20–50.

FURTHER INFORMATION

☞ Method: *Simulation.*

  Scenario: *Shanty settlement upgrading.*

⌁ *Reducing Risk.*

☆ Roger Bellers, Nick Hall.

Future search conference

Future search conferences are highly structured events, usually lasting 2.5 days, at which a cross-section of community members or 'stakeholders' create a shared vision for the future. They are more suited for dealing with general issues than specific sites.

Time lines
Participants create personal, community and global histories by writing key events on large strips of paper on the walls. This helps to make history visible, discover patterns and understand what the past means.

"I've not heard so many great ideas expressed in such a variety of clever and articulate ways... I don't know what benchmarks you use but by my lights this is the most useful, tangible, actionable output that I've ever seen."
Dennis Alter, Chairman & CEO, Advanta Corporation
Future Search Website intro, 1999.

"Staging a future search means changing our assumptions about large, diverse groups. In these meetings we learn that most people can bridge lines of culture, class, gender, ethnicity, power, status and hierarchy if they will work as peers on tasks of mutual concern."
Marvin Weisbord and Sandra Janoff
Future Search Website intro, 1999.

■ People representing the widest possible range of interests, or 'stakeholder' groups, are brought together in one room, usually for 2.5 days. The ideal number is considered to be 64 since this breaks down into 8 groups of 8. For larger groups, conferences can be run in parallel. The agenda is: 'The Future of _____ 5 to 20 years on'.

■ A highly structured 5-step procedure is adopted (as summarised in the sample timetable, right). This is designed to encourage people to think globally, focus on the future, identify common ground and make public commitments to action.

■ People carry out tasks individually, in small self-managed workshops and as a whole group.

■ The results are recorded openly on flipcharts.

✎ At least one experienced facilitator is essential plus a committed group to plan the event in advance and follow it up afterwards. The conference must be part of a wider and longer process.

✎ Discourage non-participating observers. All those present should take an active part.

$ Main costs: venue, meals and facilitation fees. Can range from US$4,000 to $60,000. $8,000–$16,000 is common.

Future Search Conference Timetable

Sample to use as a basis for designing your own.

DAY 1

13.00–18.00 Introduction.

Review the past
Participants explore key events in the histories of themselves, their community and the world, and present them on three time-lines.

Explore the present
Trends affecting the community are explored and illustrated by creating a mind map. Groups share what they are proud of and sorry about.

DAY 2

9.00–12.00 Continue with exploring the present.

12.00–18.00 **Create ideal futures**
Visions developed in small groups and acted out to everyone. Barriers to the visions identified.

Identify common ground
Shared vision identified, first by small groups and then by everyone. Projects to achieve it identified.

DAY 3

9.00–13.00 **Make action plans**
Projects planned by self-selected action groups. Public commitments to action.

Ideal numbers
64 (8 tables of 8).

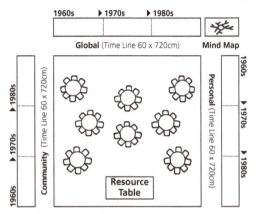

Ideal room layout
Eight tables with eight chairs per table; a resource table (for marker pens, notepads, etc); large sheets of paper on the walls for drawing three time-lines and a mind map.

Mind mapping
A large 'map' of present trends and linkages is created on the wall with coloured marker pens. Participants then fix sticky coloured dots onto those they think most important. This helps everybody focus on talking about the same issues. (☞p58 for mind map detail.)

FURTHER INFORMATION

☞ Scenario: *Whole settlement strategy.*

✎ *Future Search* (contains sample worksheets and checklists which are highly recommended).

✉ New Economics Foundation. Future Search Network.

Gaming

Games are a good way to help people understand the planning process and other people's viewpoints. They are also an enjoyable way to get people working together. They are particularly useful at an early stage of any community planning activity or to prepare people for a specific challenge ahead.

Board game
One way of discovering about the housing development process. The game uses hurdles, gates and tradeoffs which players negotiate as they proceed through the planning process. Designed to be played at the start of a planning workshop to inform and "break the ice" between participants (see the book Action Planning for Cities *for details).*

- Games are devised to mirror real life planning scenarios or to teach specific skills.

- The games are mostly played in groups, usually helped by a facilitator or someone who has played them before. Many games involve role play; people acting as if they were someone else.

- There is usually no specific output other than increased awareness but they may produce preliminary design proposals or an agenda for future initiatives needed.

Theatre
Powerful architect on stilts confronts a determined tenant in a performance on a housing estate designed to engage residents in conversation about their environment.

- When role playing, wearing badges with the name or title of the person being imitated and even suitable hats can help people feel at ease.

- Make people play someone with a very different role to themselves. For example, a planner could play being a poor child; a female tenant could play a male housing officer.

- Sometimes it can be interesting to have the person playing a role being advised by the real thing; ie the resident playing at being a planner being advised by a real planner.

- Games are good energisers and help overcome shyness.

$ Main costs in use: facilitator's fees. Developing and producing some games can be expensive in time and artwork.

Urban design role play game format

Format for a role play game allowing people to explore planning issues that may arise in the coming years.

1 Pick an issue
Facilitator introduces game and helps people to agree on an issue or site as the focus of the game (eg local transport improvements). (10 mins)

2 List interests
All the parties with an interest in, or affected by, the issue are listed on a flipchart (eg pedestrians, bus drivers, transport planners, cyclists, etc). (5 mins)

3 Give out roles
Everyone is given a role which is written on their name badge. (5 mins)

4 List desires and concerns
People think about what someone in the role they have been given would want. (10 mins)

5 Presentation
Everyone in turn presents their points to the whole group with visual explanation if possible. (20 mins)

6 Dealing
People mingle freely and attempt to make deals with each other. (30 mins)

7 Report back
Everyone reports back to the whole group on what they have achieved. (15 mins)

8 Next steps
General debate on how to take things forward. (15 mins)

Running time: 110 mins
Ideal numbers: 10–20 per workshop

Game types

Board games
Adaptations of popular board games to simulate planning and design scenarios.

Picture analysis
Getting people to say what they see in a picture and comparing notes.

Role play
Acting out being in someone else's shoes.

Storytelling
Reciting real or imaginary tales as a way of exploring hidden perceptions.

Theatre
Performing plays to characterise real life and stimulate debate.

Acting someone else's role
Local resident pretending to be a public official speaking at a planning hearing. Exercise designed to help residents deal better with a forthcoming hearing about their area.

FURTHER INFORMATION

☞ Method: *Simulation.*

⟳ *Action Planning for Cities. Participatory Learning and Action.*

☆ Urban design game format devised by Drew Mackie.

Have your say drop-in

Have your say drop-in events provide an opportunity for people to explore ideas on an issue or place and make their views known in an informal setting. Also described as Speak Outs or Community Planning Workshops, they are a useful early step in any planning activity.

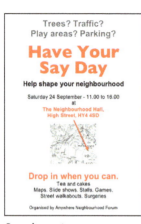

Sample poster
What, when, where, the issues

Sample 'A' board
What, when, where

- A convenient venue and time is selected, usually in a familiar local community facility, often as part of a larger community event.

- A range of interactive displays and activities is prepared to stimulate ideas and obtain feedback.

- The event is widely advertised and people are invited to drop in at any time during the scheduled opening hours.

- Results are written up and circulated to all who attended and made available on the internet.

✎ The same event can be repeated in different places, for instance different neighbourhoods in the same town. Make display material and signage portable.

✎ Encourage build up to the event by circulating a newsletter and perhaps a questionnaire.

✎ Allow plenty of time to set up and do a practice run.

✎ Worth having the event set up so that everything is visually self-explanatory. Facilitators are likely to get tied up in lengthy conversations.

✎ Be prepared to hold an impromptu workshop session if there is a critical mass of participants who want to debate.

$ Main costs: venue hire, display material, refreshments, recording and disseminating results.

FURTHER INFORMATION

☞ Methods: *Briefing workshop. Community planning forum. Open house event.*

ⓐ *SpeakOut.*

☆ Paul Barrett, Ian Coleman, Jane Freund, Mike Gibson

Wall says it all
Participants review material that has built up on the wall during the day.

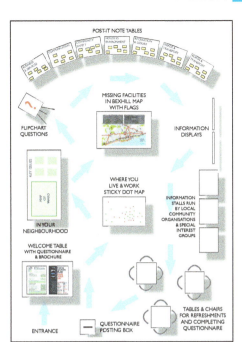

Event layout
An example event layout in a community hall.

Display and activity options checklist

☐ **Children's corner**
Give parents a break.

☐ **Decision board**
Vote on priorities using sticky dots.

☐ **Flipchart**
Respond to questions such as 'What I can do to help'. An alternative to post-it boards.

☐ **Mapping**
Identify things on maps and plans (missing facilities, resources, likes, dislikes, ideas for improvement, etc).

☐ **Opportunities**
Display or slide show with images from elsewhere.

☐ **Post-it boards**
Seek views on a range of topics (eg leisure, travel, facilities, likes, dislikes, ideas for improvement, etc).

☐ **Refreshments**
Tables for people to eat, drink, chat and complete questionnaires.

☐ **Stalls**
By local organisations showing what they can offer.

☐ **Surgery desks**
One to one conversations with local officials, councillors, professionals, specialists.

☐ **Walkabouts**
To look at local issues and features.

☐ **Welcome desk**
Information, survey forms, stickers, leaflets.

☐ **Where do you live and work?**
Put a sticky dot on the map (helps people orientate themselves, good icebreaker).

Ideas competition

Ideas competitions are a good way of stimulating creative thinking and generating interest and momentum. They can be designed to allow everyone a chance to put forward their ideas or be just for professionals.

■ Ideas competitions are normally held at the start of the development process or when there is opposition to a proposed scheme. They can be simple and immediate or highly complex.

■ A brief is produced, clearly setting out the task, entry format and deadline, judging procedure, eligibility and relevant background. The task can be to produce general ideas for improving an area or proposals for a specific site, building or problem.

■ Judging can done by a panel or through using a public voting system (see box, right). Alternatively different organisations can make separate awards.

■ Winning entries are widely publicised and published to secure momentum for implementation.

✎ Getting the public to judge entries encourages people to present better and provides credibility for the winning entries. If you have a judging panel, make sure it is not dominated by professionals.

✎ Specify a format which is accessible to non-professionals and easy to store and copy, eg A4 or A3 maximum. Models or large panels are good for exhibitions but difficult to keep, so photograph them properly. Think about publication from the outset.

$ Simple competitions for local sites can be organised very simply and cheaply. High profile competitions will involve considerable time and expense. Main costs: administration; publicity; prizes; publishing end results. Plenty of scope for sponsorship.

ANYTOWN 2050

Visions for Anytown Competition

Open competition for the best ideas for improving the environment of Anytown

What could be done to make your street, your neighbourhood, your town centre fit for the year 2050?

How can we create a new sense of vision to give our town a much needed boost?

Over £1000 in prizes to be won

Categories:
Under 8, 8-11, 12-17, 18-24, 25 and over.

Words, drawings, or photos on one sheet of A3 paper. Name, address and age on reverse. As many entries as you want.

Entries by 6 May to: Jumbo, 20 High Street.

Exhibition and judging by the general public all weekend on 7 and 8 May at the Hexagon.

The best ideas will be published in a special supplement of the local paper.

Organised by Anytown Forum in association with Darwin plc

Open ideas competition
Sample promotion leaflet.

Simple public judging rules

Register at the desk and get your sticky dots. Each person has three votes in each age category.

- ● Red = first choice (3 points)
- ● Yellow = second choice (2 points)
- ● Green = third choice (1 point)

Stick your dots on the entries.

The entries with the most points by 7pm win. Prizes to be presented by the Mayor at 7.30pm

Judging in public, by the public, on site
Passers-by use sticky dots to register their preferences for proposals for a derelict site which are pinned up on the site hoarding.

Standard format
Asking entrants to draw their proposals on prepared bird's eye view site outlines can help people make comparisons but may restrict creativity.

Two-stage competition format

Sample timetable for a fairly elaborate 2-stage competition combining an open competition for the public with a closed competition for professional teams.

Jan Preparation
Formation of co-ordinating body. Planning.

Mar Printing
Brief and publicity material.

April Launch
Widespread publicity. Detailed brief and conditions sent to those who respond.

July Stage 1 deadline
Stage 1 open to all with separate categories for professionals as well as for children.

Aug Public exhibition
Judging by public or panel. Small prizes.

Sept Stage 2 announced
Limited number of winning entrants provided with a budget to develop their schemes further.

Nov Stage 2 deadline

Dec Public exhibition
Judging by public or panel. Winners announced.

May Publication
Winning entries published.

FURTHER INFORMATION

☞ Scenarios: *Derelict site re-use. Regeneration infrastructure.*

✉ Architecture Centres Network. Royal Institute of British Architects.

Interactive display

Interactive displays allow people to engage in the issues and debate, on their own and in an enjoyable way, by making additions or alterations to pre-prepared exhibits.

Tools for participants
Post-it notes, sticky dots (several colours), coloured felt-tip pens and ballpoint pens.

Flip chart comment sheet
More visible than a book.

ISSUES / PROBLEMS

Cumulative comments
Adding points to those typed up from a previous workshop.

- Interactive displays can be used as part of a forum, workshop, exhibition, conference or other event.

- The displays can range from blank sheets with simple one-line questions to drawings or models of complex development proposals.

- A dynamic develops as people's comments build up on the displays over time.

- Thoughtful design is required to ensure that the information is presented simply and clearly and that people's responses are recorded in such a way that they can be used afterwards.

✎ Have facilitators on hand to help people get going. Once responses start to build up, the process develops its own momentum.

✎ Shop front or on-the-street venues work well as people are attracted by others taking part (☞ Street Stall).

✎ Photograph displays – or use other ways of recording them – before dismantling them.

$ Main costs: artwork and materials. Simple displays can be designed and prepared within a few minutes and need little equipment. Employing graphic or exhibition designers improves effectiveness immensely, particularly for getting responses to complex design ideas but will normally cost a considerable amount in fees.

Sticky dot display *Voting for liked and disliked buildings and spaces.*

Post-it board ideas

Headings for four blank boards which people can stick Post-it notes on (or use scraps of paper and drawing pins):

- What do you LIKE about the area?
- What do you DISLIKE about the area?
- What IMPROVEMENTS could be made?
- What can YOU do to help?

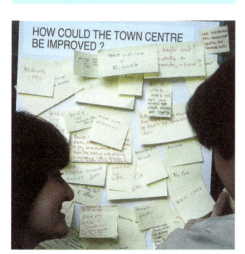

Post-it board *Comments build up in response to a simple question.*

Interactive display ideas

Verbal likes, dislikes and ideas
Put up large sheets of blank paper with suitable headings (see box, left) and get people to put their responses on Post-its.

Visual likes, dislikes and ideas
Ask people to mark their most and least favourite buildings and spaces on maps or photos using Post-its or sticky dots.

Comments on proposals
Get people's views on development proposals or options by placing sticky dots or Post-its on prepared cards linked to plans or drawings.
☞ *Table scheme display.*

General thoughts
Use flipcharts or comment books to get general comments.

FURTHER INFORMATION

☞ Methods: *Community planning forum. Elevation montage. Open house event. Street stall. Table scheme display.*

Scenarios: *Community centre. Whole settlement strategy.*

The internet

The internet has changed the way we do almost everything and community planning is no exception. The power of the web is helping people get more actively involved in improving their own communities in a great many ways.

- The internet allows people to engage from the comfort of their own homes or offices at times convenient for them.

- People are mostly free to remain anonymous if they wish but do not have to do so.

- Websites provide a cost effective way of providing access to data and archives. This is particularly useful for planning which is frequently a long and complex process.

- It is still early days and new and innovative ways of engaging people using the internet are constantly being developed.

- Some tools have been developed on the internet specifically for community planning. But there is also huge scope for using tools developed for other purposes to make community planning more efficient and effective.

✎ The internet is a hugely important resource for community planning but is rarely a substitute for gaining and sharing practical experience on the ground or for face-to-face community engagement.

✎ Do not assume everyone has internet access or feels comfortable using it. Ensure there are alternative ways of engaging.

✎ Jump in feet first. Many internet tools are daunting and it is often hard to find people who can help you use them. The best way to learn is to experiment.

Ways of using the internet for community planning

Examples of all these can be found in the second tab at:
www.communityplanning.net/methods/the_internet.php

☐ **Brainstorming**
Generating ideas and patterns. Mindmapping.

☐ **Campaigning**
Securing support for a particular viewpoint or campaign.

☐ **Communicating**
Making presentations, booklets, newsletters.

☐ **Development control**
Helping people to view and comment on planning applications and policy.

☐ **Event organising and scheduling**

☐ **Fundraising**
Raising funds for a project or initiative.

☐ **Gaming**
General awareness raising of planning and development through simulation.

☐ **Historical research**
Finding out how a place developed and is now.

☐ **Local networking**
Social media websites encouraging interaction at a local level.

☐ **Maintenance**
Providing ways for the public to report local maintenance issues to the relevant authorities.

☐ **Mapping**
Plotting information on maps, often using Geographical Information Systems (GIS).

☐ **Media sharing**
Sharing photos, film, powerpoint presentations, audio.

☐ **Method sites**
Websites set up to promote a single method.

☐ **Modelling**
3D visualisations helping people comprehend proposals and respond to them.

☐ **Neighbourhood websites**
Local community websites can provide valuable information about an area and help get people involved.

☐ **Organising**
Project management and personal organisation.

☐ **Project consultation**
Providing online information about a project and obtaining feedback.

☐ **Project websites**
Creating a website for a project to provide information and an archive of material.

☐ **Property management**
Improving communications between stakeholders (eg tenants, landlords).

☐ **Social media**
For generating interest, promoting events, getting feedback.

☐ **Stakeholder identification**
Finding out which organisations exist in an area and how to contact them.

☐ **Surveys**
Conducting surveys and producing reports on the results.

☐ **Toolkits**
Accessing good practice toolkits and resources.

☐ **Viewing property**
Viewing maps and photographs of property.

☐ ....

✎ Remember that many people access the internet through phones and other mobile devices.

$ Very cost effective way of engaging with people unless you have to pay for hardware, software or technical expertise.

FURTHER INFORMATION
Website: *ParticipateDB*
David Barrie, Slider Studio

Ketso kit

Ketso is a colourful, hands-on and re-usable toolkit for creative engagement. It enables people with differing levels of confidence and ability to engage and share ideas. Ketso can be used at many stages in a project: from developing a brief, to design and planning, to developing and implementing an action plan. The word 'Ketso' means 'Action' in Lesotho, Southern Africa, where the kit was pioneered.

Using the kit
Participants write their ideas and comments on colour-coded shapes, and place them on a central, felt workspace. Everyone can see the group's thoughts taking shape, encouraging cooperation and dialogue.

Numbers
Ketso extends your capacity. If you are new to running a workshop, it gives you simple stages and something to do with participants. If you are more experienced, it means you can run creative workshops with many people at once.

- A Ketso kit provides a set of table-top materials that can be used to capture and display people's ideas. Participants, in a workshop setting, write their ideas and comments on coloured 'leaves', and place them on a central, felt workspace before sharing them. The 'branches' on the kit can be used to give themes for participants to think about.

- A carefully designed facilitation process enables all participants' views to be expressed and stimulates both individual and group thinking, which is needed for any successful project.

- The kit is highly portable – at the end of a workshop, it folds quickly and easily into a carrying bag. The results can be written up or photographed, fed back to participants and used as the basis of a report. The kit pieces rinse clean in water, ready for reuse.

- Extensive online backup is provided free: workshop plans that can be adapted for different contexts; examples; case studies; analysis templates; training videos – www.ketso.com.

Sample Ketso workshop process

1. Arrivals and warm-up
People sit at tables of 6-8. Facilitator introduces the kit by asking participants a warm-up question and inviting them to write their answers on 'leaves' (already on the tables). Typical question: 'In an ideal world, what would you like to see in this area?'

2. Introductions
Facilitator explains aims, the Ketso approach, people invited. Participants introduce themselves at their tables.

3. Assets and possibilities
Facilitator asks a question and participants write or draw ideas on leaves, then take it in turns to share their ideas as they place them on the felt workspace. Questions might be:
- Existing Assets – what is good about the area? What is working well that we should make the most of (on brown leaves)?
- Future Possibilities – what could be done differently? Creative thinking, not worrying about practicalities at this point (green leaves).

4. Table Swap
Participants change tables and see another group's ideas. These can be highlighted or commented on (using special icons). Participants return to original tables.

5. Break

6. Generating actions
- Key challenges – what are the barriers to the desired future possibilities (grey leaves)?
- Solutions to challenges – more creative thinking, specifically about how to overcome the challenges identified (green leaves).
- Identify priorities – decide as a group which of the ideas on the workspace are most important (icons).
- Develop goals – what goals are suggested by the priorities identified (yellow leaves)?
- Next steps & actions – towards achieving the goals (using the Ketso Planner).

7. Final plenary

8. Feedback
The kit is packed up. Later it can be photographed to make a record of the ideas generated, or written up for a report to feed into future events or planning. The Ketsos or Actions from the workshop may also be taken forward into a future workshop, starting from where the first workshop left off.

Running time: 2–4 hours. Ideal numbers: **15–25**. With larger numbers, additional facilitation assistance is required

---

$ A Ketso kit can be rented or bought. A Ketso 8 (enough for a workshop of 8) costs $80 per month to rent and $420 to buy. A Ketso 24 (enough for a workshop of 24) costs $115 per month to rent and $825 to buy (2013 prices). (If a kit is bought following a rental, then the rental price is deducted from the purchase cost.) Please enquire for prices in other currencies.

$ Other costs may include: venue hire; refreshments; fees for an external facilitator (if used).

FURTHER INFORMATION
Ketso
☆ *Elaine Speakman, Dr Joanne Tippett,*

Local design statement

Local design statements are a way for local people to provide guidelines for new development in their area. They can be incorporated in local planning policy and provide a valuable way for local people to make a positive input into the planning process at an early stage. They are particularly useful in areas where local character is threatened by insensitive development.

- A local design statement is drawn up by a specially formed team of local volunteers, preferably supported by local planners and national agencies.

- The team secures the views of as many people as possible through publicity, holding workshops and circulating draft statements for comment.

- The statement will include guidance for future developers based on the character of the landscape setting, settlement patterns, building forms and transport networks.

- The statement is adopted by the local planning authority (as 'supplementary planning guidance' in the UK) and can be used to approve or reject planning applications from developers.

✎ The area covered by a statement can vary but the process works best at a village or neighbourhood level where people recognise each other. Break larger areas up and, if possible, combine with a *Countryside Design Summary* (☞ Glossary).

$ Direct costs likely to be around US$5,000 if local skills and services used. More if elaborate printing involved. Need to have a budget for reprints, especially in areas of development pressure.

Any Village Design Statement

Produced by the
Any Village
Design Group

Approved as Supplementary Planning Guidance in 1998 by Any District Council

Contents
1 Introducing Any Village
2 Brief history
3 Community strengths
4 Economy and commerce
5 Landscape and wildlife
6 Settlement patterns
7 Building types and forms
8 Conservation areas
9 Plot boundaries
10 Highways and footpaths
11 Street furniture
12 Trees

Supported by the National Neighbourhood Commission

Sample report cover
Contents and style can vary according to local needs.

"You saw the village in a completely different way than you ever had before. You really started to look at every single gable end, bit of tarmac and cobblestone. That was the most exciting thing, you learnt so much. It was an all round good exercise."
David Unsworth, Cartmel Village Design Group
Village Views video, 1996.

Reviewing progress
Villagers review pages with photographs and captions prepared during a local character workshop.

Sample local design statement process

1 Establish design team
Small group of local people. Read handbooks. Discuss with planning authority. Prepare publicity. (1 month)

2 Go public
Launch publicity. Draw in more participants. Prepare for workshop. (1 month)

3 Local character workshop
One-day event open to all. Main stages:

A Mapping in groups to identify key walks, areas and landmarks on base maps. (☞ *Mapping*).

B Photographic survey in groups taking photos which capture the character of the area (☞ *Photo survey*). Lunch while photos are developed.

C Character assessment. Each group prepares presentation on character of the area using photos and maps.

D Presentation and discussion. Groups present their work. General discussion on local character and the next steps.

4 Prepare design statement report
Expand design team. Refine and complete survey. Draft report. Consult on draft (☞ *Participatory editing*). (3 months)

5 Consult with local planning authority
Agree draft with planners and planning committee. (2 months)

6 Print report
Print report and distribute widely. Keep it in print and available. (2 months)

Total running time: 9 months minimum. Can take up to 18 months.

FURTHER INFORMATION

☞ Methods: *Mapping. Photo survey. Participatory editing.*

Scenario: *Village revival.*

Mapping

Mapping is an effective non-verbal way of finding out how people view their area. It is a good way to gather and present site-specific data, understand differences in perception and stimulate debate as a basis for joint planning.

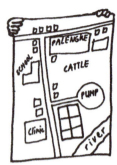

- Individuals or groups create physical maps of their neighbourhood or city using pen and paper, digital mapping software, lines in the sand, cloth, chalk or other materials to hand.

- A framework is provided to focus people's thoughts, eg places you visit often, landmarks, boundaries, places you dislike, things you would like to see.

- The maps are discussed and analysed as a basis for understanding differing viewpoints and developing proposals.

- Records of maps and debates are made for future reference.

Different perspectives
Two maps of the same place, one drawn by a woman, one by a man. Guess which is which. (Maps redrawn from originals.)

Using symbols and colour
Mapping various aspects of a community's capacity to cope with natural disasters helps planning to reduce their impact.

✎ A good place to start, especially with large groups, can be geographically accurate base maps on which people draw their issues and ideas.

✎ Using tracing paper to build up layers can be useful, getting different information on each layer. This mirrors the way that much digital mapping software works. Use symbols rather than words, especially if participants are unable to read.

✎ Creating your own maps online is becoming increasingly easy with websites like OpenStreetMap and Google Maps. But some training is worthwhile to get useable results.

✎ Mapping the same thing at different times is a good way of monitoring progress.

✎ Maps made or left in a public place provide a good focus for discussion. Particularly good in schools – children love maps.

✎ Maps can be very attractive. With some thought they can become permanent exhibits or even made into postcards!

$ Depends on materials used and cost of facilitation. Need not cost anything.

Group mapping process

1 Purpose
Decide what the map or maps should show (eg land use, hazards, resources, mobility, social facilities) and the best display method.

2 People
Gather people who know the area and are willing to share their knowledge. Decide whether to work individually or in groups.

3 Place and materials
Choose a suitable place (ground, table, wall, computer terminal) and materials (sticks, stones, seeds, pencils, felt-tips, chalk, base map, mapping software).

4 Map making
Facilitators might help people get started but then withdraw.

5 Discussion
Presentation of maps. Discussion on comparisons and lessons drawn. Notes of discussion made on flipchart or in notebook.

6 Record
Photograph maps for later use.

7 Planning
Use the maps to start developing proposals.

Running time: 1–2 hours
Process also works for diagramming. Replace word 'map' with 'diagram'.
☞ *Diagrams*.

Map types and uses

Activity map
Shows where people do things, which places they visit. Useful for planning future facilities.

Art map
Aims to be a work of art for displaying at exhibitions, making into postcards and so on.

Hazard map
Shows vulnerability to natural or environmental hazards and identifies risks and capacities. Useful for disaster mitigation.

Land use and resources map
Shows what happens where.

Mental map
Shows how people perceive their area (as opposed to being geographically accurate). Useful insight into perceptions.

Community mapping
Making a village map on the ground using powder. Community mapping allows the less articulate to express their views.

FURTHER INFORMATION
☞ Methods: *Electronic map. The internet. Local design statement. Risk assessment.* Scenario: *Village revival.*
◓ *Reducing Risk. From Place to Place.*
▣ *Common Ground.*
☆ Drawings taken from 4B.

Art map
Part of a 'parish map' used as a postcard (☞ 'Parish mapping' in glossary).

Microplanning workshop

Microplanning is a comprehensive community planning procedure for producing development plans for upgrading settlements. Originally designed for use in developing countries, it is based on regular intensive workshops which involve a minimum of preparation, materials and training.

Structured group working
Participants complete charts on large sheets of paper which are then displayed on the walls.

People needed

☐ **Community representatives**
Cross-section of local population. 8–12 people.
☐ **Logistics officer**
Provides training materials. Government officer.
☐ **Projects Officer**
Responsible for implementing results. Local government officer.
☐ **Specialists**
Technical experts (eg health, engineering, social development). As many as appropriate.
☐ **Team facilitator**
Directs procedure. Practitioner or academic.
☐ **Workshop facilitators**
Conduct small workshop groups (usually 3 needed). Selected from participants.

■ The microplanning procedure involves 8 to 12 community representatives working closely with a small team of experts and facilitators for several days.

■ A sequence of activities (see example in box, right) is worked through to arrive at a development plan and work programme.

■ The process is structured by charts on large sheets of paper which are completed and kept as a record.

■ The workshops are repeated every year or so to monitor progress and plan the next stages.

✎ Facilitators must have the confidence of all participants and should participate in a workshop to understand its dynamics before running one themselves.

✎ Hold workshops in the community rather than in government offices to make local people feel more in control.

✎ Do not treat the chart format as a straitjacket. If the one you planned does not seem to work, revise it as you go along.

$ Costs are minimal apart from organisers' and participants' time.

Sample microplanning process

STAGE 1: IDENTIFY PROBLEMS

a) Reconnaissance. Survey of locality.
b) Prepare list of problems.

Problem	Why?	To who?	Where?
_____	____	_____	_____
_____	____	_____	_____

c) Prioritise problems

Agreed summary list of problems
1 _____
2 _____

STAGE 2: IDENTIFY STRATEGY OPTIONS

a) List possible strategies (perhaps in small groups).

Problem	Short-term Strategy	Long-term Strategy
_____	_____	_____
_____	_____	_____

b) Compare different groups' priorities.

Strategy	All agree	2 teams agree	1 team agrees
_____	☐	☐	☐
_____	☐	☐	☐

c) Agree strategy priorities.

Agreed summary list

Problem	Strategy
1 _____	_____
2 _____	_____

STAGE 3: PLAN ACTIONS NEEDED

a) List actions needed to achieve each strategy. Consider options, eg high and low cost.

Strategy

Actions needed	high cost	low cost
_____	☐	☐
_____	☐	☐

b) Negotiate and select agreed options.

Strategy

Agreed actions needed
1 _____
2 _____

STAGE 4: ALLOCATE TASKS

a) List tasks required to achieve each action.

Action

Tasks	Who	What	When	How
1 _____	____	____	____	____
2 _____	____	____	____	____

b) Locate improvements
Make plans, sections, sketches.

STAGE 5: MONITOR AND EVALUATE

This stage takes place weeks, months or years later. Also perhaps at the beginning to review any previously planned actions.

a) Describe the status of each action.

Action planned	Progress
_____	_____
_____	_____

b) Draw lessons.

Action planned	Corrective action needed	Lessons learned
_____	_____	_____
_____	_____	_____

Running time: 2–5 days

FURTHER INFORMATION

☞ Scenario: *Shanty settlement upgrading.*
✑ *Action Planning for Cities.*
✉ Centre for Development and Emergency Practice (CENDEP).
☆ Nabeel Hamdi

Mobile unit

Mobile units can make it easier to provide the technical support necessary for community planning activity. They are particularly useful for working in communities lacking facilities or where a series of similar events are planned in several locations.

Mobile planning aid
Volkswagen van used for transporting exhibition material and model-making equipment to communities as part of a planning aid service.

- Mobile units can range from a van used to transport an exhibition to a mobile home or trailer converted into a fully equipped design studio.

- The choice of vehicle is determined by its intended use, the size required and whether it needs off-road capability.

- The units are fitted out with facilities and equipment necessary for the activities planned (see box, right).

- Suitable graphics are applied to the outside to create the desired image.

✎ Can create a sense of presence and credibility as well as being a useful technical resource.

✎ New technologies in document production may reduce the need for such a facility or at any rate change the requirements. Could end up as an expensive toy. Plan carefully.

$ Costs of conversion can vary. Running costs of maintenance and insurance need to be considered. Savings can include costs of hiring premises and travel costs.

Mobile studio facilities

☐ Computers for word processing, layout and internet research (perhaps with modem via mobile phone).
☐ Printer (for photos, flyers and large drawings).
☐ Drawing boards.
☐ Exhibition panels (perhaps for display on the outside of the unit).
☐ Flipcharts.

☐ Library of technical literature.
☐ Light box.
☐ Paper cutter or guillotine.
☐ Photocopier.
☐ Print machine (for large drawings).
☐ Stationery cupboard (notepads, Post-it notes, etc).
☐ Storage for drawings and photos.
☐ Toilet and washroom.
☐ Video camera and player.
☐ ....

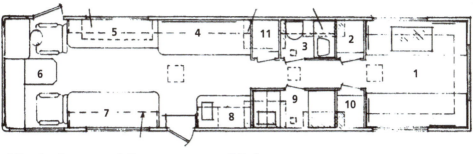

1 Drawing Centre
2 Storage cupboard
3 Bathroom
4 Reproduction area
5 Computer centre
6 Cockpit
7 Typing area
8 Kitchen
9 Darkroom
10 Storage cupboard
11 Equipment cupboard

Mobile design studio
Custom converted 38-foot recreation vehicle used as a design studio for community planning workshops in rural areas in the USA in the 1990s. The internal layout is shown in the drawing above and includes items not now likely to be necessary due to technical advances.

FURTHER INFORMATION

☞ Scenario: *New neighbourhood.*

✉ Ball State University.

☆ Tony Costello

Models

Models are one of the most effective tools for getting people involved in planning and design. They are particularly useful for generating interest, presenting ideas and helping people think in three dimensions.

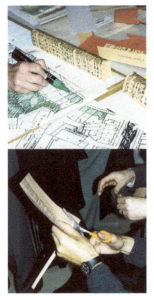

Making models
A very good way to gain an understanding of how a building or city is put together.

■ Models can be made from a wide variety of materials. They can be highly elaborate, aiming to be as realistic as possible, or simple and illustrative. The choice will depend on the purpose of the model and the resources and time available.

■ Models are often adaptable so that alternative proposals or options can easily be shown by moving parts around.

■ The construction of models is highly educational and enjoyable and is often done in groups as part of the planning and design process.

✎ Slick presentation models are good for presenting proposals but are usually hard to adapt and so inhibit creativity. Think through the options for construction carefully at the outset. Generally, use materials that are easily available and simple to cut up, shape, fix, colour and move about. Pasting base-maps or plans onto a rigid board is a good way to get started, and it ensures that you get the scale right.

✎ Models are an ideal centrepiece for exhibitions, workshops and venues such as architecture centres.

$ Models can cost very little if scrap materials are used. Presentation models can be extremely expensive. The main cost involved though is time. One innovative way of paying for detailed models of a neighbourhood is to get building owners to pay for the cost of having their own buildings upgraded from simple blocks or cut-outs to being fully detailed and painted.

Neighbourhood model
Buildings made from wood blocks and glued onto a wooden baseboard. Good for displaying outside and generating attention. Very durable. Need a workshop to make one.

Street model
Buildings made out of folded cardboard and glued onto a cardboard base board. Very flexible but not durable. Good focal point for design workshops and interactive exhibitions.

House model
Large-scale model using cardboard, allowing people to be involved in designing their homes to a high level of detail.

Room layout model
Simple cardboard model scaled to help people design room layouts. The one shown was used by blind people designing a new centre for the blind.

FURTHER INFORMATION
☞ Method: *Planning for Real.*
Scenarios: *Community centre. Housing development.*

Neighbourhood planning office

Neighbourhood planning offices provide an important local focal point for community planning activity and make it easier to follow up and sustain initiatives. Ideally every neighbourhood should have one, but they are particularly valuable in rundown areas or where there is a lot of building activity.

Local presence
Architects set up office in a flat on a housing estate which they are rehabilitating.

- Neighbourhood offices should be in a prominent location, preferably with a shop frontage, and have opening hours convenient for local people.

- They provide a working base for all professionals dealing with an area, a venue for meetings and workshops and a first point of contact for local people on planning and building issues.

- They should be staffed by people with project management skills able to take a pro-active role in pursuing improvement initiatives, and by locals.

✎ Neighbourhood planning offices often work best if managed by an independent body or partnership. Avoid total community control or total local authority control.

✎ Useful to base an office in a rundown building which can be renovated as a pilot project to stimulate other local improvements. Great scope for volunteers and trainees to run an office once it is set up.

✎ Combining a neighbourhood planning office with an environment shop, community design centre or architecture centre can be a powerful combination.

Demonstration project
Before and after of a shop used as a neighbourhood planning office and as a demonstration for improving street frontages.

$ Main costs: salaries, rent, heating, lighting, furniture and equipment. Costs can be reduced by seconding professional and technical staff and using volunteers to handle general enquiries and administration. From US$15,000 to $150,000 per annum.

Neighbourhood planning office information systems

- ☐ Community profile information
- ☐ Development plans
- ☐ Local history
- ☐ Local organisations and contacts
- ☐ Maps: varying scales
- ☐ Photos: aerial, historical, current
- ☐ Planning applications
- ☐ Product catalogues
- ☐ Project files: A–Z
- ☐ Property files: Building or plot
- ☐ Statutory plans
- ☐ ....

Resident resource
Local residents looking through product catalogues to specify design work on their homes.

Professional base
An architect helps residents at a weekly surgery at an office manned by trainees and volunteers.

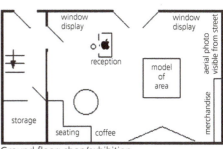

Ground floor: shop/exhibition

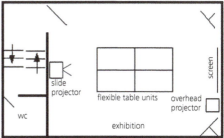

First floor: meetings room

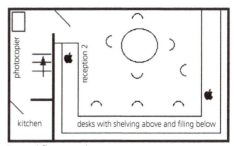

Second floor: workspace

Sample layout
Ideal layout for a well-resourced neighbourhood planning office with public shop/exhibition area, semi-public seminar room and private workspace. Minimum tolerable size: 375 square feet per floor (15 x 25). Even better if all facilities are on ground floor. If resources are not available, make do with whatever space you can find.

FURTHER INFORMATION

☞ Methods: *Architecture centre. Community design centre. Environment shop.* Scenario: *Local neighbourhood initiative.*

Newspaper supplement

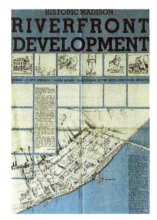

Public profile for planning
Supplement cover (above) and inside page illustration (below) showing analysis of an area.

"Newspapers can play an innovative role in citizen awareness of the planning and design process. They avoid the stigma of being considered an outsider's 'propaganda sheet' – a phrase sometimes attached to planning documents and special publications."
Anthony Costello, Professor of Architecture, Ball State University
Small Town, Jan/Feb 1983.

Newspaper supplements are one of the most effective ways of spreading planning and design ideas to large numbers of people and generating public debate. They are particularly useful for presenting proposals from community planning events, especially if combined with other coverage before and afterwards.

■ A working relationship is established between those promoting community planning initiatives and the local paper's editors and journalists.

■ Standard newspaper coverage is used to publicise activities and generate debate: news stories, feature articles, letters, legal notices, guest columnists.

■ Special supplements are used to provide in-depth coverage of planning proposals and community planning activities.

■ Feedback is generated through the letters pages, readership polls and follow-up features.

✎ Persuade editors to allow design teams to help lay out supplements. This forces architects and planners to communicate better and will cut the newspaper's costs. It can also provide a useful educational experience for students.

✎ Order extra copies and distribute to schools and to specific audiences.

$ May well be free if newspaper treats supplement as a commercial venture and incorporates advertising. Subsidy may be required, particularly if extra copies are wanted. Full cost still cheap compared with printing a special report. An 8-page supplement in black and white might typically cost around US$650 for 6,500 copies, ie 10 cents per copy.

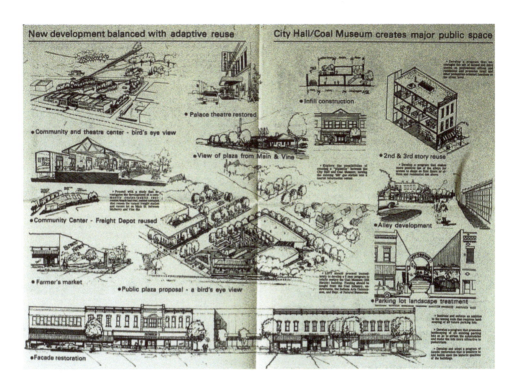

New development balanced with adaptive reuse

City Hall/Coal Museum creates major public space

- Infill construction
- Palace theatre restored
- Community and theatre center - bird's eye view
- View of plaza from Main & Vine
- Community Center - Freight Depot reused
- 2nd & 3rd story reuse
- Alley development
- Farmer's market
- Public plaza proposal - a bird's eye view
- Parking lot landscape treatment
- Facade restoration

Advantages of a supplement

Cheap. Inexpensive compared with producing and distributing a special report.

Coverage. Reaches a very high proportion of the population (in most areas).

Credibility. Has greater credibility than a report produced by consultants.

Familiarity. Feels less threatening than most specially produced planning reports.

Format. Large format allows drawings to be published at a reasonable scale.

Immediacy. Very quick publication and distribution. The results of one day's workshop can be distributed the next day.

Skills. Brings expert journalistic skills to bear.

Clear graphics
Double-page spread from a special 8-page supplement produced during a 3-day planning weekend. Published and distributed with the local paper on the final day of the weekend, a few hours before a public presentation by the design team. Key features: concise writing; clear and understandable drawings; simple sequence.

FURTHER INFORMATION

☞ Methods: *Design assistance team. Participatory editing. Planning weekend.*

   Scenario: *New neighbourhood.*

✉ Ball State University.

☆ Anthony Costello.

Online consultation

Online consultation provides a channel of communication with a developer or government body that is accessible, convenient, interactive and auditable. Particularly useful for issues and projects that affect a large geographical area or large population such as major property developments and renewable energy projects. A good way to engage a broad audience in consultation, including people who do not typically get involved.

- Issues and proposals are presented online in a user-friendly, visual, interactive way.

- Visitors to the website are able to read and digest all information and proposals and then opt to make a response if they wish.

- People wishing to respond register and provide some personal details so responses can be analysed.

- Participants are given the option to be kept up-to-date via email about the consultation and the project.

- A full audit trail of activity and communication is maintained. Feedback is stored in a secure database where it can be viewed, responded to and reported on by the organisers.

- Reports are generated on activity, feedback and key issues raised for further analysis.

Sample contents of online consultation website

- ☐ Home page
- ☐ About us (the developer or agency)
- ☐ About the place (location of proposed development)
- ☐ The proposals
- ☐ Benefits
- ☐ Planning history
- ☐ Issues (eg Housing, Environment, Energy)
- ☐ News
- ☐ Frequently asked questions (FAQs)
- ☐ Information bank (Links, Downloads)
- ☐ Have your say
- ☐ Register
- ☐ Contact us

"Informative website. I'm all in favour of anything which will help the environment and protect it for future generations."

"It is fantastic to hear that there is a proposed windfarm. It is a much more efficient way of creating electricity than the usual power station method."

Comments recorded via online consultations

"30.1 million adults in the UK (60%) use the internet every day or almost every day. The percentage rises to 99% for users aged 16 to 24."
Report by the UK Office of National Statistics, August 2011.

Get involved page
For Viking Energy Wind Farm.
Client: Viking Energy.
www.vikingenergy.co.uk

Project information page
For proposed Snetterton Biomass Plant.
Client: Iceni Energy.
www.snettertonbiomassplant.co.uk

✎ Run online community consultation alongside traditional community planning activities – such as workshops, exhibitions, postal surveys – to give everyone the chance to join in.

✎ Publicise online consultations well ie in local newspapers, newsletters and websites. Send personal invitations to key stakeholders, possibly with a special code to allow them to register more quickly.

✎ Keep information simple but make technical/planning documents available for download for those that want them.

✎ Ensure the registration process is quick and simple. Mostly just request a name, email address and postcode.

✎ Ensure your online questionnaire matches with your 'offline' questionnaire.

✎ Keep the online consultation content, and the people who have signed-up, regularly updated.

✎ Consider search engine optimisation, marketing and social media platforms to raise awareness of and drive visitors to online consultations.

✎ Ensure feedback can be reported on effectively, filtering where needed to drill

down to the views of those most affected (e.g. certain postcodes) or to isolate key topics (e.g. visual impact, wildlife, access).

✎ Use interactive maps and masterplans or films to bring proposals to life.

$ A specialist company will be able to develop an online consultation system that you can update yourself – using a simple publishing system – and use to generate reports on feedback. Alternatively they will be able to update it for you for an additional charge.

$ Some systems can be used to store and manage all consultation data / feedback – not just that collected online.

$ Average costs for a decent online consultation system: US$8,000 to $25,000. But could be up to $80,000 for top end site with multiple reporting capabilities.

FURTHER INFORMATION

☞ Methods: *The internet.*

✉ Consense.

☆ *Jessica Topham.*

Open house event

Open house events allow those promoting development initiatives to present them to a wider public and secure reactions in an informal manner. They are less structured than a workshop and more informal than a traditional exhibition.

- Open house events can be organised at any stage of the design and development process by any of the parties. They can last from a few hours to several weeks.

- The venue will be arranged with a number of displays on the proposals and options using a variety of interactive display techniques (see plan, right). Organisers will be present to deal with queries and engage in informal debate.

- Material collected will be analysed afterwards and used to further develop the initiative.

✎ Good way to gauge initial public reaction to development proposals or options. Particularly useful for getting public involvement in proposals from a design workshop or planning day.

✎ There is no need to present drawings in an elaborate way, but careful thought needs to be given to highlighting the main points and on determining how reactions are obtained. Well worth engaging professional exhibition design skills if available.

✎ Prominent on-site venues work best, for instance an empty shop.

$ Main costs: hire of venue and exhibition material; staff time; design time (3 person days).

Inviting people in
Pavement sign encouraging passers-by to visit an open house event in a vacant shop on the future of the area.

"I've been a councillor for 12 years and I've never been involved in an exercise like this before. We should be doing this for all of our towns instead of development control which is awful."
Leader of Waverley Borough Council
after a design workshop and open house event, 1997.

Relaxed atmosphere
People move freely from display to display and hold discussions with the organisers.

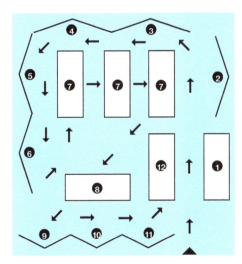

Sample layout in shop unit

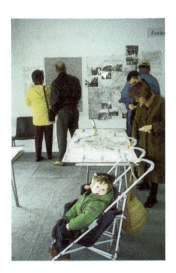

1 **Entry desk.** Take Post-its, pens, sticky dots (Red=Dislike. Green=Like. Yellow=Not sure).

2 **Welcome panel.** Read about history and aim of present initiative.

3 **Participant data.** Stick dots on panels to show where you live/work, age group and other relevant statistics.

4 **Issues, goals and action needed.** Use Post-its to make additional points to those listed.

5 **Likes and dislikes.** Put stickers on map to show favourite and least favourite buildings/spaces.

6 **Visions.** Add Post-it comments to sketches of area visions (preferably before and after).

7 **Table scheme displays.** Use sticky dots to make your views known on proposals already drawn up. ☞ *Table scheme display.*

8 **Draw your own.** Sketch your own ideas with felt-tips on tracing paper laid over base plans.

9 **What next.** Read about it.

10 **Help.** Sign up if you can offer any assistance.

11 **Comments.** Write on flipcharts any comments not already covered.

12 **Further information.** Write your name and address if you want to receive further information as things develop.

Open Space workshop

Open Space workshops provide a highly democratic framework for enabling any group of people to create their own programme of discussions on almost any theme without much preparation. They are particularly useful for dealing with policy issues, community building, complex change, for generating enthusiasm and for dealing with urgent issues needing quick action.

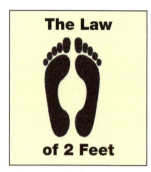

The 'Law of 2 feet'
If at any time you feel you are neither learning nor contributing, move elsewhere.

The five principles

- Whoever comes are the right people.
- Whenever it starts is the right time.
- When it's over, it's over.
- Whatever happens is the only thing that could happen.
- Wherever it happens is the right place.

Five principles
In other words: participation is voluntary; be relaxed about timetabling and venues; move on when there's no more to say; let go of expectations.

"It was fantastic. I felt really heard. I learnt lots I didn't know about my local area, and we created some brilliant ideas of what to do. There's a real sense of community now, and I'm ready for action!"
Open Space participant
Hammersmith & Fulham.

- A theme, venue and time are determined and publicised by the organisers.

- Participants start by sitting in a circle and deciding for themselves the issues to discuss, using a simple procedure (see format, right) usually guided by a facilitator.

- Workshop sessions are self-managed by the participants within a framework of simple principles and a 'law' (see margin, left). Each session produces a brief written report of the conversation and usually recommended actions.

- The recommended actions are prioritised.

✎ The framework is flexible and can easily be adapted by the facilitators or participants. The 'principles', 'law' and timetable can be adjusted to take account of local conditions and experience.

✎ Good facilitation is important for setting up the workshop and getting people started. Once up and running, the facilitator can become almost invisible.

$ Main costs: venue, refreshments, stationery (A4 paper, large marker pens, Post-it notes, flipchart paper and masking tape) and facilitator's fee (if any).

Open Space workshop format

with likely minimum timings.

1 Preparation

Set up the space as shown in sketch, right.

2 Opening circle – introduction

Participants sit in a circle. Facilitator explains the theme and procedures. (10 mins)

3 Opening circle – declaring issues

Participants are invited to identify issues relating to the theme they want to convene sessions on. People write their issue on a sheet of paper with their name, read it out ("My name is.... My issue is ......") and place the sheet on the Bulletin Board, adding a Post-it note stating time and place for that conversation. (30 mins)

4 Signing up

Everyone gathers round the Bulletin Board and signs up for the workshops they wish to take part in. (15 mins)

5 Workshop sessions and reporting

First sessions take place. People may use 'The Law of 2 Feet' to move from session to session. Notes are taken of the conversations – usually with recommendations for taking that issue forward. These notes are posted on The News wall. (60 mins).
This step is repeated as time allows.

6 Action planning

Participants prioritise recommendations (using sticky dots) and decide who will take forward what and when. (20 mins)

7 Final plenary circle

Participants share any reflections they wish, to complete the event. (15 mins)

8 Report circulated

At the end of the event or soon after. Contains action points, next steps and responsibilities.

Running time: half day – 5 days
Ideal numbers: 5 to 500.

Starting point
Open circle of chairs; Bulletin Board for posting workshop topics with timing and location; posters of 'principles', 'law' and Open Space theme for event. Breakout spaces of open circles of chairs may be created in the plenary space after the opening, or separately.

Creating an agenda
Participants sign up for which issues they want to discuss in workshop groups, selecting from the menu created by the participants themselves. Straight after each session, a report of the conversation is posted on The News Wall, so everyone can benefit from all the sessions.

FURTHER INFORMATION

- ☞ Scenario: *Local neighbourhood initiative.*
- 🖳 *Open Space World.*
- ⌀ *Open Space Technology.*
- ✉ Wikima.
- ☆ Romy Shovelton.

Participatory editing

Participatory editing allows people to help shape reports and news-sheets without necessarily leaving their own homes. Reports have a crucial role to play in crystallising the results of community planning initiatives and communicating to others.

- The nature and structure of the product are determined by the organisers. A draft is drawn up by writers, editors, designers and illustrators.

- Drafts are circulated, or displayed, for comment. Participants make comments on the draft with coloured pens or Post-it notes.

- Editors go through the comments and produce a revised draft which is approved by the organisers. The process is repeated as necessary.

✎ Explain the process clearly at the outset. Stress that comments are not automatically included but help the editors make improvements. Appoint one person as editor-in-chief to avoid lengthy wrangling in the event of disagreements. Collective editing sounds good in principle but rarely works well in practice.

✎ Secure a good cross-section of participants. It is quite extraordinary how few comments will normally be duplicated, even with many people responding.

✎ Holding an 'editing workshop' can generate ideas that would not emerge from individuals. Use pages pinned up on the walls as a basis for discussion (☞ p289).

✎ Always circulate material as close as possible to its final form. Sending out text without pictures for instance has limited use.

$ Main costs: photocopying; binding; postage; time.

Dear.............

FOREST ACTION REPORT
COMMENTS PLEASE

A draft mock up of the report arising from the recent design workshop is enclosed / attached.

Please let me have your comments by midday Friday 4 May by tel., fax, post or email.

Any reactions would be useful. But the best help would be if you could mark up all comments as proposed alterations in red pen on the draft / tracked changes and return. And, if possible, let me have any long sections of new copy by email so I can cut and paste it to reduce the chance of typing errors.

The editing team will produce a revised draft and there will be a final opportunity to see and discuss this on Saturday 5 May from 2 to 6 at the warden's office on Hill Street.

Your help will of course be acknowledged unless you let me know that you prefer otherwise.

sincerely

Report Editor

Participation by post and email
Sample letter / email inviting comments on a report.

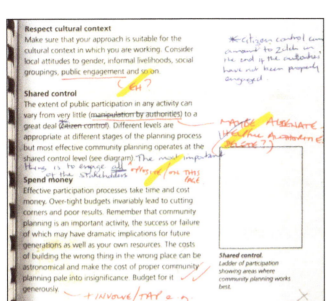

Respect cultural context
Make sure that your approach is suitable for the cultural context in which you are working. Consider local attitudes to gender, informal livelihoods, social groupings, public engagement and so on.

*[handwritten annotation: * Citizen control can amount to Zilch in the end if the authorities have not been properly engaged.]*

[handwritten annotation: GH?]

Shared control
The extent of public participation in any activity can vary from very little (manipulation by authorities) to a great deal (citizen control). Different levels are appropriate at different stages of the planning process but most effective community planning operates at the shared control level (see diagram). *[handwritten: The most important thing is to engage all of the stakeholders]*

[handwritten annotation: MAYBE ALTERNATE HEATRE ANOTATONE DELETE?]

[handwritten annotation: this page]

Spend money
Effective participation processes take time and cost money. Over-tight budgets invariably lead to cutting corners and poor results. Remember that community planning is an important activity, the success or failure of which may have dramatic implications for future generations as well as your own resources. The costs of building the wrong thing in the wrong place can be astronomical and make the cost of proper community planning pale into insignificance. Budget for it generously.

[handwritten: + INVOLVE/TAP e g PARISH COUNCILS + OTHER LOCAL AUTHORITIES]

Think on your feet
Once the basic principles and language of participatory

Shared control.
Ladder of participation showing areas where community planning works best.

Making comments
Specific suggestions for alterations marked on a draft are more useful than general comments (example shown is from a draft of this book). Various digital sofware versions of the same process are available, eg Acrobat Professional, and there is internet based software, eg Google Editor.

Tips on producing reports

- Keep the structure simple.
- Be concise. People don't read much. Lengthy reports are only useful for massaging egos. Concentrate on getting the argument right. Using bullet points and headings will help this.
- Be visual. Good images are worth thousands of words. 'Before and After' images are particularly good for conveying proposed changes.
- Using short quotes or 'soundbites' from people can be very powerful.
- Make sure you credit everyone accurately.

Sample report structure
Simple format which works in most situations.

1 **Recommendations** (1,2,3 etc. The only thing many people will read)
2 **The Way Forward** (issue 1, issue 2 etc. summary paragraphs)
3 **Background** (why the report is necessary and how it was produced)
4 **Issues** (main issues in depth – optional)
5 **Ideas** (everything suggested even if not agreed by everyone – optional)
6 **Proposals** (what should happen – in detail)

Appendices (may be separate document)
A Workshop notes
B Credits
C Other relevant info

Workshop report structure
Simple format to avoid tedious blow-by-blow accounts and assist with compiling reports.

1 Workshop title.
2 People present – name and organisation.
3 Issues raised – heading and bullet points.
4 Proposals – heading and bullet points.

FURTHER INFORMATION

☞ Methods: *Design assistance team. Local design statement.* Scenario: *Planning study.* See also editing workshop format on page 289.

Photo survey

Photo surveys help groups develop design ideas by taking and discussing photos of their existing environment. They can be used as part of a wider community profiling or community planning event or as an independent exercise.

- Participants go around their neighbourhood individually or in teams, taking photos of places and images according to a general or specific theme.

- The photos are sorted, selected and prints are placed on large sheets of blank paper or maps. Photos can be grouped or cut up and comments may be added using Post-it notes or felt tips.

- The completed sheets or maps are used as a basis for discussion, analysis and design.

Taking photos
Making images of what is important for you in the local environment for sharing with others.

✎ Undertaking the whole exercise in one stretch builds a useful momentum but requires polaroid cameras or digital cameras and computers. Letting people take photos individually over a week can allow more thought but requires more self-discipline.

✎ If not done automatically, record file numbers on the back of prints before they are used.

✎ Before and after photos can be highly effective. Dig out historical photos and take new ones from the same spot.

✎ After the photo survey is completed it can be useful to introduce photos from other places and make comparisons.

"I was surprised how the photographs added a new dimension to everyone's perception."
Ning Tan, facilitator
Philippine workshop, 1995.

$ Assuming you have computers available, the only cost is making prints. Investing in disposable cameras may sometimes be worthwhile.

Photo survey process

Assuming digital cameras and computers with printing facilities. If not, use polaroid cameras or split into 2 sessions.

1 Briefing. Agree priorities
Briefing by facilitator. Agreement of objectives, timescales and themes. Theme examples:
- memorable places and images;
- beautiful places, ugly places;
- places to be alone, to socialise, to play;
- private places, public places;
- ugly buildings, beautiful buildings;
- threats.
Divide into teams and hand out cameras. (30 mins)

2 Take photographs
Teams go round taking photos. (Teams can have the same or different themes.)
(1–3 hours, depending on size of area)

3 Download images during lunch break
Prints produced – standard size are fine. (1.5 hours)

4 Prepare presentation
Teams arrange photos on boards or paper sheets. Symbols and words added on Post-its to record comments, feelings and evaluations. Relevant photos grouped together. When completed (or time up) photos pinned or glued down. Sheets named and put up on wall. (1 hour)

4 Exhibit
Viewing of exhibits. Tea break. (30 mins)

5 Presentation
Each team presents their images and conclusions to a plenary session. Debate and discussion. Areas of agreement and disagreement recorded. (1 hour)

Ideal numbers: **6 teams of 6–8 max**

Running time: **5.5 hours minimum.**

Sorting photos
Villagers place photos of their own houses on a large map as an early step in a week-long planning workshop.

Cutting up photos
Photos being cut up and pasted on a large map to create a jigsaw display. Using this technique, people contribute photos which they think characterise their particular area. These are cut up to fit the given area of the map (perhaps a parish or plot). The end result is a vivid pictorial comparison of how people see their locality.

FURTHER INFORMATION

☞ Methods: *Elevation montage. Local design statement. Mapping.*

Scenario: *Village revival.*

☆ Peter Richards, Deike Richards, Debbie Bartlett.

Promotion leaflets
Ingredients: Title; Area covered; What planning aid is; What kind of help can be given; How much it will cost; Examples of help given; Who to contact.

Planning aid scheme

Planning aid schemes provide free and independent planning advice to groups or individuals who cannot afford to employ a consultant. They aim to give people the knowledge, skills and confidence to deal with the planning system and to become involved in wider planning issues.

■ Planning aid schemes are normally set up and run by national or regional professional institutions.

■ A register of qualified professional planners prepared to volunteer their time is established.

■ People needing help are put in touch with the nearest suitable volunteer on the register.

■ The volunteer assists as much as possible, referring queries to the authorities or consultants if appropriate.

■ As schemes become well established they may employ paid workers, establish telephone helplines, produce publications and become more pro-active in encouraging community participation.

✎ Government grant assistance is useful for setting up and administering planning aid systems.

✎ Producing information sheets on the planning system and common problems and issues can make the volunteer's job much easier.

✎ Need not be restricted to planners. 'Architectural aid', 'Surveying aid' and so on can also be very valuable.

$ Setting-up costs: administration in compiling register; distributing publicity material. Ongoing costs: dealing with enquiries.

Planning aid advice services checklist

☐ Appealing against a refusal of planning permission.
☐ Appearing at a public inquiry.
☐ Applying for planning permission.
☐ Drawing up community or neighbourhood plans and local design statements.
☐ Guidance on development proposals and specific site problems.
☐ How the planning system works.
☐ How to find information and contact the right people.
☐ Objecting to or supporting a planning application or planning appeal.
☐ Putting forward your own views when local plans are being prepared.
☐ The rights of an individual or group on planning matters.
☐ The need for planning permission.
☐ Understanding enforcement procedures.
☐ Understanding the many types of development plans.
☐ Using the most effective public participation methods.
☐ ....
....

Government funding

National office
Overall scheme publicity and funding.

Regional offices
Register of local professional volunteers. Local publicity.

Professional volunteers

Planning aid network
The scheme is coordinated by the national office of a professional institution. Regional branches publicise the scheme locally and maintain registers of professional planners willing to work in a voluntary capacity.

Benefits for professionals

• Opportunity to take part in a wide range of activities including environmental education.
• Satisfaction in helping people participate in the development of their communities.
• Useful source of continuing professional development.
• Valuable insight into the planning system from a user's point of view.

FURTHER INFORMATION

☞ Scenario: *Regeneration infrastructure.*

✉ Royal Town Planning Institute (National Planning Aid Co-ordinator).

Planning day

Planning days are a good way for getting the key parties to work creatively together to devise and explore options for a site, neighbourhood or city.

■ Participants will normally be personally invited by the event instigators. The aim is to have a cross-section of main stakeholders.

■ A briefing pack is sent to all those attending. As well as setting out the aims of the day, the pack will contain background information about the area and the development process so that everyone starts the day with the maximum up-to-date knowledge.

■ Workshop formats are designed to encourage the development of creative ideas (☞ *Design workshop*).

■ Facilitators will often be from outside the area to provide a measure of independence.

■ A printed summary is produced as soon as possible afterwards and the proposals may be exhibited to a wider public (☞ *Open house event*).

✎ Personal invitations can ensure a balanced attendance. But avoid criticism of exclusivity by having spare places for others.

✎ One-day events can generate a wealth of information and ideas which can easily be lost. Make sure there are resources available for recording, presenting and following up the results.

✎ Holding an 'awareness raising' day (☞ glossary) a couple of weeks beforehand can be helpful to generate momentum.

$ Main costs: venue, catering, organiser's time (10 person days minimum), facilitator's fees.

Dear_____,

I have pleasure in inviting you to participate in a special planning day on Tuesday 25th April at 25 High Street. A timetable, guest list and briefing pack will be sent out prior to the event.

The aim is to help develop practical but exciting development options for the area and encourage further collaboration between those concerned. The outcome will form the basis for wider public consultation shortly afterwards.

The format of the day has been carefully designed to achieve results. As well as all major local stakeholders we are also inviting a few specialist advisors to provide the breadth of input required. If there are others you think should be present, please let me know, though space is limited.

To help us in making arrangements, please confirm that you can attend.

Yours sincerely

Sample invitation letter

"We need more events like this."
Participant, Planning day
Oxpens Quarter Initiative, Oxford, 1997.

Workshop sessions
Participants divided into groups working round tables with flipchart to one side.

Plenary sessions
Reporting back from the workshops with drawings and flipchart sheets pinned on the wall.

Sample planning day timetable

Ideal numbers: 40–80
Larger numbers comfortable if enough space and facilitators; 10 max per workshop.

10.00 Arrivals and coffee
Viewing of display material.

10.30 Introductions and briefings

11.00 Briefing workshops: issues and opportunities
Participants allocated to one of four workshop groups, eg:
1 Transport (access and movement)
2 Activities (land uses)
3 Strategic issues (regional context)
4 Quality of life (environment)

12.15 Plenary session
Report back from workshops

12.45 Lunch and site walkabouts

14.00 Design workshops: options and proposals
Participants work in one of several design workshop groups focusing on different aspects of the site, eg:
1 Regional context **2** Town context
3 The site **4** River edge **5** New square?

15.15 Plenary session
Report back from workshops.

15.45 Tea

16.15 Next steps
Planning future activity.

17.30 Presentation
To councillors, press.

18.00 Reception

FURTHER INFORMATION

☞ Methods: *Briefing workshop. Design workshop. Newspaper supplement.* Scenarios: *Inner city regeneration. Planning study. Town centre upgrade.*

Suggestion cards
These can be pre-prepared with blanks for people to add any ideas of their own. The use of colour and visual symbols makes the process accessible to those with low literacy levels.

Priority cards
These are used to record all suggestions and their locations.

"Compromise and consensus become easier because everyone's line of vision converges on the subject matter – the model itself – allowing for practical ways of non-threatening communication and participation."
Neighbourhood Initiatives Foundation
leaflet, 1997.

Planning for Real

Planning for Real uses simple models as a focus for people to put forward and prioritise ideas on how their area can be improved. It is a highly visible, hands-on community development and empowerment tool, which people of all abilities and backgrounds find easy and enjoyable to engage in.

■ A large 3-dimensional model of a neighbourhood is constructed, preferably by local people, using cardboard cut-outs for buildings pasted onto a base plan fixed to polystyrene or cardboard.

■ The model is used at pre-advertised sessions held in various locations in the community.

■ Participants place suggestion cards on the model indicating what they want to see happen and where (eg playground, parking, standpipe, tree, shopping).

■ The cards are sorted and prioritised to establish an action plan which is followed up by working groups.

✎ Kits with building cut-outs and cards can be purchased (☞ further info), or you can make up your own using available materials.

✎ Events work best if facilitated by someone who has done it before but the basic idea is easy to pick up from the kits. The kits' manufacturers – the Neighbourhood Initiatives Foundation – recommends that users should be fully trained by them.

✎ The model kits are good for generating interest and creating an initial vision. After that they need some creative adaptation if they are to be used for detailed design.

$ From US$800 (venue and materials) to $24,000 (trained facilitator to prepare for several months).

Typical Planning for Real process

1 **Initiation.** Define area. Set up Steering Group. Get support. Purchase model pack (optional) or gather materials. (3 months)

2 **Make model.** A collective exercise by Steering Group, often with school children or students. Usually to a scale of 1:200 or 1:300 – which allows people to identify their own homes – and in sections so that it is easily transportable. (2 days)

3 **Publicise activity.** Take model around the area to generate interest. (2 weeks)

4 **Training session.** Run through process with Steering Group. (2 hours)

5 **Open sessions.**
One or more times in different locations.
- People gather around model. **Introduction** by facilitator explaining objectives and process. (10 mins)
- Participants individually place **suggestion cards** on the model. Professionals watch and answer questions but do not take part. (30 mins)
- Participants **discuss results** and rearrange cards until collectively happy with the result. (30 mins)
- Participants **record results**, usually on priority cards setting out the suggestion and its location. (30 mins)
- Participants **prioritise suggestions** by placing priority cards on Now, Soon or Later boards and identifying who should take action. (30 mins)
- **Discussion on next steps** and establishing working parties on the main issues. (20 mins)

(Total: 2.5 hours – possibly broken up into a series of separate drop-in 'suggestions' sessions, and then a prioritising session.)

6 **Working parties.**
Follow up suggestions. (2 months)

7 **Feedback.**
Circulation of newsletter. (1 month)

Making suggestions
Participants mill around the model, and make their views known by placing pre-written or self-completed suggestion cards onto it.

Prioritising
Working in small groups, participants order the suggestions by placing cards onto a chart which is divided into three bands –'Now', 'Soon', 'Later' – on one axis and those who should be responsible for taking action on the other.

FURTHER INFORMATION

☞ Method: *Models.* Scenario: *Inner city regeneration.*

⌥ *The Power in our Hands.*

✉ Planning for Real Unit.

☆ Margaret Wilkinson. 'Planning for Real'® is a registered trademark of the Neighbourhood Initiatives Foundation.

Planning weekend

Planning weekends are an elaborate but highly effective way of generating momentum for change and getting all parties involved in producing a masterplan or plan of action for a site, neighbourhood or city.

Briefing
Team members are briefed by community leaders and officials at the start of a planning weekend.

Public presentation
Team members present their proposals for the area to a public meeting after four intensive days of workshops, brainstorming and team working.

■ Planning weekends comprise an intensive and carefully structured programme of activities spanning a weekend. They usually last for 5 full days – Thursday to Monday – but may be longer or shorter. The main workshop sessions are open to the general public.

■ The weekends are facilitated by a multidisciplinary team. This may be comprised of outsiders or locals or a combination of the two.

■ The end result is a set of proposals for action which is presented to the community on the last evening and produced in exhibition and print form.

✎ Planning weekends – often called *community* planning weekends – work best when there is at least 6 months preparation time and a commitment by all parties to follow up afterwards.

✎ The most effective long-term results are likely to be when events are organised locally with back-up and support from people who have done it before.

"In many ways, the process has transformed the way that Americans shape community development policies and take those actions that most directly affect their community's growth or change."
American Institute of Architects
R/UDAT Handbook, 1992.

✎ Employing a local resident as event co-ordinator can help ensure local support and follow-up.

✎ Have paper tablecloths at meals and encourage inpromptu sketching.

$ Average costs: US$30,000 excluding organisers' time and assuming team members come free. Professionally organised events can cost over $100,000. Locally organised events can be done for under $15,000.

Planning weekend timetable
Sample for a 5-day event. Customise.

DAY 1 THURSDAY — BRIEFING
08.00 **Setting up**
Room layout. Delivery of equipment and supplies. Erection of banners and signs.
12.00 **Team assembles**
13.00 **Buffet lunch**
Welcome by hosts and sponsors.
14.00 **Reconnaissance**
By team of area by bus, train, plane or on foot.
16.00 **Political briefings**
By local politicians.
17.00 **Community briefings**
By local inhabitants.
18.00 **Technical briefings**
By planners, engineers, developers.
19.00 **Team briefing**
By Chairperson on Team working processes.
19.30 **Launch event** (optional)
Public meeting and/or dinner/reception.

DAY 2 FRIDAY — ISSUES
09.00 **Team briefing and preparation**
10.00 **Setting the scene**
Presentations by local interests.
11.00 **Topic or 'Briefing' workshops**
Open to all, punctuated by lunch and tea breaks. Several parallel topic-based groups ending with plenary report back (or one single open plenary workshop).
17.00 **Team review**
Detailed problem definition.
18.00 **Breather**
Minute writing, reading, exercise.
20.00 **Team dinner**

DAY 3 SATURDAY — SOLUTIONS
09.00 **Team briefing and preparation**
10.00 **Report back on Day 2**
By Chairperson and/or Team members.
10.30 **Lessons from elsewhere**
Presentations by Team members.
12.00 **Design workshops**
Open to all, punctuated by lunch and tea breaks and ending with plenary report back. In parallel groups of 10-15.

17.00 **Team review**
Developing central themes.
18.00 **Breather**
Minute writing, reading, exercise.
20.00 **Team brainstorm dinner**
Imaginative solutions.

DAY 4 SUNDAY — TEAM WORKING
10.00 **Team preparation**
11.00 **Team editorial meeting**
Report, presentation and production structure.
12.00 **Report and presentation production**
Writing, editing, drawing, Powerpoint show. Review meetings as necessary. Team only. Sleep and eat as and when possible.

DAY 5 MONDAY — PRESENTATION
07.00 **Printers deadline**
Report and/or broadsheet to printers.
All day **Presentation preparation**
Image and text selection. Exhibition mounting. Hall arrangements.
All day **Clearing up**
Tidying up, packing equipment and supplies.
17.30 **Press briefing**
19.00 **Public presentation**
Powerpoint show followed by discussion and formal thanks. Distribution of report or broadsheet.
21.00 **Farewell social event**

Ideal numbers: 100–250. Team: 10–30
Larger numbers can be catered for if enough space and workshop facilitators.

FURTHER INFORMATION

☞ Methods: *Briefing workshop. Design workshop.* Scenarios: *Inner city regeneration. Local neighbourhood initiative. Newspaper supplement.* Case study: *Caterham Barracks Village, UK.*

🕮 *The Charrette Handbook. The Community Planning Event Manual. Creating a Design Assistance Team for Your Community.*

☆ Charles Campion, John Thompson & Ptnrs.

Prioritising

	NOW	SOON	LATER
We can do it on our own	■ ■		■
We can do it with a little help		■ ■	
We can do it with help plus some money	■	■ ■	
We can do it jointly with the local authority	■		■
We cannot do it but can tell the local authority or other agency what needs doing	■ ■ ■	■	■
Who else could help?	■	■	■

Prioritising projects
Matrix for placing cards identifying possible projects or actions needed.

Prioritising is a way of placing in order of priority what needs doing and when. This is an important aspect of all decision making and often needs to be done as a group activity if the results are to be generally agreed on.

■ The various options are worked out using brainstorming, surveys or other methods.

■ A graphic format is selected to allow the prioritising of options to be simply and visually displayed. There are many ways of doing this, including the three examples shown on these pages (and on pages 38–39, 85 and 96–97).

■ After discussion of the issues, and perhaps presentations, participants make individual choices using stickers or cards.

■ The results are analysed and provide the basis for decision making or further discussion.

✎ Often worth allowing people an opportunity to change their votes after seeing how others vote and discussing the results. This allows people to think through situations which are often quite complex.

✎ Facilitator's skill is finding the appropriate graphic format for the issues being considered.

✎ Great scope for using computers to process results, especially where large number of people and choices are involved.

$ No significant costs involved apart from facilitator's fees if any.

Wheel of fortune group prioritising method

Way for a group of people to collectively rank up to 20 competing priorities. Suitable for a workshop or public meeting.

1 Preparation

Large sheets of paper are taped together to create a big square on the floor or a table. The bigger the group, the larger it needs to be. A large circle is drawn on the paper, divided into as many slices as there are options. Each slice is labelled.

2 Coloured sticky notes

Participants are each given 3 cards or Post-it notes. Different colours can be given to people representing different interest groups.

3 Voting

Participants vote for their top three priorities by placing their cards or Post-its in the relevant slice.

4 Discussion and recording

Votes are counted and recorded for further discussion.

The process is repeated with different groups.

Ideal numbers: 10–15
Running time: 20 minutes

Fence prioritising method

Way for a group to arrive at a majority view on issues where there are conflicting options. Likely to be done after presentations, and discussion of the issues involved.

1 A list of issues is prepared, perhaps by a consultant.
2 The issues are illustrated graphically on lines with a 'fence' in the middle (see below).
3 Participants discuss each issue in turn. After discussion, each participant places a dot somewhere along the line. A dot placed towards the end of a line indicates strong agreement for the given option. A dot in the middle indicates no strong views either way (ie 'sitting on the fence').
4 The strongest concentration of dots (or the mean position of the sum of all the dots) is taken as the collective view.

Example below: planning a new settlement.

	FENCE	
Neighbourhoods. Based on 5-minute walk (400m)		No identifiable neighbourhood structure
Shopping. Small retail centres you can walk to		Larger retail centres you can drive to
Roads. New road with 50km/hr speed limit		New road as by-pass with 80km/hr speed limit
Streets. Interconnected streets with calmed through-traffic		Curvilinear street system with cul-de-sac streets
Working/Living. Mixing working and living places		Separate working and living places
Integration. Development linking with surrounding area		New self-contained communities

---

FURTHER INFORMATION

☞ Methods: *Design workshop. Ideas comp. Microplanning. Planning for Real.*

☆ Matrix: Neighbourhood Initiatives Foundation. Wheel of fortune: Robin Deane, 1066 Housing Association. Peter Richards, Deicke Richards Architects.

Process planning session

Process planning sessions allow people to work together to determine the most suitable public participation process for their particular situation. It is particularly useful to hold them at an early stage in a community planning initiative and then at periodic intervals.

- As many as possible of the key interested parties or 'stakeholders' are invited to ensure that the outcome is supported by all parties.

- Participants are introduced to the various options available and helped to design a process of their own, usually by an external facilitator.

- A formal workshop format is normally followed (example in box, right) to make the procedure equitable and transparent.

- Sessions are held periodically whenever there is a need to review the overall process.

✎ Make people feel comfortable and relaxed. Spanning lunch can work well for officials and business people with participants seated around circular tables. Evening sessions spanning a buffet supper will normally work better for residents.

✎ Be on guard for sabotage by those who don't want any kind of process to take place.

✎ Showing slides or videos of methods in use is usually a good way to generate enthusiasm.

✎ Invite external facilitators to present options, but keep ownership local from the start.

$ Main costs: venue; catering; fee for presenter.

ANYWHERE FORUM

COMMUNITY PLANNING FOR ANYWHERE REGENERATION?

All members of the Anywhere Forum are invited to a slide show and workshop to plan a strategy for involving local people in regeneration initiatives

Monday 17 February 7–9.30pm at Anywhere Community Centre

THIS MEETING IS IMPORTANT FOR THE FUTURE OF ANYWHERE

Please come if you can
Contact: Joan Simms, Secretary, Anywhere Forum, 227 Farley Way
Tel: 444777

Sample flyer
Key components: issue; time and location of event; stress importance, contact details.

Evening session
Police, residents and other stakeholders taking part in an evening process planning session in a community centre. It led to a community planning weekend seven months later.

Process planning session sample format

1 Introductions
Facilitator explains event objectives and structure. Everyone says briefly who they are and what their hopes are for the session. (15 mins)

2 Presentation
Slide show or video of possible processes to provide inspiration. (45 mins max)

3 Aims
Short debate on overall objectives and specific constraints. (15 mins)

4 Refreshment break

5 Individual ideas
People fill in a process planner (☞ box, right, p219 or p224) OR develop their ideas on a blank sheet of paper. (10 mins minimum)

6 Group ideas
People are divided into groups (4–8 ideal). Individuals present their idea to group. Group votes to pursue one idea only and develop it further. (20 mins min)

7 Report back
Each group makes semi-formal presentation of their idea to plenary of all participants. (5 mins each group)

8 Selection
Vote on which idea to pursue and then discuss improvements and next steps. (10 mins minimum).

Ideal numbers: 16–20.
Larger numbers no problem.

Running time: 2–4 hours.
3 hours comfortable.

Note: This format can also be used for general training purposes with no specific location or issue in mind.

Lunchtime session
One of four tables at a working lunch for key players (property owners, authorities, amenity groups) to determine a development process for a major town centre regeneration initiative. It led to a design workshop and open house event one year later.

Sample process planner
Customise and leave space for responses.

Aims
1 What do you want to **achieve**? _____
2 What are the main **issues**? _____
3 What geographical **area** are you concerned with? _____

Process
4 What **methods** do you favour? _____
5 **When** should activities take place? _____
6 **Who** are the key people to involve? _____
7 What **expertise** do you need? _____

Organisation
8 Which **organisation/s** should lead? _____
9 Who else should **help**? _____
10 How much will it **cost** and **who pays**? ___
11 Who does **what next**? _____

12 **Other** thoughts and ideas _____

FURTHER INFORMATION

☞ Getting started p8. Useful formats p219 and p224.

Scenarios: *Local neighbourhood initiative. Planning study. Town centre upgrade.*

Reconnaissance trip

Reconnaissance trips involve direct inspection of the area being considered by mixed teams of local people and technical experts. They are used to familiarise everyone with the physical environment and key issues at the start of many community planning processes and to review progress at intervals.

Tour of neighbourhood
Well planned route map with important features marked (above). Viewing from the air, with the media and on the ground (below).

■ A route is carefully planned to include key local features and issues. The route may be walked or toured by bus, boat or other forms of transport. It may include visits to buildings or facilities.

■ The trip is undertaken by a mixed group of local people and technical experts. Usually a team leader will direct the group and determine the pace.

■ The group make notes, sketches, take photos and talk informally to people in their own setting. They may check existing plans for accuracy.

■ At the end of the trip a debriefing is held, and the notes and other materials compiled into a form useful to the next stage of the planning process.

✎ Where little information exists, the route can be planned with a view to producing a specific 'transect' diagram or map *(see right)*.

✎ Groups of more than 15 can be unwieldy. Split into smaller groups, perhaps taking different routes and comparing notes afterwards.

✎ Viewing from a hill or high tower is particularly useful. If funds allow, a trip in a helicopter or light aircraft can be worthwhile.

✎ Good opportunity for engaging with media, especially TV.

$ Main costs: transport; organiser's time.

Reconnaissance trip timetable

Sample for a complex trip lasting most of a day with advance planning.

1 **Briefings.** By a number of key parties (in a hall or meeting room).

2 **Bus.** Tour of wider area. Commentary by local residents and planners. Stops at high viewing point and key buildings and sites.

3 **Lunch.** In a local bar with business people.

4 **Walk.** Around central area. Semi-structured interviews with traders. Detailed checking of land use plan.

5 **Tea.** At a community centre with local residents. Discussion.

6 **Visit.** To arts centre. Viewing of local crafts exhibition. Discussion with artists.

7 **Team meeting.** Debriefing and review.

Transect walk format

For a simple walk where little information exists and with little advance planning.

1 **Select people.** Decide who will do the walk. Ensure a cross-section of interests.

2 **Decide route and issues.** Plan a route which covers the issues under consideration (eg land use changes, development pressures, hazards).

3 **Walk.** Walk the route making sketches, taking notes, holding informal interviews, taking photos.

4 **Construct profile.** Compile all notes and sketches. Prepare a profile in map or diagram form.

5 **Display.** Use profile as a basis for consultation and planning.

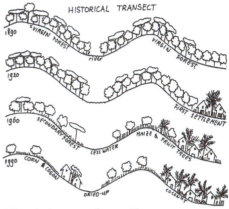

Historical community profile
Diagram resulting from a transect walk showing the evolution of the landscape over the last century.

Looking round
Exploring and discussing a site proposed for development and a factory in a proposed conservation area.

FURTHER INFORMATION

☞ Methods: *Diagrams. Design assistance team. Mapping. Planning weekend. Review session.*
Scenario: *New neighbourhood.*

Review session

Review sessions are a useful way of monitoring progress and maintaining momentum. They can be held weeks, months, or even years after an action planning event or other community planning initiative.

Reunion
Cakes made by a local resident set the tone for team members returning to the scene of an action planning event for a review session.

Was it a useful thing to do?

What did it achieve?

How could we have done it better?

What happens next?

Sample brief
For a review session on a community planning event.

- Background material is produced evaluating the outcome of initiatives and reviewing progress.

- All those involved in previous activity are invited back to a session, normally lasting for one day. Invitations can also be sent to those who may wish to become involved in the future.

- A programme is designed to review progress, evaluate earlier initiatives and determine the next steps (see sample timetable, right).

- A report of the session is written up and circulated.

✎ Timing is important. Holding a review session too soon will be pointless. Left too long and you may lose momentum.

✎ Make it an enjoyable event by including opportunities for socialising and networking.

✎ Evaluating precisely what outcomes have resulted from any particular initiative is always difficult because there are so many variables. No one is likely to have the whole picture. Produce a draft of the Progress Monitor (p223) and circulate it for comment.

✎ Good opportunity to get new people and groups on board, particularly those feeling excluded by not being involved previously.

$ Main costs: venue, preparation, travel costs, refreshments.

Review session timetable

10.00 **Arrivals and refreshments**
Viewing of display material.

10.30 **Walkabout**
To observe progress on the ground.

11.15 **Report back**
By those undertaking initiatives.

12.15 **Evaluation sessions**
General review as a group.

12.45 **Lunch**
(plus evaluation sessions for special groups, eg external team members).

14.00 **Next steps**
List actions needed now and by who.

15.15 **Refreshments and networking**

Ideal numbers: 30–40

Reviewing progress
Team members and participants of a community planning week meet 16 months later to review progress and plan further initiatives.

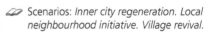

FURTHER INFORMATION
Scenarios: *Inner city regeneration. Local neighbourhood initiative. Village revival.*
Useful formats: *Progress monitor. Evaluation form.*
☆   Dick Watson

Risk assessment

Risk assessment involves analysing threats (or 'hazards') facing a community. It should ideally be used in all planning – since most communities face some kind of threat. But it is most necessary for vulnerable communities prone to natural or human-made disasters.

- Risk assessment comprises three elements:
  - **hazard analysis** – understanding what hazards exist, the likelihood of them occurring, their likely intensity and their effect.
  - **vulnerability assessment** – understanding who or what is vulnerable to the hazards.
  - **capacity assessment** – understanding what capacities exist within the community to reduce vulnerability.

- A range of methods can be used to make it easy for communities to make their own risk assessments as a basis for taking action to reduce risks (see box right). Most involve group work, preferably with trained facilitators.

- The end result is a clear understanding by the community of the nature and scale of the risks it faces. It is then possible to determine what is needed to reduce the risk; for instance new local initiatives, outside resources, technical expertise.

✎ Big benefit is in obliging planning to consider natural and human-made hazards and infrequent threats all too often ignored.

✎ Involve local emergency services; an invaluable source of knowledge.

$ Varies depending on approaches adopted and numbers involved.

Is your community ever threatened by:

- ☐ Accidents (car, rail, air)
- ☐ Armed conflict
- ☐ Civil unrest
- ☐ Cyclone
- ☐ Deforestation
- ☐ Drought
- ☐ Earthquakes
- ☐ Environmental degradation
- ☐ Epidemics
- ☐ Fire
- ☐ Flooding
- ☐ Migrations (forced)
- ☐ Over-development
- ☐ Pests
- ☐ Pollution
- ☐ Tidal waves
- ☐ Tornadoes
- ☐ Tourism (excessive)
- ☐ Traffic congestion
- ☐ Tribal wars
- ☐ Typhoon
- ☐ Volcanic eruption

Hazards checklist
Typical hazards that may face a community but are often ignored until it is too late. They range in seriousness but the same principles for assessing and reducing risks apply to all.

Vulnerability and capacity matrix

POTENTIAL HAZARD *Flooding*	VULNERABILITIES	CAPACITIES
PHYSICAL and MATERIAL What is vulnerable? What resources exist to address vulnerability?	· Houses & farmland in low lying areas. · Water supplies easily contaminated by floods. · Food supplies get cut.	· People have boats to save belongings. · Identifiable evacuation centre exists.
SOCIAL and ORGANISATION Who is vulnerable? What resources exist to make them less so?	· People in outlying areas (15 families). · Migrant workers. · People unable to swim (particularly women).	· People's organisation at community level. · Warning system exists. Disaster response committee functions.
MOTIVATION and ATTITUDE What attitudes lead to vulnerability? What capacities exist to improve the situation?	· Individualism. · Lack of community spirit/cooperation.	· New positive attitude by young people. · Voluntary organisations.

Some participatory risk assessment methods

Hazard and risk mapping
Locating hazards on maps along with people, buildings and infrastructure at risk from those hazards (☞ *Mapping*).

Simulation exercises
Acting out the effect of possible hazards. Either to assess the impact of new initiatives on existing risk levels or to understand the impact of past hazards (☞ *Simulation*).

Hazard or threat ranking
Prioritising the importance of various hazards according to community perceptions and needs (☞ *Community profiling*).

Vulnerability and capacity analysis
Compiling a matrix of a community's vulnerabilities to, and capacities to cope with, each hazard identified (see example, above).

Completing a vulnerability and capacity matrix
General and risk-specific information from secondary sources and community profiling sessions is ordered into categories and placed in a matrix as shown above. This is usually done in group sessions using a large wallchart. A separate matrix is completed for each hazard. Separate charts can be completed for men and women and for different ethnic groups. Completed matrices can be used to test a proposed initiative's impact on a community's vulnerability and capacity, and to monitor it during implementation.

FURTHER INFORMATION
☞ Method: *Community profiling. Mapping. Simulation.* Scenarios: *Disaster management. Shanty settlement upgrading.* ⱬ *Rising from the Ashes* ☆ Roger Bellers. Nick Hall.

Roadshow

Sample advertising leaflet
Key components: map showing sites; times and locations of workshops, exhibitions and symposium; details of organisers, sponsors etc; aims and objectives.

Roadshows combine a series of workshops, exhibitions and a symposium to generate professionally produced urban design proposals based on local people's wishes. They are a good way of generating a critical mass of energy for securing wide debate and an impetus for implementation.

■ An overall theme is agreed by the organisers (such as vacant sites or rundown estates) and a number of sites in a neighbourhood selected for attention.

■ Teams of professionals are selected by open competition to prepare improvement schemes for each of the selected sites.

■ The chosen teams facilitate design workshops with local residents, prepare proposals and present them in an interactive exhibition.

■ A final, highly publicised symposium is held to debate the results and generate momentum for the scheme's implementation.

"It's a wonderful format; this teach-in on matters that we all have opinions about with people who are knowledgeable. It's started a discussion that's desperately needed about taking control of our own environment. May the debate roll on."
Roger de Freitas, Hammersmith Society
Summary Symposium, Architecture Foundation Roadshow, 28 May 1998.

✎ Roadshows are most likely to succeed if organised by an independent body with the active support of the local authorities and community groups.

✎ Other publicity and involvement activity undertaken at the same time (eg school workshops, video soapboxes, radio phone-ins) can help generate momentum.

$ Main costs: organisers' time (3 person months at least); publicity material, fees for design teams (optional); venue for symposium.

Sample roadshow timetable

Jan–Mar **Preparation.** Decide on area, theme and sites. Secure support from key groups, and funding. Prepare format and logistics.

Apr **Announce competition for design teams.** Open competition to select professional teams.

June **Select teams.** Based on ability to work with local communities as well as on technical ability.

July **Official public launch.** To secure media publicity.

Aug–Sep **Public workshops.** To brief design teams (one workshop for each site). **Schools programme.** Workshops generating proposals from children. **Video soapbox.** Prominently located to gain views of wider public.

Oct **Design time.** All-day crit for all design teams and key local stakeholders to share approaches prior to finalising proposals.

Oct **Exhibition of proposals.** With provision for people to comment. Preferably held at on-site locations as well as at a locally prominent venue where the symposium is to be held.

Oct **Symposium.** With high profile speakers and media.

Nov **Scheme revision.** In the light of comments.

Dec **Report published.**

Ideal numbers: 10 sites and design teams
Total time period: 1 year

Exhibition of proposals
Proposals from the design teams are publicly exhibited to encourage discussion and dialogue which is continued at a public symposium.

FURTHER INFORMATION

☞ Methods: *Design workshop. Ideas competition. Interactive display. Design fest. Video soapbox.*

✉ Glass-House Community Led Design.

Simulation

Simulation can be used to act out a real event or activity, helping both participants and observers gain information and insights prior to formulating plans. It can also be used to test draft plans.

Look at the sky, the clouds are dark. It may be a storm coming. Let's turn on the radio.

Local radio channel: "Flood warning No 3."

Quick, let's go home and sandbag our house.

I'll go and move the animals to higher ground.

Tell grandpa to come and stay at our house - just in case the stream banks burst.

Do you think we could move our belongings into the school hall if things get too bad?

Not sure. Drop in at the store on the way back and ask.

- An event or activity to be simulated is chosen. This could be a natural or human-made hazard – such as an earthquake – or daily life in a street or building.

- People who have experienced the event or activity from a variety of perspectives are brought together for a workshop session.

- People act out the event or activity as a drama, individually or in groups. Usually, a carefully structured exercise is prepared in advance by a facilitator (see example in box, right).

- Key information and issues arising are recorded for future use.

- Recommendations are identified for future actions.

✎ Enjoyable way of getting information that would be hard to obtain any other way.

✎ Good process for team building and clarification of roles.

✎ People may need time to prepare, so the method should be explained in advance.

✎ Allocate time for discussion after each simulation exercise to allow people to reflect on their own performance.

$ Minimal costs involved for materials, plus facilitator's fees if any.

Sample simulation exercise

1 Determine event or activity to simulate
Eg: A recent flood.

2 Design the exercise
Objectives. Process. Materials required.

3 Assemble participants/cast of characters
Eg: A cross-section of the local community
affected in different ways by the flood,
plus officials and technical experts dealing
with flood relief and avoidance measures.

4 Explain purpose
Eg: To understand how people reacted to
the recent flood in order to decide on
measures to reduce the impact of future
ones. (10 mins)

5 Divide into groups
Ask each group to prepare to act out a
different aspect of the event or activity in
the form of a drama. Eg: Before the flood;
during the flood; after the flood. Each
group also to appoint a reporter. (10 mins)

6 Group working
Each group prepares its drama through
discussion prompted by responding to key
questions. Eg: "When and how did you
know a flood was coming?" "What did
people do and when?" Reporter notes
main issues arising. (60 mins)

7 Plenary: dramas and presentation
Each group acts out its drama followed by
a presentation by the reporter summing up
the main issues. General discussion.
(60–90 mins)

8 Review (perhaps later or after a break)
Review of issues and concerns raised.
Discussion on next steps. (30 mins)

Ideal numbers: 18–24 (3 groups of 6–8)
Running time: 140–170 mins (plus 30
mins for review)
Note: The same exercise could be used to
simulate an event that has not yet
happened but might do in the future.

Acting out an event
*Local residents dramatising how they were
affected by a recent typhoon during a field
workshop to improve disaster management.*

Street stall

Street stalls are interactive displays held out of doors. They make it possible to secure the views of larger numbers of people than is normally possible indoors. They are especially useful where the views of people using a particular street or public space are required.

Bath News

PRECINCT'S FUTURE: hundreds stop to answer revamp questions

Shoppers speak out on Southgate ideas

- A highly public location is selected and exhibition and interactive display material mounted for a selected period.

- Facilitators are on hand to encourage people to make comments and engage in debate.

- The event may be advertised in advance but this is not essential.

"The street stall proved to be an invaluable and invigorating experience for us all. We were overwhelmed by the interest taken... and all subsequent developments of our scheme were made against the backdrop of what the people of Bath wanted to see."
Student report, Prince of Wales's Institute of Architecture
Bath Project, 1996.

"The day had a certain verve which boosted – and was reinforced by – the strong level of interest of passers-by. It was good for the Trust to be involved in something as popular and constructive – we are often portrayed as being elitist and negative."
Timothy Cantell, Chairman, Planning Committee, Bath Preservation Trust
letter, March 1997.

✎ Arcades, colonnades and supermarket foyers are good venues as they provide shelter from the rain. Ideal if you can also have the use of a shop.

✎ Can benefit from, and be attractive for, radio and television coverage. Leaflets can also be handed out to passers-by and placed in shop windows.

✎ Be careful when using Post-it notes and leaflets if windy conditions are likely – they may blow away!

✎ Getting formal permission to set up a stall in a public area can take forever. Plan well ahead or just do it and be prepared to move if necessary.

✎ Likely to attract a broader range of people than an indoor event, but marginalised groups or reticent individuals may still need special inducement to participate. Have a 'postbox' so that people can make contributions anonymously.

$ Main costs: display material; staff time.

Taking to the streets

Shoppers join in a debate on the future of the town centre by writing on Post-it notes, sketching their own ideas and holding discussions with the organisers. Over 2,000 Post-it notes were posted up over 5 hours on a cold winter day and two books filled with comments. The results were used to prepare a scheme for one of the most important development sites in the town.

FURTHER INFORMATION

☞ Methods: *Interactive display. Open house event. Table scheme display.* Scenario: *Community centre.*

Table scheme display

Table scheme displays allow large numbers of people to understand and make an input into development proposals, with or without engaging with others. They can be used as part of an exhibition or open house event.

- Drawings or models of a proposed scheme are placed on a table with the main elements identified on separate voting sheets around the edge.

- Separate tables can be used for different scheme options.

- People vote on what they like or dislike by placing sticky dots on the voting sheets.

- More detailed comments can be made using Post-it notes, either on the same tables or on separate displays.

- The results are analysed afterwards to inform the next stages of the planning process.

✎ Good way of introducing people to the design process. Works particularly well for getting comments on rough sketch schemes developed at design workshops. Redrawing is not usually necessary though it can help if time allows.

✎ Useful debate will invariably take place around the tables. It can be helpful to have organisers present at each table to respond to questions and to take notes.

✎ Have a spare table with a blank plan for those wanting to draw up their own ideas in more detail.

$ Few costs involved unless proposals are professionally redrawn.

THE MAIN ELEMENTS OF THE SKETCH SCHEMES ARE HIGHLIGHTED.

Please indicate whether you agree or disagree with the ideas by using the stickers provided.

● Green = Agree

● Red = Disagree

● Yellow = No opinion

YOU MAY HAVE YOUR OWN IDEAS OR SUGGESTIONS.

Please write these on the comment sheet or sketch them on the blank plan provided. It will help if you add your name and address.

Sample instructions

Table scheme display
Voting with sticky dots on town centre improvement ideas proposed by a design workshop focusing on transport. Part of a one-day open house event.

FURTHER INFORMATION

☞ Methods: *Interactive display. Open house event.*

Scenario: *Community centre.*

Task force

Urban design task forces are multidisciplinary teams of students and professionals which produce proposals for a site or neighbourhood based on an intensive programme of site studies, lectures, participatory exercises and studio working, normally lasting several weeks. They are an efficient way of securing high quality design proposals at the same time as providing a first-rate educational opportunity.

Urban Design Task Force

Anytown, Anycountry
5–26 July 2015

Team members wanted
Contact Urban Design Task Force
10 High Street, Anytown

Recruiting team members
Sample poster for a task force.

"The task force is valuable because when people come from outside they have a special vision, with a certain objectivity, and they see things we don't see. That vision is very very good for developing new approaches."
Yves Dauge, Mayor of Chinon
France, 12 August 1994.

"Before the Task Force, all discussion about the future of the city – what should happen, when and where – took place in small rooms with one or two people. Now everyone is discussing it."
Lorenzo Piacentini, engineer
Viterbo, Italy, 1994.

"It was an absolutely exceptional experience. We were exposed to so many inspiring people and it was very intensive. It had a great influence on my life."
Joanna Wachowiak,
architecture student, 1994.

■ Task forces combine an academic and practical training in urban design with the development of realistic proposals for improving a site, neighbourhood or city.

■ Staff and student team members will come from a range of backgrounds, ages and, normally, countries.

■ The programme begins with academic input and skills training and then moves into engaging with the community and producing urban design proposals (see sample format, right).

■ Task forces are likely to be organised by academic institutions in partnership with local agencies.

✎ Plan at least one year in advance in order to have time to secure support from all relevant local organisations and make the necessary logistical arrangements.

$ Cost dependent on numbers involved. Main costs: travel; accommodation; staff time; presentation materials. Cost for a 4-week event likely to be around US$130,000. Contributors: host city, student members, academic institutions. Scope also for sponsorship and international exchange funding.

Task force sample format

1 Building a skill base
Seminars, practical experience and visits
for the team designed to develop skills in:
- observational drawing and painting
- urban analysis
- local building crafts
- measuring buildings
- modelmaking
- team working
- participatory design

(1 week)

2 Small live projects
Developing urban design proposals for
small sites. These may be of real practical
value but are primarily designed to develop
skills in urban design, presentation and
team working. (1 week)

3 Public engagement on large live project
Public lectures, meetings or workshops
with various interest groups, community
planning event (eg *Community planning
forum*). (3 days)

4 Studio working
Developing urban design proposals.
(2 weeks)

5 Presentation
Exhibition and public presentation of
proposals with newsletter. (1 day)

6 Publication
Publication of book or report of proposals.
(6 months)

Ideal numbers: 20–30 students
10 tutors

Running time: 3–6 weeks

Public engagement
Finding out local views on the city.

Studio working
*Task force members prepare proposals in a
temporary locally-based studio.*

Presentation
*Task force members explain their proposals to
local politicians at the final presentation.*

FURTHER INFORMATION

☞ Methods: *Community planning forum.
Urban design studio.* Scenario: *New
neighbourhood.*

☏ *Viterbo; Santa Maria in Gradi.*

✉ Prince's Foundation.

☆ Brian Hanson and Richard John.

Urban design studio

Urban design studios are special units attached to a university or other educational establishment which undertake environmental project work, usually in the immediate locality. They can provide both a valuable educational experience for students and an important resource for local communities.

Academic rigour
Combining theory and practice.

"It allowed me to apply things I learned in school in a no-longer fictitious environment. It's not the community being treated as a laboratory for students to exercise their creative will. Both sides are getting something out of it."
J B Clancy, student
Yale Urban Design Workshop
New York Times, 19.11.1995.

"Students are increasingly interested in what it means to be a participant in the public realm. The idea of a citizen architect is back."
Alan Plattus, Director
Yale Urban Design Workshop
New York Times, 19.11.1995.

■ Urban design studios are set up by an educational establishment, usually at a school of architecture or planning. They will normally be independent units.

■ The studios have access to all the resources of the establishment: staff, students, researchers, facilities and equipment.

■ Relationships will be built up with local agencies and community organisations and a variety of project work will be undertaken.

■ Once established, the studios will start advertising their services and take on consultancy work.

✎ Independence is essential to overcome the incompatibility of curriculum and real project timetables. Academics and administrators sometimes find such units threatening because students often enjoy the work more than academic studies. Also, live projects generate their own momentum and are hard to dovetail into predetermined time slots. Studios rarely survive unless given enough time to build up a reputation, so making it possible to attract funding for projects and become self-sufficient.

✎ Core staff are needed to maintain momentum of projects during school vacations and other times when students are unavailable.

✎ Studios may work best if student involvement is voluntary.

$ Main costs are staff, travel and equipment. Initially funded as part of architecture school. Later, can secure consultancy fees.

Urban design studio typical projects

Activities which can be educational and easily carried out by an education institution.

- ☐ **Community planning events**
  Organisation of community planning forums, design days and task forces.
- ☐ **Design guides**
  Research and production of guides for local areas.
- ☐ **Design proposals**
  Preparing design ideas for specific sites or a masterplan for a whole area.
- ☐ **Model-making**
  Making models of buildings or neighbourhoods.
- ☐ **Surveys**
  Assisting communities with surveys and analysis of community needs.
- ☐ **Visualisation**
  Assisting communities with visual aids including computer imaging.

Academic resource
Students, academics and community members use a school of architecture to debate and solve real local planning issues. Strange though it may seem, this is not a normal occurrence in most architecture schools.

FURTHER INFORMATION

☞ Methods: *Community planning event. Local design statement. Task force.*

Scenarios: *Derelict site re-use. New neighbourhood.*

✉ Ball State University. Yale Urban Design Workshop.

User group

The creation or strengthening of user groups is a key element of most community planning. They act as clients in championing the views of those who will use the end product and keep the momentum going, often for many years.

- User groups should be as representative as possible of the end users of any initiative, including as many interests and viewpoints as possible.

- Initially user groups are likely to be informally organised and dominated by self-selected enthusiasts. As projects develop, the groups may need to become more formally organised with democratic voting procedures and, perhaps, legal status.

- For larger projects, several different groups may be useful at various times and groups will have sub-groups and working parties for specific issues.

✎ It is important to work closely with existing organisations but each project needs its own dedicated group. Otherwise projects simply become 'another item on the agenda' of an existing body and will probably be mediocre or flounder.

✎ If enough people are interested, set up sub-groups and working parties. The more people that can be involved and given roles the better.

✎ Make sure the nature of any group is clearly understood. It is always worth writing down 'terms of reference' setting out a group's purpose, powers, accountability, funding, meeting schedules and so on.

$ Main costs initially: printing and publicity. Most groups will raise money through membership fees and fundraising events.

INAUGURAL MEETING

Anytown Transport Forum
7pm Friday 4 June
Baptist Hall, John Street

A new organisation to coordinate and encourage initiatives to make travelling around Anytown easier for everyone.

AGENDA
1 Why a new organisation?
3 What kind of Forum?
4 Who should be on it?
5 How to administer it?
6 Election of steering group
7 Dates of future meetings.

Refreshments available

ALL WELCOME

Starting up
Sample leaflet advertising a meeting to set up a new group.

Common user group types

Action group
Informal issue-based campaigning group for interested individuals.

Community association
Represents the interests of a geographical neighbourhood or cultural entity. Includes residents, workers, businesses, etc.

Development and community land trust
Formally constituted organisation with a range of interests, usually with charitable status. Has development capability.

Forum
Liaison body for representatives of constituent organisations and interests. May be area- or issue- based.

Friends of ....
Loose support network of people supporting a particular place or cause.

Housing cooperative
Organisation of people who want to build or manage housing together.

Management committee
Formal organisation for managing a project.

Project group
Group set up to deal with one specific project (eg a new sports hall).

Residents association
Organisation representing residents in an area.

Steering group
Informal group set up to progress matters.

Working party
Informal group dealing with a specific topic.

Forum participant checklist

People who might be involved in a neighbourhood improvement forum.

- ☐ Architects/planners/designers
- ☐ Health workers
- ☐ Local authority staff
- ☐ Local business people
- ☐ Local residents' representatives
- ☐ Local shopkeepers' representatives
- ☐ Local teachers
- ☐ Play workers
- ☐ Police liaison officers
- ☐ Religious leader/s
- ☐ Social workers
- ☐ ....

Working together
Families who formed themselves into a working party and then a housing cooperative to plan and manage the construction of their own homes.

FURTHER INFORMATION

☞ Methods: *Development trust.*

Scenarios: *Local neighbourhood initiative. Town centre upgrade.*

✉ Community Matters.

Signing up
Starting a new user group at a workshop.

Video soapbox

Video soapboxes allow members of the public to broadcast their opinions on video screens erected in public places. They are particularly useful for generating public interest and debate for high profile events such as a roadshow.

If there were facilities, then the kids would get better and so would the world.

We need more activity centres like swimming pools and ice-rinks.

There are no public toilets!

Youth speaks
Young people using the soapbox facility to say what they think.

■ The basic technology required is a video camera, a projection facility and a screen. These can be used independently or incorporated into a special construction to make a prominent street feature (as in the example illustrated, right).

■ People are filmed making comments on an issue and these are projected for public viewing. This can be done simultaneously, or facilities can be included to allow for editing and captioning (see photos, left).

■ Video tapes can be kept for future screenings and can be analysed as a survey of public opinion.

✎ Video is a great medium for getting people to participate. Young people especially often find it more comfortable than meetings for expressing ideas and opinions.

✎ Get people making their own videos of their neighbourhood using small hand-held camcorders. These can very useful for getting a debate going at a workshop.

✎ Video footage of local neighbourhoods and community planning activity, preferably edited, can be useful for sponsors or decision-makers who may not be able to visit at the right moments. They can bring a funding application to life.

$ Basic video equipment can be bought for a few hundred dollars although editing equipment is more expensive. Education establishments often have facilities which can be used. Elaborate constructions like the one illustrated cost thousands of dollars but provide good opportunities for sponsorship. The one shown was paid for by a telephone company.

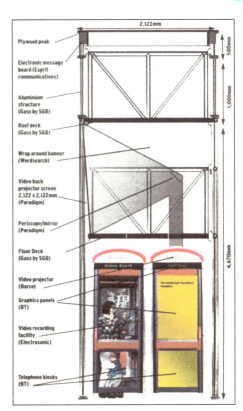

Public viewpoint

A resident's comments on the state of the local area are screened prominently in a shopping street. Passers-by can add their views to the debate by stepping into one of the converted telephone booths, picking up the handset and pressing 'record'.

Design details

Four telephone boxes are modified for people to record their views. Each booth contains a telephone handset which triggers the automatic video recording programme. Simple written and spoken operating instructions are provided. The scaffold tower above has a message board using moving text to invite the public to participate, a light cube with images relevant to the issue being considered and a back projection video screen on which the recorded messages are projected.

FURTHER INFORMATION

☞ Method: *Roadshow.*

✉ The Glass-House Community Led Design.

☆ Example shown designed by Alex de Rijke as part of an Architecture Foundation Roadshow. Illustration and screen shots courtesy of *Building Design.*

Community mapping,
Yunan, China, 1997

Scenarios A–Z

A range of scenarios covering some common development situations. Each illustrates one way in which methods can be combined in an overall strategy. For latest see:
www.communityplanning.net/scenarios/scenarios.php

Use for inspiration, not as blueprints. It is important to stress that in each case, there are many other ways of achieving the same objective. Note also that the timescales shown may be over-optimistic in some contexts as they assume that securing permissions, raising finance and setting up organisational frameworks takes place fairly smoothly.

Community-led plan

Although cumbersome, the label is self-explanatory. These are plans produced by, not for, the community.

The scenario outlined here is a step-by-step process that enables all citizens to participate in, and contribute to, improving their local area. It is dependent on initiation and leadership by committed local volunteers but works best if carried out in partnership with local authorities and other key stakeholders.

There are nine steps in four main phases of what is sometimes known as the LEAD process: **L**aunch; **E**vidence; **A**gree; **D**eliver.

It will be up to each community to decide how best to undertake each step and how long to take over it. The 18-month timescale indicated on the scenario timeline is fairly tight and most community-led plans will take longer as people assume responsibilities, get used to working with each other and learn a variety of new tasks.

The process becomes cyclical, being repeated every few years as necessary to ensure that plans remain up-to-date and responsive to local needs.

FURTHER INFORMATION

☞ Methods:
*Community profiling.
Community planning
event. Draft plan
consultation. Open
house event. Online
consultation. Process
planning session.
Review session.*

Scenarios:
*Neighbourhood
Development Plan.*

🖥 *Community Led
planning.*

⊘ *Community Led
Planning Toolkit*

✉ Action with Communities
in Rural England.
Action for Market Towns.

☆ Phillip Vincent.

Note: This scenario is based on a process that has been undertaken by over 4,000 communities across England. It has been developed, and promoted, by two umbrella organisations, Action with Communities in Rural England (ACRE) and Action for Market Towns (AMT).

Community-led plan

Producing a parish plan, local action plan, community plan or neighbourhood plan from the bottom up.

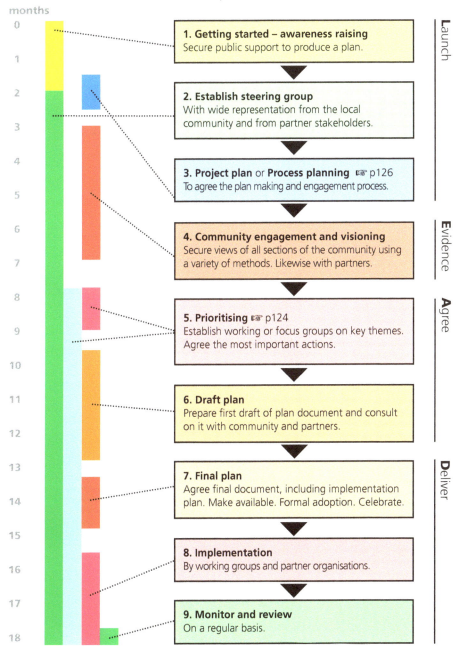

months

1. Getting started – awareness raising
Secure public support to produce a plan.

Launch

2. Establish steering group
With wide representation from the local community and from partner stakeholders.

3. Project plan or **Process planning** ☞ p126
To agree the plan making and engagement process.

4. Community engagement and visioning
Secure views of all sections of the community using a variety of methods. Likewise with partners.

Evidence

5. Prioritising ☞ p124
Establish working or focus groups on key themes. Agree the most important actions.

Agree

6. Draft plan
Prepare first draft of plan document and consult on it with community and partners.

7. Final plan
Agree final document, including implementation plan. Make available. Formal adoption. Celebrate.

Deliver

8. Implementation
By working groups and partner organisations.

9. Monitor and review
On a regular basis.

Community centre

This scenario applies to the design and construction of any building for community use.

The conventional approach would be for a local authority to commission architects to plan and design a building which is then managed by that authority. All too often such facilities are inappropriate and uneconomic. Sometimes they are rejected by the local communities they are intended for. Occasionally they are even vandalised and destroyed.

In the scenario shown here, the need for the building is established by the community. Planning and design are then coordinated by a special project group which involves everyone interested at key stages.

The end result is a facility which has been shaped by members of the community to suit their needs and is then looked after by the people who use it.

FURTHER INFORMATION

☞ Methods:
Community planning forum. Community profiling. Feasibility fund. Interactive display. Open house event. User group.

☞ *Plan, Design and Build. User Participation in Building Design and Management.*

Community centre

A community needs a new social centre, sports facility, school, health centre or village hall.

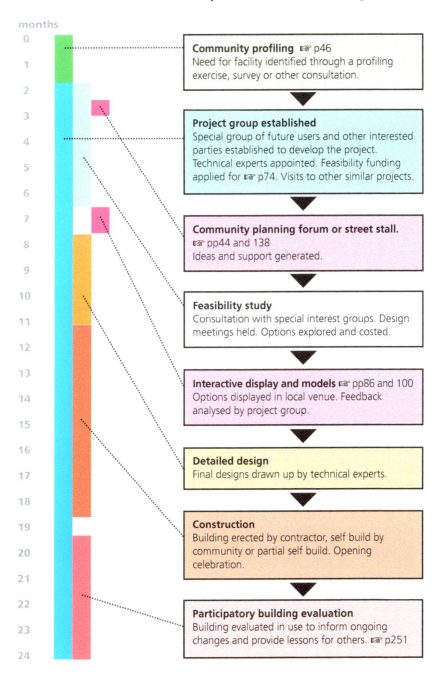

months

Community profiling ☞ p46
Need for facility identified through a profiling exercise, survey or other consultation.

Project group established
Special group of future users and other interested parties established to develop the project. Technical experts appointed. Feasibility funding applied for ☞ p74. Visits to other similar projects.

Community planning forum or street stall.
☞ pp44 and 138
Ideas and support generated.

Feasibility study
Consultation with special interest groups. Design meetings held. Options explored and costed.

Interactive display and models ☞ pp86 and 100
Options displayed in local venue. Feedback analysed by project group.

Detailed design
Final designs drawn up by technical experts.

Construction
Building erected by contractor, self build by community or partial self build. Opening celebration.

Participatory building evaluation
Building evaluated in use to inform ongoing changes and provide lessons for others. ☞ p251

Congestion charging

Congestion charging schemes are always controversial because of fears that they will disrupt lifelong habits and harm business.

The scenario shown here emphasises the importance of identifying who will be affected and working with them in a variety of different ways to mitigate any adverse impacts.

A relatively leisurely process is envisaged to allow time for people to reflect on, and prepare for, the changes in behaviour required and for feedback to be processed and incorporated in revised proposals as the scheme evolves.

The scenario assumes that the process is instigated by politicians and managed by a technical team guided by a steering group.

There are four broad phases of engagement:

1. Initial consultation to identify affected parties and understand their viewpoints;
2. Informal consultation on specific options;
3. Formal consultation on proposed scheme;
4. Ongoing monitoring and fine tuning.

FURTHER INFORMATION

☞ Methods:
E-voting. Draft plan consultation. Open house event. Planning day.

☆ Devised by Sarah Speirs, WSP.

© Milena Marega, Sarah Speirs and Nick Wates. Created as part of a Civitas Elan training programme, 2010.

Congestion charging

An initiative to set up a system for charging motorists for driving into the city centre at peak times.

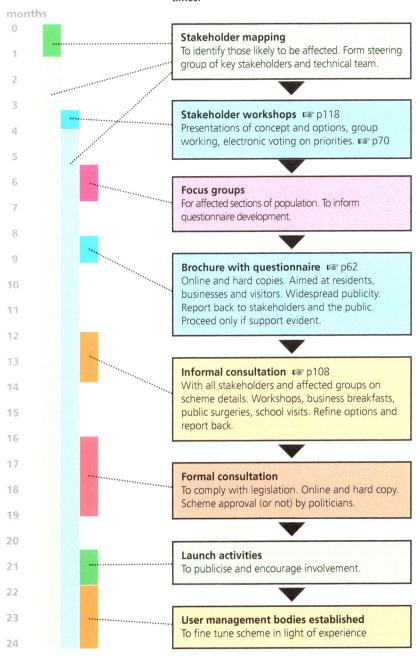

months

0
1
2
3
4
5
6
7
8
9
10
11
12
13
14
15
16
17
18
19
20
21
22
23
24

Stakeholder mapping
To identify those likely to be affected. Form steering group of key stakeholders and technical team.

Stakeholder workshops ☞ p118
Presentations of concept and options, group working, electronic voting on priorities. ☞ p70

Focus groups
For affected sections of population. To inform questionnaire development.

Brochure with questionnaire ☞ p62
Online and hard copies. Aimed at residents, businesses and visitors. Widespread publicity. Report back to stakeholders and the public. Proceed only if support evident.

Informal consultation ☞ p108
With all stakeholders and affected groups on scheme details. Workshops, business breakfasts, public surgeries, school visits. Refine options and report back.

Formal consultation
To comply with legislation. Online and hard copy. Scheme approval (or not) by politicians.

Launch activities
To publicise and encourage involvement.

User management bodies established
To fine tune scheme in light of experience

Derelict site re-use

This scenario shows an initiative to make use of a derelict area of land in public ownership. Such land exists everywhere, usually attracting rubbish and having a depressing effect on the local neighbourhood.

Often, sites are left vacant for many years. Alternatively, local authorities may carry out some landscaping or sell the land to the private sector for development.

The scenario here shows how a popular use for the site can be generated and implemented, starting off with an ideas competition.

The initiative can be taken by anyone: a local authority, regeneration agency, community group, individual or urban design studio at a school of architecture or planning.

FURTHER INFORMATION

☞ Methods:
Art workshop.
Ideas competition.
Open house event.
Street stall.
Urban design studio.

Derelict site re-use

An initiative to make use of a derelict urban site in public ownership. Timescale assumes relatively simple option adopted such as a pocket park. A building would take longer to construct.

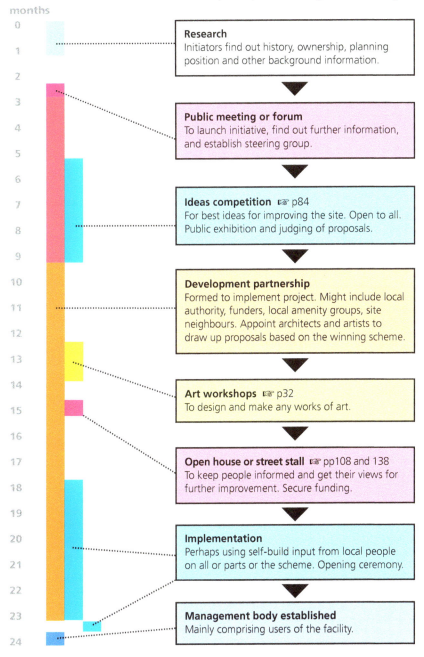

months

0
1
2
3
4
5
6
7
8
9
10
11
12
13
14
15
16
17
18
19
20
21
22
23
24

Research
Initiators find out history, ownership, planning position and other background information.

Public meeting or forum
To launch initiative, find out further information, and establish steering group.

Ideas competition ☞ p84
For best ideas for improving the site. Open to all. Public exhibition and judging of proposals.

Development partnership
Formed to implement project. Might include local authority, funders, local amenity groups, site neighbours. Appoint architects and artists to draw up proposals based on the winning scheme.

Art workshops ☞ p32
To design and make any works of art.

Open house or street stall ☞ pp108 and 138
To keep people informed and get their views for further improvement. Secure funding.

Implementation
Perhaps using self-build input from local people on all or parts or the scheme. Opening ceremony.

Management body established
Mainly comprising users of the facility.

Disaster management

This scenario applies particularly to communities facing the threat of natural or human-made disasters such as floods, earthquakes, wind storms and industrial accidents.

Disasters tend to happen to people at risk. They are at risk because they are vulnerable to hazards. This vulnerability can best be reduced by increasing people's capacity to deal with a range of social, cultural, economic and physical factors.

The key to successful disaster management is ensuring that victims and potential victims are involved. Much formal disaster management does not do this and is often unsustainable, costly and ineffective.

Participatory community-level disaster management involves a cross-section of people and interests in researching, planning and implementing projects. Because the projects are developed for and by local people, there is more interest, understanding and success in reducing suffering and losses.

The key principles of this approach are:

- **Communities themselves are best placed to prioritise threats and take effective risk reducing actions.**
- **The best time to reduce the impact of disasters is before the next disaster occurs.**
- **The identification of hazards and who and what may be affected by them is necessary before risk reduction plans can be made.**
- **Progress has to be well publicised to maintain interest and strengthen the culture of disaster reduction.**

FURTHER INFORMATION

☞ Methods:
Prioritising.
Risk assessment.

𝄐 *Disaster Mitigation.*

✉ Federal Emergency Management Agency (FEMA).
South Bank University.

☆ Roger Bellers, Nick Hall. Based in part on Project Impact programme run by FEMA.

Disaster management

Making communities more disaster-resistant by involving citizens, officials and business. Applicable worldwide. Timescale for low risk situation. Can be speeded up significantly in emergencies.

months

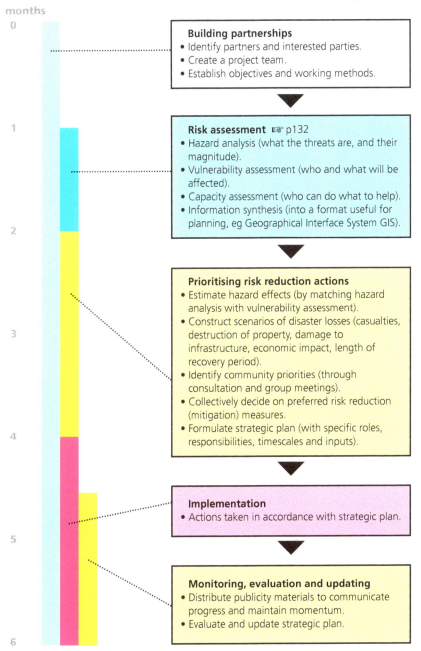

Building partnerships
- Identify partners and interested parties.
- Create a project team.
- Establish objectives and working methods.

Risk assessment ☞ p132
- Hazard analysis (what the threats are, and their magnitude).
- Vulnerability assessment (who and what will be affected).
- Capacity assessment (who can do what to help).
- Information synthesis (into a format useful for planning, eg Geographical Interface System GIS).

Prioritising risk reduction actions
- Estimate hazard effects (by matching hazard analysis with vulnerability assessment).
- Construct scenarios of disaster losses (casualties, destruction of property, damage to infrastructure, economic impact, length of recovery period).
- Identify community priorities (through consultation and group meetings).
- Collectively decide on preferred risk reduction (mitigation) measures.
- Formulate strategic plan (with specific roles, responsibilities, timescales and inputs).

Implementation
- Actions taken in accordance with strategic plan.

Monitoring, evaluation and updating
- Distribute publicity materials to communicate progress and maintain momentum.
- Evaluate and update strategic plan.

Energy saving and generation

This scenario shows how a community can start planning to reduce its consumption of energy. It starts with the formation of a local energy group, usually by enthusiasts, although this will hopefully be supported by the authorities and energy companies.

The group's first task will be to understand the various technologies involved and the funding

Energy saving and generation

A neighbourhood of around 5,000 homes wants to reduce its energy consumption and carbon footprint. Urban or rural.

months

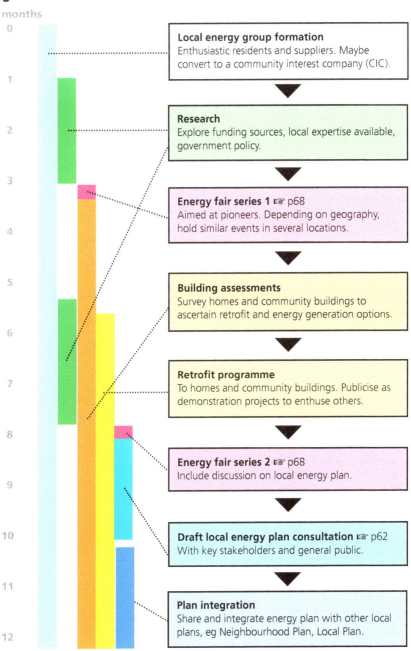

0

Local energy group formation
Enthusiastic residents and suppliers. Maybe convert to a community interest company (CIC).

1

2

Research
Explore funding sources, local expertise available, government policy.

3

Energy fair series 1 ☞ p68
Aimed at pioneers. Depending on geography, hold similar events in several locations.

4

5

Building assessments
Survey homes and community buildings to ascertain retrofit and energy generation options.

6

Retrofit programme
To homes and community buildings. Publicise as demonstration projects to enthuse others.

7

8

Energy fair series 2 ☞ p68
Include discussion on local energy plan.

9

Draft local energy plan consultation ☞ p62
With key stakeholders and general public.

10

11

Plan integration
Share and integrate energy plan with other local plans, eg Neighbourhood Plan, Local Plan.

12

Environmental art project

This scenario is about constructing environmental artworks.

The conventional approach would be for a local authority or landowner to appoint an artist to undertake the work. The artist might be given a completely free hand or, more likely, would submit designs for approval to the 'client'. Although this process has led to some fine environmental artworks, it has also resulted in artworks that are neither wanted nor respected by local inhabitants.

The scenario shown here makes it possible to create something that belongs to the community. Within a framework managed by artists, local people are involved in designing and making artworks and their work becomes part of the local landscape.

FURTHER INFORMATION

☞ Methods:
   Art workshop.

☆ Candid Arts Trust.
   Freeform Arts Trust.

Environmental art project

An initiative to improve the public environment by constructing a major sculpture, mosaic or other work of art.

months

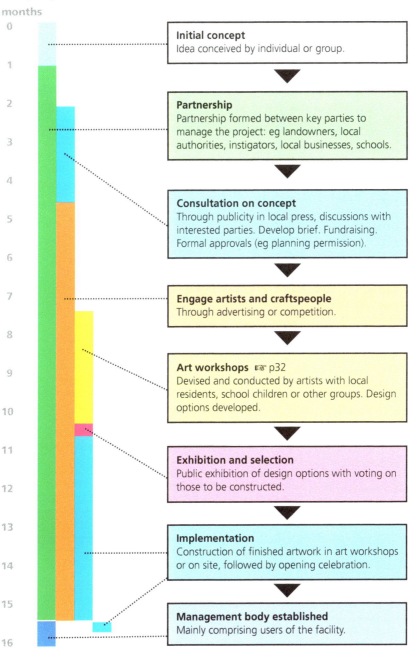

0

Initial concept
Idea conceived by individual or group.

Partnership
Partnership formed between key parties to manage the project: eg landowners, local authorities, instigators, local businesses, schools.

Consultation on concept
Through publicity in local press, discussions with interested parties. Develop brief. Fundraising. Formal approvals (eg planning permission).

Engage artists and craftspeople
Through advertising or competition.

Art workshops ☞ p32
Devised and conducted by artists with local residents, school children or other groups. Design options developed.

Exhibition and selection
Public exhibition of design options with voting on those to be constructed.

Implementation
Construction of finished artwork in art workshops or on site, followed by opening celebration.

Management body established
Mainly comprising users of the facility.

Freight delivery

The delivery of freight is not something that most people give much thought to. But especially in historic high density urban areas it can be very difficult to devise a system which is convenient for business and acceptable to residents. The solutions are likely to involve a combination of organisational and technical mechanisms and relate to national, regional and local policy.

Recognising the highly specialist nature of this kind of planning and the limited amount of public interest, the scenario shown here assumes that the process is driven by a technical team either within a local authority or engaged as consultants.

Freight delivery

Developing a strategy for the delivery of freight in an urban or rural area.

months

Stakeholder mapping
To identify those likely to be affected. Establish steering group of key stakeholders. Briefings.

Stakeholder workshops
Presentations on current problems and issues, vision, strategy options. Circulate feedback.

Planning sessions ☞ p54
For key stakeholders and technical team. Develop freight strategy action plan. With freight map showing strategic and local routes, weight restrictions, complementary measures.

Stakeholder conference ☞ p118
Presentations on plan followed by discussion in breakout groups. Request written responses within fixed period (eg 4 weeks). Refine plan, develop monitoring strategy.

Publicity
For industry and public.

Formal consultation ☞ p62
With stakeholders and public. Mainly online. Feedback to decision makers and consultees. Formal adoption (or not).

Education & training
For the industry and general public. Produce flyer with freight map. Maybe an exhibition.

Establish Freight Quality Partnership
Of key stakeholders as a forum to monitor progress and promote good practice.

Housing development

This scenario covers the building of a new housing development for a large number of people.

Conventionally, large housing developments are undertaken by governments or private developers. In both cases architects and contractors are appointed who mostly design and construct homes without knowing who they are for. As a result the new housing is frequently bland, wasteful and unsuited to the occupants. Occasionally it even has to be demolished because nobody will live in it.

In the scenario shown here, the future occupants are identified in advance. They may be owner-occupiers or tenants. They form themselves into an association or housing cooperative, appoint their own architects and work through the design and construction process together.

In this way people get the customised housing they want and develop a sense of community even before they have moved in. The experience of working together enables people to go on to develop other projects such as education, employment and social facilities.

FURTHER INFORMATION

Housing development

A large new housing development is built with the future occupants involved from the outset.

Timescale assumes rapid approvals and efficient main contractor.

months

0
1
2
3
4
5
6
7
8
9
10
11
12
13
14
15
16
17
18
19
20
21
22
23
24
25
26
27
28
29
30
31
32
33
34
35
36

Occupants form group
Families come together and form an association or cooperative with help from advisors. Funding mechanism agreed. Committees formed. Architects appointed.

Briefing
Visits to other projects, illustrated questionnaires, slide shows, skills survey, briefing workshops ☞ p36.

Site office
Design base established in local hall or shop ☞ p102.

Design meetings
Regular sessions between architects and occupants' committees using models ☞ p100, choice catalogues ☞ p38 and drawings to determine scheme concept and layout.

Design surgeries
Between architects and individual occupants to agree room layouts, fixtures and fittings using models ☞ p100, mock-ups and choice catalogues ☞ p38.

Construction
Regular site visits. Possibly self build of all or part of the scheme.

Other projects started
Such as child care facilities, social facilities, employment projects.

Industrial heritage re-use

This scenario applies where industrial buildings become redundant, particularly if they have heritage value or could be used for other purposes.

Typically, as industrial buildings cease to be used, they will be left empty and become derelict. The area where they are situated becomes increasingly run down, and other businesses and landowners suffer. Unless an initiative is taken the buildings will eventually fall down or there will be little option but to demolish them and start again from scratch.

Industrial areas often contain fine, sturdy structures which contribute to local character. Often they are ideally suited for conversion for other purposes. The difficulty is in making a sufficiently bold transformation of an area to change its image, attract new uses and persuade landowners and others to invest.

In this scenario, a partnership is established between the main parties, and an academic institution plays a key role in raising the profile of the area, assembling expertise and helping organise an action planning event to firm up a strategy agreed by all.

FURTHER INFORMATION

☞ Methods:
Community planning event. Design assistance team.

☆ John Worthington.

Industrial heritage re-use

An academic institution helps a local authority regenerate a run-down industrial area in a variety of ownerships.

months

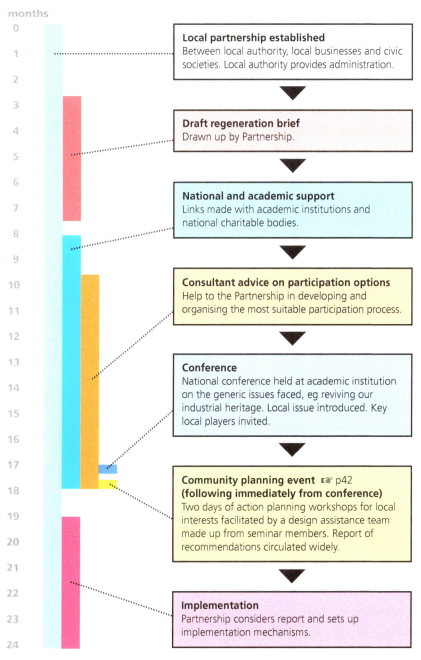

0

1

Local partnership established
Between local authority, local businesses and civic societies. Local authority provides administration.

2

3

4

Draft regeneration brief
Drawn up by Partnership.

5

6

7

National and academic support
Links made with academic institutions and national charitable bodies.

8

9

10

Consultant advice on participation options
Help to the Partnership in developing and organising the most suitable participation process.

11

12

13

14

Conference
National conference held at academic institution on the generic issues faced, eg reviving our industrial heritage. Local issue introduced. Key local players invited.

15

16

17

18

Community planning event ☞ p42
(following immediately from conference)
Two days of action planning workshops for local interests facilitated by a design assistance team made up from seminar members. Report of recommendations circulated widely.

19

20

21

22

Implementation
Partnership considers report and sets up implementation mechanisms.

23

24

Inner city regeneration

This scenario shows how a deprived inner city area can transform itself over a period of almost a decade.

Starting by tenants gaining control of the management of their housing, a series of initiatives are taken as local people and their advisors become increasingly confident and competent in managing the regeneration process and forming partnerships. These include an improvement programme for existing housing estates, new housing development on infill sites, landscaping of open spaces, community arts and youth projects and, finally, the development of a community masterplan for attracting the private sector to invest in new housing, leisure and commercial projects, so leading to the creation of a balanced and sustainable community or 'urban village'.

FURExHER INFORMATION

☞ Methods:
Community planning event. Art workshop. Choice catalogue. Design game. Development trust. Neighbourhood planning office. Planning day. Planning for Real. Review session.

☆ Dick Watson.

Inner city regeneration

Rejuvenation of a deprived inner city area dominated by blocks of local authority flats and lacking amenities.

months

Tenant management organisation formed
Authority hands over management of flats to tenants. Tenants appoint community architect.

Neighbourhood planning office opened ☞ p102
For tenant committees and consultants.

Housing estate improvement programme
Scheme developed using Planning for Real ☞ p120 and choice catalogues ☞ p38.

New housing
Designed and built by a local housing association after a planning day ☞ p118.

Open space projects
Devised by special projects committee using design games ☞ p52.

Community arts and young people's projects
Using arts workshops ☞ p32 and projects in schools.

Community planning event ☞ p42
To take stock and produce a strategy for future action. With outsider and local design assistance team members. Lasting several days.

Review session ☞ p130.

Masterplan
Drawn up by development partnership and local development trust ☞ p56.

Local neighbourhood initiative

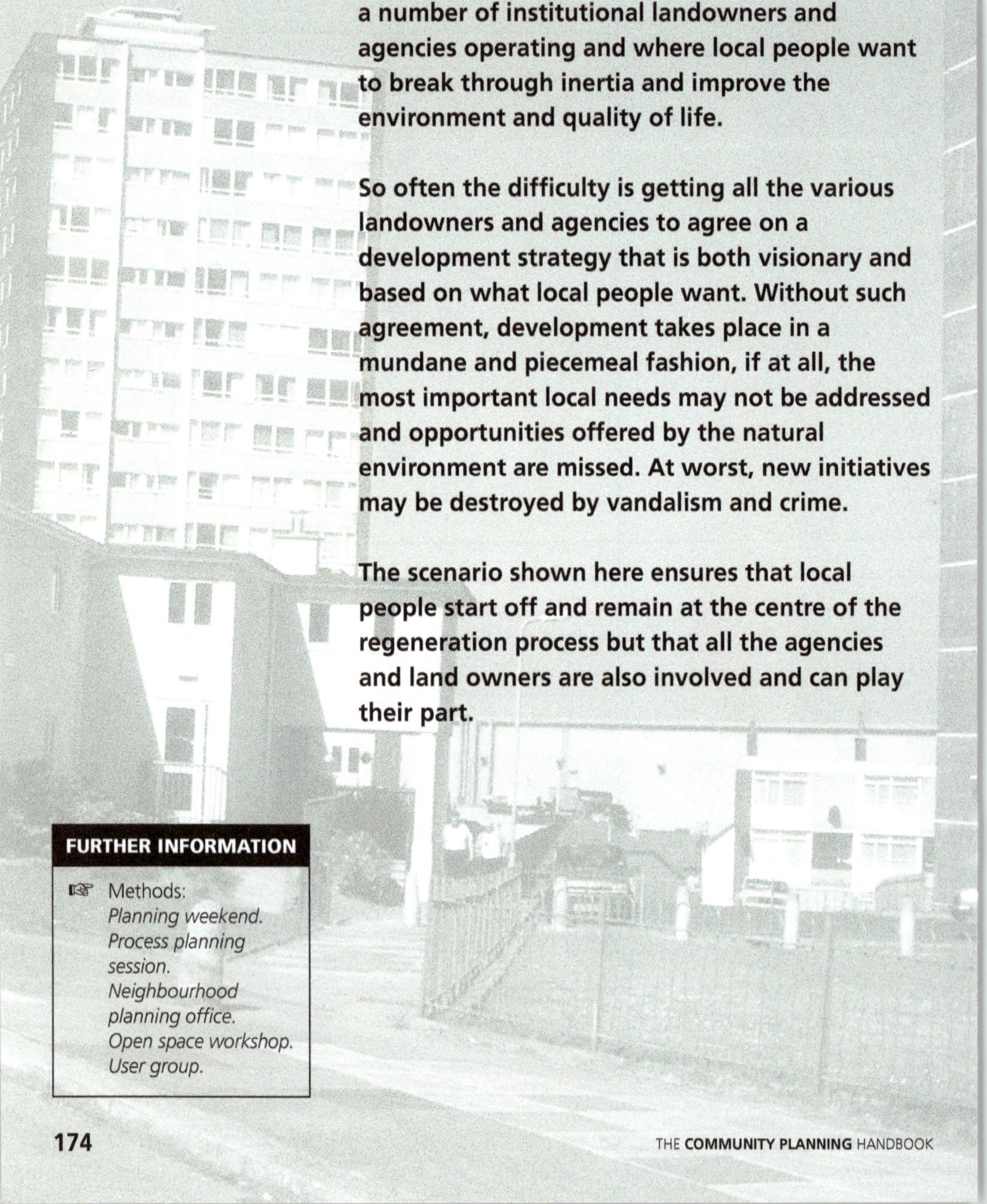

This scenario applies to any area where there are a number of institutional landowners and agencies operating and where local people want to break through inertia and improve the environment and quality of life.

So often the difficulty is getting all the various landowners and agencies to agree on a development strategy that is both visionary and based on what local people want. Without such agreement, development takes place in a mundane and piecemeal fashion, if at all, the most important local needs may not be addressed and opportunities offered by the natural environment are missed. At worst, new initiatives may be destroyed by vandalism and crime.

The scenario shown here ensures that local people start off and remain at the centre of the regeneration process but that all the agencies and land owners are also involved and can play their part.

FURTHER INFORMATION

☞ Methods:
  Planning weekend.
  Process planning session.
  Neighbourhood planning office.
  Open space workshop.
  User group.

Local neighbourhood initiative

Local people in a rundown neighbourhood and agencies working with them take the initiative to speed up the regeneration process.

months

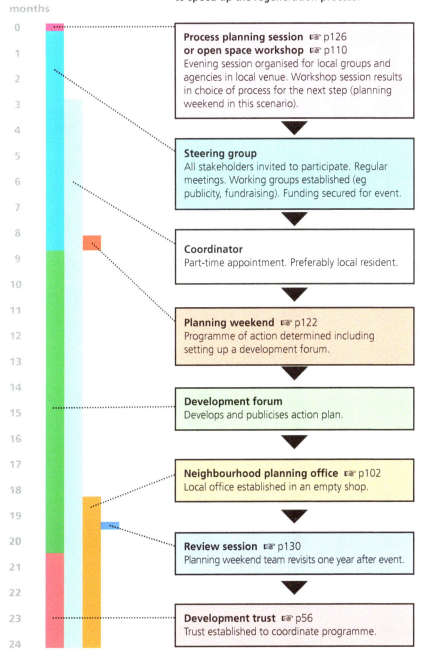

Process planning session ☞ p126
or open space workshop ☞ p110
Evening session organised for local groups and agencies in local venue. Workshop session results in choice of process for the next step (planning weekend in this scenario).

Steering group
All stakeholders invited to participate. Regular meetings. Working groups established (eg publicity, fundraising). Funding secured for event.

Coordinator
Part-time appointment. Preferably local resident.

Planning weekend ☞ p122
Programme of action determined including setting up a development forum.

Development forum
Develops and publicises action plan.

Neighbourhood planning office ☞ p102
Local office established in an empty shop.

Review session ☞ p130
Planning weekend team revisits one year after event.

Development trust ☞ p56
Trust established to coordinate programme.

Local plan production

Local spatial plans are the key mechanism for making decisions about the future of an area and require creative engagement from all sections of the community.

This scenario is designed to put communities in the driving seat of local planning by setting out ways in which they might do the visionary thinking and provide the local knowledge and ideas that more bureaucratic processes fail to deliver. The way of working between communities and government becomes one of dialogue and creativity rather than one of isolation and reaction often leading to frustration or even hostility.

The scenario is based on experience in England of producing Local Development Frameworks (Local Plans) for which it will be especially relevant.

FURTHER INFORMATION

☞ Methods:
Process planning session.
Community profiling.
Community planning event. Online consultation.
Open house event.

☆ Kelvin McDonald.

Note: The timescales shown in the scenario timeline are ideal but perhaps over optimistic. In practice, the time taken to prepare local development frameworks is dependent on the planning authority's resources and political priorities and may vary enormously. (The 'Local Development Scheme' (LDS) on an English local authority's website will provide details of the timings for the different stages in your local plan.)

Local plan production

Getting involved in producing a spatial plan for a local area (sometimes known as a Local Development Framework).

months

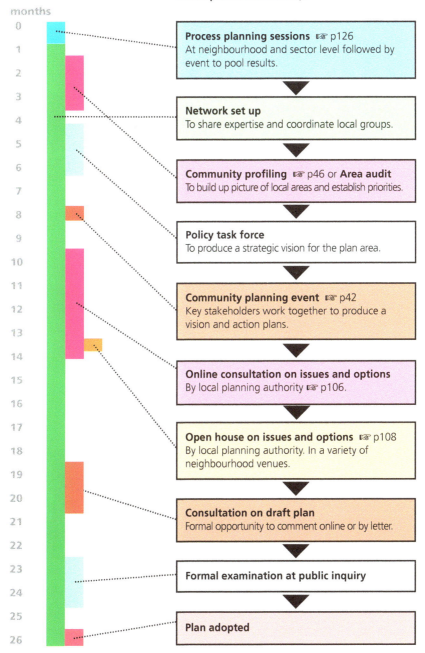

0

Process planning sessions ☞ p126
At neighbourhood and sector level followed by event to pool results.

Network set up
To share expertise and coordinate local groups.

Community profiling ☞ p46 or **Area audit**
To build up picture of local areas and establish priorities.

Policy task force
To produce a strategic vision for the plan area.

Community planning event ☞ p42
Key stakeholders work together to produce a vision and action plans.

Online consultation on issues and options
By local planning authority ☞ p106.

Open house on issues and options ☞ p108
By local planning authority. In a variety of neighbourhood venues.

Consultation on draft plan
Formal opportunity to comment online or by letter.

Formal examination at public inquiry

Plan adopted

26

and neighbourhood planning is a good opportunity to enhance that. But the regulations require a certain minimum amount of consultation and this is what is shown here. A limited amount of community engagement may sometimes be appropriate if there has already been a history of community-based planning in the area – such as producing a Village Design Statement or a Parish plan for instance – and where the neighbourhood development plan's purpose is to provide a statutory land use planning version of these.

At the time of going to press (early 2014) few neighbourhood plans have been completed so the scenario illustrated here is based on limited experience with frontrunners and advice from those devising the process. The timescale will vary and for some, the timescale shown here may be optimistic.

FURTHER INFORMATION

☞ Methods:
 Draft plan consultation.

 Scenarios:
 *Community led plan.
 Local plan.*

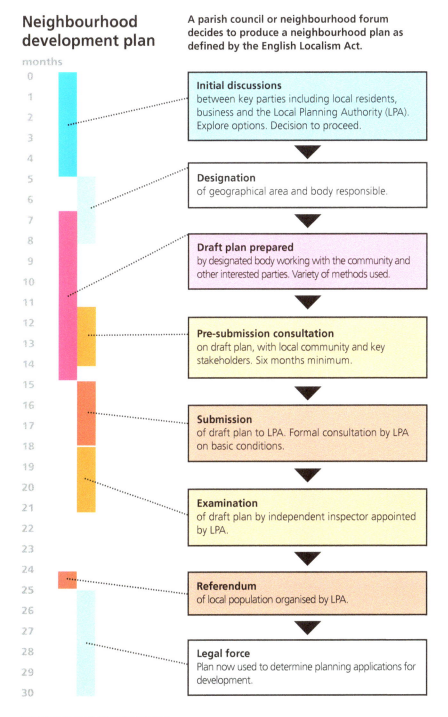

Neighbourhood development plan

A parish council or neighbourhood forum decides to produce a neighbourhood plan as defined by the English Localism Act.

months

0
1
2
3
4
5
6
7
8
9
10
11
12
13
14
15
16
17
18
19
20
21
22
23
24
25
26
27
28
29
30

Initial discussions
between key parties including local residents, business and the Local Planning Authority (LPA). Explore options. Decision to proceed.

Designation
of geographical area and body responsible.

Draft plan prepared
by designated body working with the community and other interested parties. Variety of methods used.

Pre-submission consultation
on draft plan, with local community and key stakeholders. Six months minimum.

Submission
of draft plan to LPA. Formal consultation by LPA on basic conditions.

Examination
of draft plan by independent inspector appointed by LPA.

Referendum
of local population organised by LPA.

Legal force
Plan now used to determine planning applications for development.

New neighbourhood

This scenario shows how creative proposals can be developed for a new neighbourhood, extension to a neighbourhood or completely new settlement.

Mostly with such developments, it is left to the private sector to come up with proposals, or else consultants might be invited to prepare a masterplan for consideration by the authorities. In both cases, the crucial design conception stage tends to take place without engaging local people or a sufficiently broad range of expertise. When consultation does finally take place, it is too late for all but minor changes to be incorporated.

In the scenario shown, initial proposals are developed, at relatively little cost, by a task force of experts and students from a wide range of disciplines and backgrounds, in close consultation with local interested parties. These are then refined through further local input and drawn up in detail by a professional team.

The organisers are likely to be an urban design consultancy, architecture centre or urban design studio at a school of architecture or planning.

FURTHER INFORMATION

☞ Methods:
Architecture centre.
Newspaper
supplement.
Mobile unit.
Open house event.
Reconnaissance trip.
Task force.
Urban design studio.

New neighbourhood

Devising proposals for a new neighbourhood by involving a task force of experts and students working closely with local interested parties. Timescale assumes co-operative landowner.

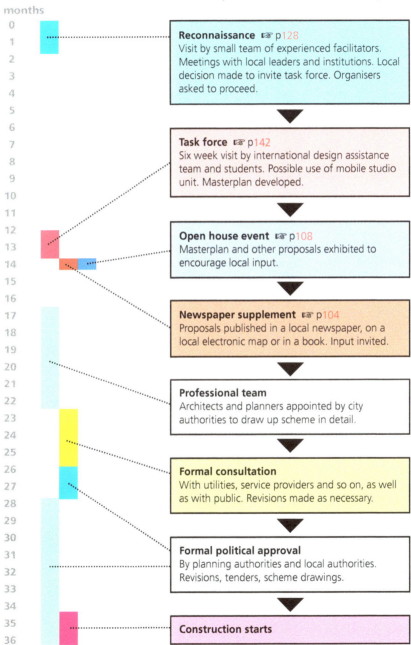

months
0
1
2
3
4
5
6
7
8
9
10
11
12
13
14
15
16
17
18
19
20
21
22
23
24
25
26
27
28
29
30
31
32
33
34
35
36

Reconnaissance ☞ p128
Visit by small team of experienced facilitators. Meetings with local leaders and institutions. Local decision made to invite task force. Organisers asked to proceed.

Task force ☞ p142
Six week visit by international design assistance team and students. Possible use of mobile studio unit. Masterplan developed.

Open house event ☞ p108
Masterplan and other proposals exhibited to encourage local input.

Newspaper supplement ☞ p104
Proposals published in a local newspaper, on a local electronic map or in a book. Input invited.

Professional team
Architects and planners appointed by city authorities to draw up scheme in detail.

Formal consultation
With utilities, service providers and so on, as well as with public. Revisions made as necessary.

Formal political approval
By planning authorities and local authorities. Revisions, tenders, scheme drawings.

Construction starts

Planning study

This scenario applies where professional planning consultants are commissioned by a local authority or landowner to produce recommendations on future development options in a relatively short period of time.

The conventional approach would be for the consultants to prepare a report based entirely on their past experience and researching available literature.

In the scenario shown here, the consultants also include a consultation process which has to be tightly time-tabled to suit their client's timescale. This ensures that the consultants' proposals are based on up-to-date knowledge of local people's views and that local people begin to become involved in the development process.

FURTHER INFORMATION

☞ Methods:
Participatory editing.
Planning day.
*Process planning
session.*

Planning study

Planning consultants are asked by a local authority to prepare a study of the potential of a large sector of a city. The timescale is short.

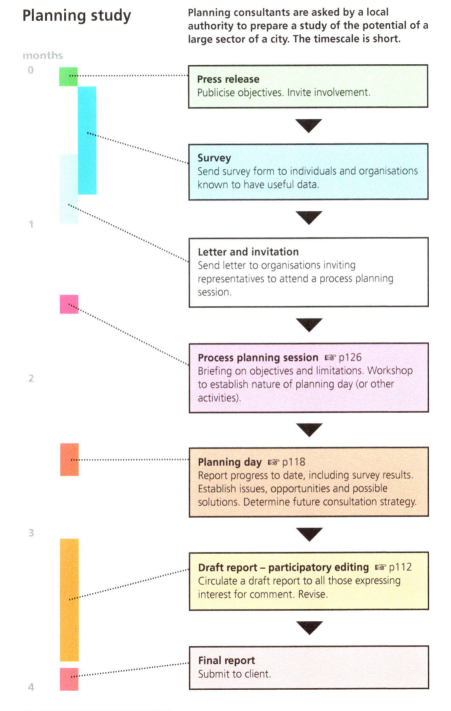

months

0

Press release
Publicise objectives. Invite involvement.

Survey
Send survey form to individuals and organisations known to have useful data.

1

Letter and invitation
Send letter to organisations inviting representatives to attend a process planning session.

2

Process planning session ☞ p126
Briefing on objectives and limitations. Workshop to establish nature of planning day (or other activities).

Planning day ☞ p118
Report progress to date, including survey results. Establish issues, opportunities and possible solutions. Determine future consultation strategy.

3

Draft report – participatory editing ☞ p112
Circulate a draft report to all those expressing interest for comment. Revise.

Final report
Submit to client.

4

Public transport corridor

Involving the public in public transport initiatives is especially important because their success will often depend on behaviour changes (e.g. people stopping driving to work in private cars) which are less likely to happen if people do not feel convinced by the approach adopted.

Four distinct phases of public consultation can be identified for most initiatives involving major transport infrastructure:

1. **Overall route consultation – to firm up aims of project and explore strategic options.**
2. **Specific neighbourhood consultation – to explore options for route and detailed planning.**
3. **During construction – to build momentum and prepare for behaviour change.**
4. **In use – to monitor progress and encourage**

Public transport corridor

A town wants to establish a route for a public transport corridor and then get people to use it. Planners and transport operators take the lead.

months

0
1
2
3
4
5
6
7
8
9
10
11
12
13
14
15
16
17
18
19
20
21
22
23
24
25
26
27
28
29
30
31
32
33
34
35
36

Publicity
Promote concept using media, websites, mailings.

Planning day for key stakeholders ☞ p118
To establish aims and explore strategic options.
Set up transport forum as steering group.

Brochure with questionnaire ☞ p62
For all town residents and travellers to secure views on route options. Establish advice helpline and branding.

Planning day for key stakeholders ☞ p118
To assess feedback from questionnaire and agree preferred route.

Open house and Mobile unit ☞ p108 & p98
In affected neighbourhoods and on transport systems to explore views on preferred route.

Formal statutory consultation
Final proposals circulated to stakeholders and on website. Scheme approval by authorities.

Education pack, toolkit, DVD
To inform on any disruption and prepare people for the new system.

Launch activities
To publicise and encourage involvement.

User management bodies established
Schemes such as 'Adopt a station', MyBus.

Regeneration infrastructure

This scenario shows how the framework for encouraging community planning can be improved by government and private and voluntary agencies. It can be applied at national, regional or even international level.

The focus is on supporting and promoting the setting up of enabling mechanisms, some of which will become self-financing after a period of time.

The costs involved are a fraction of the support normally given to regeneration programmes and the long-term benefits are likely to be far greater.

FURTHER INFORMATION

☞ Methods:
Architecture centre.
Award scheme.
Community design centre.
Feasibility fund.
Ideas competition.
Neighbourhood planning office.
Planning aid.
Useful checklists:
Initiatives needed.

Regeneration infrastructure

Leading institutions and government collaborate to set up a framework to support community planning initiatives at local level.

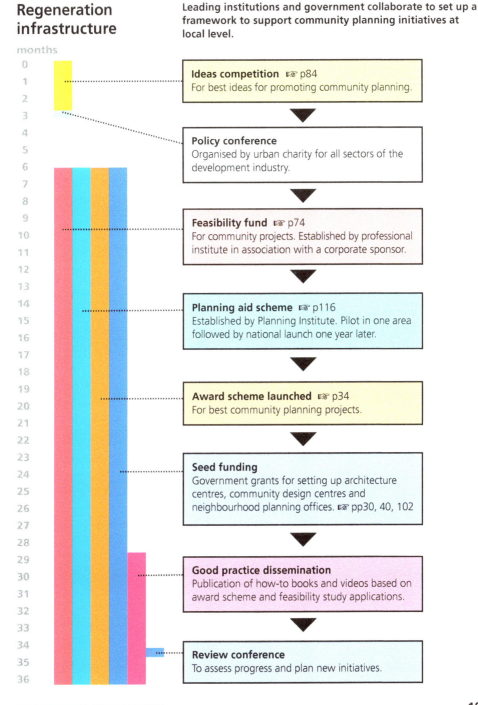

months

0
1
2
3
4
5
6
7
8
9
10
11
12
13
14
15
16
17
18
19
20
21
22
23
24
25
26
27
28
29
30
31
32
33
34
35
36

Ideas competition ☞ p84
For best ideas for promoting community planning.

Policy conference
Organised by urban charity for all sectors of the development industry.

Feasibility fund ☞ p74
For community projects. Established by professional institute in association with a corporate sponsor.

Planning aid scheme ☞ p116
Established by Planning Institute. Pilot in one area followed by national launch one year later.

Award scheme launched ☞ p34
For best community planning projects.

Seed funding
Government grants for setting up architecture centres, community design centres and neighbourhood planning offices. ☞ pp30, 40, 102

Good practice dissemination
Publication of how-to books and videos based on award scheme and feasibility study applications.

Review conference
To assess progress and plan new initiatives.

Regional plan production

The regional level of planning is the level at which new housing allocations are normally decided and at which the impact of new housing on the environment, on resources (such as water supply) and on infrastructure (such as roads and

Regional plan production

months

Getting involved in producing a plan for a region (meaning a substantial area of land including many towns and villages as well as countryside).

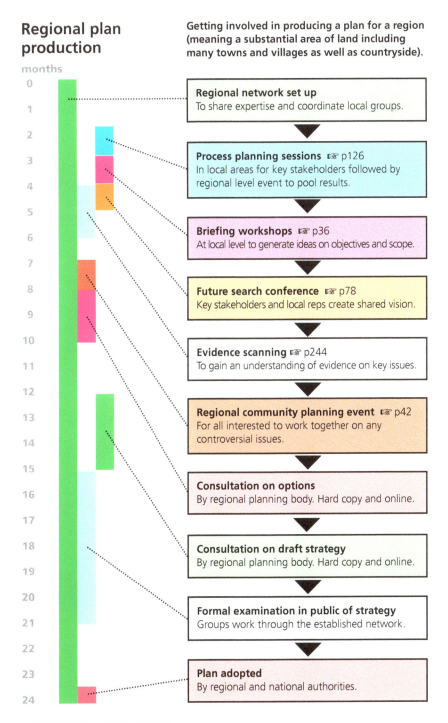

Regional network set up
To share expertise and coordinate local groups.

Process planning sessions ☞ p126
In local areas for key stakeholders followed by regional level event to pool results.

Briefing workshops ☞ p36
At local level to generate ideas on objectives and scope.

Future search conference ☞ p78
Key stakeholders and local reps create shared vision.

Evidence scanning ☞ p244
To gain an understanding of evidence on key issues.

Regional community planning event ☞ p42
For all interested to work together on any controversial issues.

Consultation on options
By regional planning body. Hard copy and online.

Consultation on draft strategy
By regional planning body. Hard copy and online.

Formal examination in public of strategy
Groups work through the established network.

Plan adopted
By regional and national authorities.

Shanty settlement upgrading

This scenario applies to the informal settlements which proliferate around many cities in developing countries. The residents may be squatters, tenants or owner-occupiers.

Often, authorities ignore such places, leaving them to their own devices. Alternatively they may attempt to have them demolished on the grounds that they are unsightly, unhealthy or unlawful.

In this scenario the authorities support the residents to upgrade their settlement by providing technical assistance. Over the years, services are installed, roads are improved and building construction standards raised.

Eventually such settlements can become almost indistinguishable from other parts of the city.

FURTHER INFORMATION

☞ Methods:
Community design centre.
Community profiling.
Field workshop.
Microplanning workshop.
Risk assessment.

⌓ *Action Planning for Cities.*

✉ Centre for Development and Emergency Practice. International Institute for Environment and

Shanty settlement upgrading

Residents gradually upgrade their homes and neighbourhood with assistance from the authorities, technical experts and support agencies.

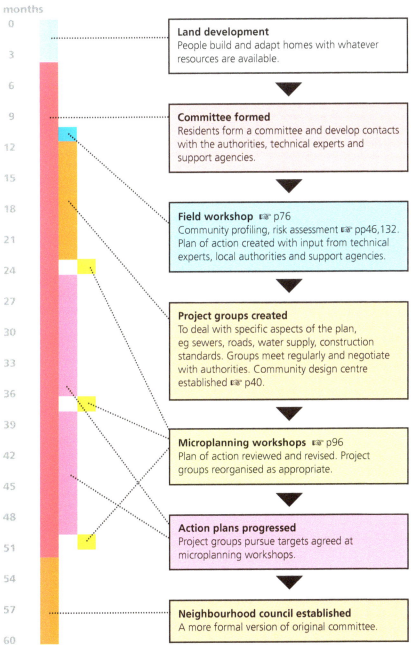

months

0

3

6

9

12

15

18

21

24

27

30

33

36

39

42

45

48

51

54

57

60

Land development
People build and adapt homes with whatever resources are available.

Committee formed
Residents form a committee and develop contacts with the authorities, technical experts and support agencies.

Field workshop ☞ p76
Community profiling, risk assessment ☞ pp46,132. Plan of action created with input from technical experts, local authorities and support agencies.

Project groups created
To deal with specific aspects of the plan, eg sewers, roads, water supply, construction standards. Groups meet regularly and negotiate with authorities. Community design centre established ☞ p40.

Microplanning workshops ☞ p96
Plan of action reviewed and revised. Project groups reorganised as appropriate.

Action plans progressed
Project groups pursue targets agreed at microplanning workshops.

Neighbourhood council established
A more formal version of original committee.

Town centre upgrade

This scenario applies when a planning authority wants to initiate improvement of a town centre area.

Many town centre areas have developed in a piecemeal fashion over a number of years. Land will be in a variety of ownerships. Buildings are likely to have been designed with little respect for overall urban design.

If the planning department does nothing, the piecemeal approach will continue and fundamental issues will never be solved.

The approach shown here allows a planning authority to involve all the many different interests in developing an overall strategy which can be incorporated into the planning framework.

FURTHER INFORMATION

☞ Methods:
   Open house event.
   Planning day.
   Process planning session.
   User group.

Town centre upgrade

A planning department initiates development of part of the town centre without the conflict between developers and citizens so common in much town centre development.

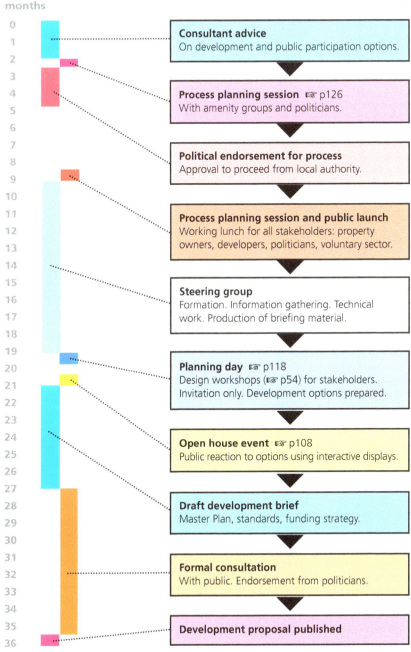

months

0	
1	**Consultant advice**
2	On development and public participation options.
3	
4	**Process planning session** ☞ p126
5	With amenity groups and politicians.
6	
7	
8	**Political endorsement for process**
9	Approval to proceed from local authority.
10	
11	**Process planning session and public launch**
12	Working lunch for all stakeholders: property
13	owners, developers, politicians, voluntary sector.
14	
15	**Steering group**
16	Formation. Information gathering. Technical
17	work. Production of briefing material.
18	
19	
20	**Planning day** ☞ p118
21	Design workshops (☞ p54) for stakeholders.
22	Invitation only. Development options prepared.
23	
24	**Open house event** ☞ p108
25	Public reaction to options using interactive displays.
26	
27	**Draft development brief**
28	Master Plan, standards, funding strategy.
29	
30	
31	**Formal consultation**
32	With public. Endorsement from politicians.
33	
34	
35	**Development proposal published**
36	

Urban conservation

This scenario covers an initiative to improve the state of historic buildings in a town.

Restoring buildings is very costly and sufficient public funds are rarely available to meet the demand. In this scenario the local authorities allocate funding for three years to start up an independent project providing technical assistance and taking initiatives. As well as administering grants to pump-prime quality repairs by private owners, the project undertakes a wide range of education programmes aimed at raising awareness and stimulating initiatives by both private individuals and community groups.

When the funding period expires, the project is converted into a development trust controlled by local people. As skills and interest grow, the trust takes on a broader and more far-reaching role.

FURTHER INFORMATION

☞ Methods:
Activity week.
Architecture centre.
Award scheme.
Community design centre.
Development trust.

Urban conservation

An initiative to improve the state of historic buildings in an area by raising awareness and stimulating a wide range of local activity.

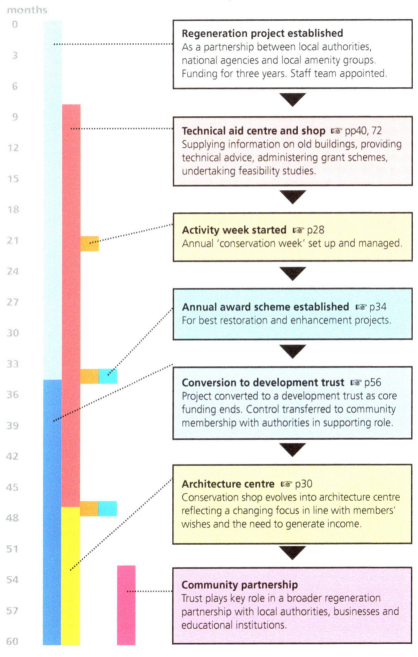

months

0	
3	

Regeneration project established
As a partnership between local authorities, national agencies and local amenity groups. Funding for three years. Staff team appointed.

Technical aid centre and shop ☞ pp40, 72
Supplying information on old buildings, providing technical advice, administering grant schemes, undertaking feasibility studies.

Activity week started ☞ p28
Annual 'conservation week' set up and managed.

Annual award scheme established ☞ p34
For best restoration and enhancement projects.

Conversion to development trust ☞ p56
Project converted to a development trust as core funding ends. Control transferred to community membership with authorities in supporting role.

Architecture centre ☞ p30
Conservation shop evolves into architecture centre reflecting a changing focus in line with members' wishes and the need to generate income.

Community partnership
Trust plays key role in a broader regeneration partnership with local authorities, businesses and educational institutions.

Village revival

This scenario covers a village developing initiatives to preserve and build on its local character.

With changes in traditional agricultural practices, many villages suffer from either development pressure or loss of population. Often political control is exercised many miles away and local people feel powerless to do anything about it.

In this scenario parish mapping is used to generate interest and understanding. Villagers then decide to develop a local design statement to guide new development and a countryside design summary is prepared to make better links with the character of the surrounding region.

Finally, with the experience of learning to work together, a number of project groups are established to develop new facilities.

FURTHER INFORMATION

☞ Methods: *Community profiling. Local design statement. Mapping. Photo survey. Review session.*

Village revival

A village community takes steps to protect the traditional character and develop new facilities.

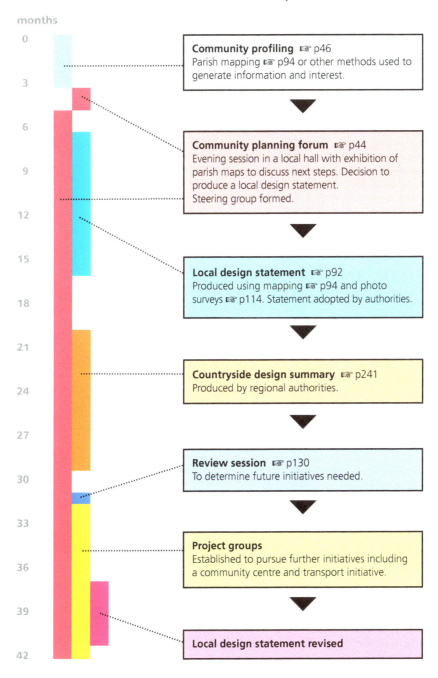

months

0

3

Community profiling ☞ p46
Parish mapping ☞ p94 or other methods used to generate information and interest.

6

9

Community planning forum ☞ p44
Evening session in a local hall with exhibition of parish maps to discuss next steps. Decision to produce a local design statement.
Steering group formed.

12

15

18

Local design statement ☞ p92
Produced using mapping ☞ p94 and photo surveys ☞ p114. Statement adopted by authorities.

21

24

Countryside design summary ☞ p241
Produced by regional authorities.

27

30

Review session ☞ p130
To determine future initiatives needed.

33

36

Project groups
Established to pursue further initiatives including a community centre and transport initiative.

39

42

Local design statement revised

Whole settlement strategy

A whole settlement strategy creates a vision for a village, town or city as a whole and sets out ways to achieve it: How does the place work? What is good about it? What is bad? What needs changing? How can we plan for a sustainable future?

A conventional approach would be for a local authority to engage town planning or development consultants to produce a plan which would then be put out to consultation, modified and adopted.

This scenario shows one way in which community participation can be incorporated into the development of such a strategy from the outset. This is a requirement set by the United Nations in its 'Agenda 21'. It also improves the likelihood that the strategy will be approved of and implemented. Whole settlement strategies can form the basis for more detailed Community Plans.

Whole settlement strategy

A local authority initiates a strategy to improve a town's sustainability, involving local people and service providers in its creation.

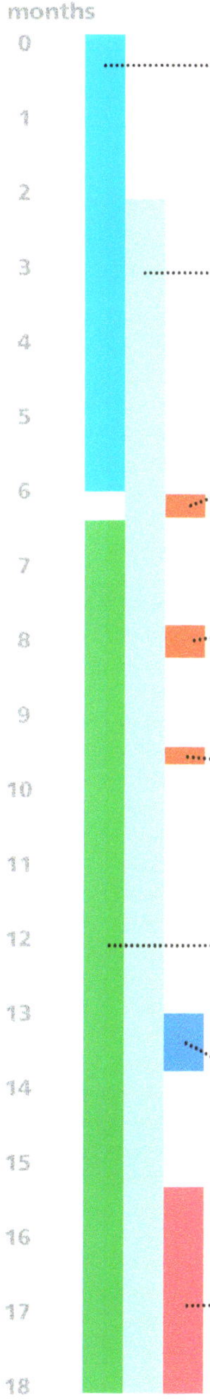

months

0
1

Working party
Established by local authorities involving as many interested parties as possible. Initial planning of process. Gathering of briefing documentation.

2
3

Consultants appointed
If necessary to advise on process. Detailed planning and organisation. Training.

4
5

Future search conference ☞ p78
Or other visioning process. Involving 60–70 people from as many different interest groups as possible.

6
7

Focus groups
Sessions to cover any groups not covered at future search conference.

8
9

Feedback conference
To report on future search conference and focus groups and decide on next steps.

10
11
12

Steering group – community partnership
Appointed at future search conference to guide the overall process. Detailed proposals drawn up by working parties with local authority officers.

13
14

Open house or interactive exhibition ☞ p108
Proposals presented to general public for comment. Feedback incorporated by steering group.

15
16
17

Formal approval
Authority formally adopts strategy and promotes implementation. Steering group monitors progress.

18

Programmes

A selection of programmes managed by governments or other institutions which use community planning for specific purposes.

This new section for the second edition is mirrored on the website at:

www.communityplanning.net/programmes/

Although devised for specific conditions in specific countries, many of the elements of these programmes are generic and can be replicated elsewhere.

Visual minuting, Planning Camp, Eden Project, Cornwall, UK, 2012

City regeneration, Taipei, Taiwan

Summary

City government led programme of community planning and creative city projects.

Purpose

- Stimulate regeneration.
- Environmental improvements that people want.
- Conservation of historic buildings and streetscape.
- Support traditional culture.

Scope

City wide but focusing on two inner city districts: Wanhua and Daton.

Key principles/elements

City government as:

- partner with community groups
- patron for civic vitality
- resource coordinator
- promoter for social enterprises
- driver for innovative regeneration
- architect for creative milieu.

Process – key elements

1995 First Urban Landscape Design Awards.
1996 Neighbourhod Improvement Programme empowers citizens to propose public realm environmental improvement projects.
1999 Community Planners Programme started to provide technical support to local communities.
2002 Young Community Planners Cultivation Project started to encourage more passionate young professionals.
2003 Community Empowerment Network Taipei centre opened in former hospital providing advice and training and providing a bridge between the public and private sectors. Mapping tools introduced to identify community assets and resources.
2008 Video and editing tools provided to communities to film documentaries.
2010 Focus on Green projects; sustainable urbanism.

2010 Launch of Urban Regeneration Station (URS) project to stimulate cultural creativity. Adopts urban acupuncture concept to revitalise key points across the city.

Support available

- Urban regeneration office with 12 staff and budget to buy buildings and implement projects; c US$2.5 million per annum;
- Close links with Architecture and Planning courses in universities;
- Visiting facilitators from overseas.

Fishbowl workshop
Key stakeholders discuss initiatives to improve the historic central districts over a meal surrounded by onlookers and in front of a map covered with Post-it notes contributed earlier by local residents.

臺北市社造盤點計畫案行政區標點圖

1999年之前（32案）

1999年~2000年（56案）

2000年之後（75案）

合計163案

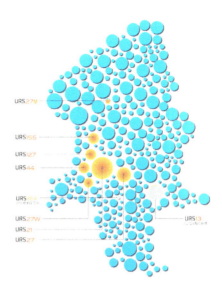

URS27M
URS15S
URS127
URS44
URS27W · URS13
URS21
URS27

Making a difference throughout the city
Neighbourhood Improvement Programmes map, 1995–2002. Includes pedestrianisation, pocket parks, landscaping, building conservation, public art, commercial district management. (Red dots, projects completed before 1999; Yellow, 1999–2000; Blue, after 2000. Total 163.)

Urban acupuncture
Urban Regeneration Stations map, 2013. Current projects are shown brown, deceased projects grey, potential projects blue.

Background

Rapid urbanisation in Taiwan in the mid 20th century caused issues such as insufficient public space, reduced quality public space and destruction of traditional neighbourhood social structures.

Impact

- 163 neighbourhood improvement projects completed between 1996 and 2010.
- 466 teams of community planners active between 1999 and 2010.
- 1,056 community planners trained between 2002 and 2011.
- 9 urban regeneration stations developed.

URS 127 – Design Gallery
Working space for young designers with attached gallery space in a traditional commercial street. The building is also home to a small theatre and an arts workshop. Formerly a shop and residence.

FURTHER INFORMATION

✉ Taipei City Urban Regeneration Office. The Urbanists Collaborative – Taipei.

☆ Thanks: Chung Chieh Lin, Director, Urban Regeneration Office, Taipei City; Song-Nien Xiao, Michelle Hou and Jin Liu, Cosmos Inc.

Heart & Soul Community Planning, USA

Summary

A foundation led programme to help people make better decisions for the future of their communities using innovative public engagement and a focus on enhancing local character.

Purpose

- To create vibrant small cities and towns through broad based citizen engagement that reconnects a town's character to its future actions.
- To help small towns describe and apply their heart and soul so that they can adapt to change while maintaining or enhancing the things they value most.

Scope

Applies to small cities, towns and neighborhoods (under 50,000 population) throughout the United States of America.

Key principles/elements

- **Include everyone** – work hard to connect with every member of a community. Making the process open, accessible and inviting to all increases the chances that everyone will support goals, solutions and actions.
- **Understand local values** – learn what matters most to residents, the shared core values that capture the essence of each place. Let the character of your community define growth and change.
- **Think holistically** – recognising a community's connectedness, develop whole-of-community strategies and solutions that weave elements and interests together rather then pull them apart.
- **Promote authentic engagement** – go beyond typical efforts and insist on deep, true engagement of citizens. Heart & Soul community planning means residents are involved in important local policies, plans and decisions from the very beginning.
- **Facilitate communication and learning** – work hard to make sure everyone has a chance to become truly informed on the issues and options at hand. Instill in residents the importance of this learning.

- **Build partnerships** – far-reaching visions and plans can be achieved only by pooling ideas, resources, skill, capacities and tools. Collaboration among local government, public, private, business, civic and community groups is key to enduring communities.
- **Strengthen local capacity** – knowledge, skills, leadership, experience and confidence are hallmarks of strong communities and must be continually cultivated in residents. Where capacity is strong, community will thrive.
- **New roles** – espouse new roles for planners and elected officials as listeners, facilitators and advisors to residents, not just enforcers and deliberators.
- **Embrace change** – not about stopping growth and change, but shaping it to support and strengthen broadly held values and characteristics – a town's heart and soul.

Process

- Four-phase, 12-step method (see diagram right)
- 18-24 month project duration
- Adaptability – Towns choose among methods within Framework
- Capacity building approach
- Community Network Analysis
- Comprehensive and ongoing engagement of residents
- Integrate storytelling and art
- Identify shared values and apply to local issues and trends
- Values-based decision making
- Take Action
- Measure and Steward Progress

Programme logo

Process wheel
The four-phase, 12 step approach.

Support available

- Online methods, tools and resources;
- Online Handbook;
- Limited staff and monetary support through rigorous qualifying process;
- Other publications.

Background

In 2008, the Orton Family Foundation began a $10 million, five-year initiative to develop a new approach to values-based community planning. It was designed to bring citizens back into the process of charting the future of their cities and towns. The approach became called "Heart & Soul Community Planning".

The programme was successfully piloted in partnership with 10 communities in the Northeast and Rocky Mountain regions, testing new methods, tools and messages. With the Heart & Soul approach, tools and techniques taking final shape, the Foundation will pilot ways to scale the programme and spread it across America.

Early days
The 10 Heart & Soul pilot towns and other communities worked with, 1995 to 2013.

Impact

Anecdotal evidence of cultural and economic growth sparked by programme. Link between economic vitality and shared understanding of what is most important to residents supported by independent study. 10 towns assisted at time of going to press.

Quotes

"When a community takes the time to get to know itself, it gains a sense of identity and purpose that informs decisions and planning. Through Heart & Soul Community Planning, the Orton Family Foundation helps towns plan for their most vibrant future."

Lyman Orton, Founder, 2008.

"The economic development is generated by the changes in community that are manifested through the Heart & Soul process. I know that for sure, and Biddeford [ME] is the evidence of that."

Donna McNeil, Arts Policy & Program Director, Maine Arts Commission, 2013.

FURTHER INFORMATION

 Orton Family Foundation www.orton.org Heart & Soul Community Planning
www.orton.org/who/heart_soul Heart & Soul Handbook
www.orton.org/resources/heart_soul_handbook

☆ Thanks: John Barstow and Rebecca Sanborn Stone, Orton Family Foundation

Neighbourhood Planning, England

Summary

An ambitious government led programme to incorporate community led planning into the statutory planning system.

Purpose

To devolve planning to local neighbourhood level in the hope that this will reduce resistance to new housebuilding and stimulate enterprise.

Scope

Scheme applies throughout England.

Key principles/elements

- A new bottom tier of the planning system governed by statute. Parish councils and designated neighbourhood forums in the driving seat.
- A new right; not a legal requirement. Part of a broader package of community rights as part of a 'localism' agenda.
- Powerful tools for local communities to shape planning policy, with safeguards to ensure compatibility with existing local plans and national planning policy – the Basic Conditions.
- Collaboration and partnership working encouraged, involving civil society, local government, business, landowners and developers.
- New role for planning authorities as facilitators and advisors.
- Flexibility for each plan to be different. No national template.
- Not about stopping development happening but shaping and influencing design, location, mix, phasing and delivery.
- Support packages for groups producing plans.

Process – key elements or the Basic Conditions

1 **Neighbourhood area designation** (what geographical area will the plan cover)
2 **Neighbourhood body designation** (what organisation will take the lead)
3 **Pre-submission consultation** (minimum 6 week period for consultation with key interested parties and local people)

4 **Submission** of draft plan to Local Planning Authority (LPA) which ensures all affected parties know about it – 6 week period)
5 **Independent examination** by professional planner to check if plan meets Basic Conditions, report produced
6 **Referendum** organised by LPA – to ensure popular support for the plan – 50% of voters must be in favour
7 **Making the Plan Order** (plan becomes part of the local development plan and gains legal weight – it will be used to determine planning applications.

Support available

- Small proactive in-house team at the Department of Communities and Local Government;

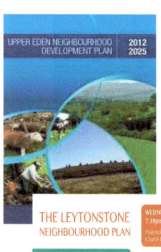

- Local authorities have legal 'duty to support' those producing plans;
- Grants to over 200 Frontrunners (£20k each);
- Grants to several national organisations in first two years to provide support to local groups, develop good practice advice and provide networking opportunities (approx. £4 million per annum);
- Funding support to Local Planning Authorities (based on key stages being reached – £5k per area designation as a forum; £5k when plan submitted to examination; £20k after successful examination)

- From 2013, a £9.5 million support programme, run by a consortium of national organisations, of practical support and grants of £7k per neighbourhood area.

Impact

Too early to tell. At time of going to press (early 2014) over 750 communities applied to be designated as neighbourhood planning areas, over 500 communities designated and producing plans, 50 draft plans produced, 15 submitted for examination, 3 plans passed referendum and been formally made.

Quotes

"When people know that they will get proper support to cope with the demands of new development; when they have a proper say over what new homes will look like; and when they can influence where those homes go, they have reasons to say 'yes' to growth."

Greg Clark MP, Financial Secretary to the Treasury, 18 November 2010.

"We are clear that local people – and local authorities – must be at the heart of planning. The Localism Act has put the power to plan back in the hands of communities, but with this power comes responsibility: a responsibility to meet their needs for development and growth, and to deal quickly and effectively with proposals that will deliver homes, jobs and facilities."

Eric Pickles, Secretary of State for Communities and Local Government, 6 September 2012.

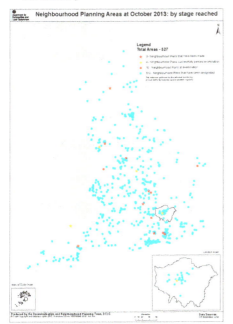

Neighbourhood Planning Areas underway in England, October 2013.

FURTHER INFORMATION

💻 www.communityplanning.net/neighbourhoodplanning/neighbourhoodplanning.php

www.mycommunityrights.org.uk

☞ Scenarios: Community led plan. Neighbourhood development plan.

☆ Thanks: Gareth Bradford and William Roden (DCLG); Mike Gibson.

Case studies

Some examples of community planning in action. Real people, real places, real results.

Case studies can very usefully demonstrate what can be achieved. But because every situation is unique it is often hard to find case studies relevant to you in their entirety. Instead you are likely to find specific elements which may be helpful or which provide inspiration.

Communityplanning.net has developed a detailed format which makes it possible to fully understand who has done what and when and to make comparisions between different approaches. The following pages provide snapshots of a small selection of these. To get the full stories visit the website where you can also download them in A4 format. **www.communityplanning.net/casestudies/casestudyintro.php**

There are also links to other collections of online case studies and a llisting of online case studies can be accessed from **www.communityplanning.net/projects/projects.php**

Key to colour coding

■	**Intense community planning activity** Events, workshops, meetings, open house events, exhibitions	■	**Key points in community planning process** Formation of organisations or partnerships, launch of initiatives, project completion
■	**Moderate community planning activity** Surveys, consultation periods	■	**Other relevant events and activities** Local election, local plan adoption, tendering
■	**Low level community planning activity** Preparation, revising documents, survey analysis, design work	□	**Nothing much happening** Waiting, breathing spaces

Community planning workshop
St Leonards-on-Sea, UK, 2003.

Caterham Barracks Village, UK

Theme
New sustainable community

Location
Caterham-on-the-Hill, Surrey, UK

Project leader:
Linden Homes with John Thompson & Partners

The Vision
Aerial drawing showing how the new scheme will relate, July 2002.

Completed development
Mixed tenure houses overlooking the Green. Building on right is for single persons, central building is family rented, buildings in background are private, 2008.

An impressive example of a private developer using consensus-led masterplanning to create a new sustainable community. Over 1,000 local people were involved in an initial vision-building planning weekend held on the site, a former army barracks with many historic buildings. The completed scheme is an economically integrated, mixed-use neighbourhood that includes housing (366 homes for sale and for rent), supermarket, offices, veterinary hospital, doctors surgery, indoor skateboard and BMX centre, landscaping and open space. A new community development trust manages leisure and business facilities and creates jobs for local people.

Process

Year	Month	Event
1998	Jan	Site purchase
	Feb	Community planning weekend – 5-day event
	Mar	
	April	Event Report published with Vision for the future
	May	Continued community and stakeholder consultation
	Jun	
	Jul	Planning application submitted
	Aug	
	Sep	
	Oct	Local support for planning application
	Nov	Buildings let for short term uses
	Dec	
1999	Jan	
	Feb	
	Mar	
	Apr	Planning approval granted
	May	
	Jun	
	Jul	
	Aug	
	Sep	
	Oct	
	Nov	
	Dec	
2000	Jan	Community Development Trust set up

Note: The skate park was opened in 2002 and the new housing was completed in 2005.

Outcomes

Successes

- Redundant Caterham Barracks turned into an enjoyable place to live and work embedded within an active community.

- Consensus-led approach helped residents understand that demands for community facilities were only financially achievable and sustainable with a higher density of new housing than they initially wanted. This led to considerable changes to the original development brief: a higher number of mixed-tenure housing units enabled the developer to fund a variety of additional facilities for the local community. The development value of the site was increased by US$80 million and community benefits of $4 million created.

- Balanced community created by providing a mix of housing tenure and prices. Of the 366 new homes, 28% (102) are affordable units provided by The Guinness Trust, and distributed within each phase of the development alongside those for private sale. Responding to local need, over 70% are 2 and 3 bedrooms properties and 24 units are sheltered. 60 homes are provided from the conversion of the original buildings, the remainder are new build.

- Sustainability of community enhanced by including a wide range of facilities on site including: Tesco supermarket (2,500 m^2 – 1,800 net), Veterinary hospital (1,068 m^2), Nursing home (with 58 beds), Health and fitness club, Children's nursery, Play area, Offices, Live/work units (as part of housing provision), Doctor's surgery, Skatepark in converted chapel, Cricket pitch and refurbished pavilion, Junior football pitches.

- Responsive, sustainable management body established. A new Community Development Trust manages leisure and business facilities on the site and uses its assets to create jobs for local people.

- Several awards received (see Awards).

Awards

Building for Life Gold Standard Award, 2005.

The Deputy Prime Minister's Award for Sustainable Communities, 2003, Finalist.

The European Urban and Regional Planning Awards, 2002, Conversion (Joint Winner).

The Royal Town Planning Institute National Awards for Planning Achievement, 2000: Award for Planning for the Whole Community.

British Urban Regeneration Association Community Award, 2000: Caterham Barracks Community Trust.

Quotes

"This is a unique event in a unique place. The Barracks have a special place in the hearts of the people of Caterham."

"It's not just about bricks and mortar; it's about people's lives, building a community that gets on well together."

Participants at the community planning weekend, *1998.*

Reviews

'The Village at Caterham demonstrates how a consensus-led approach can deliver substantial rewards for all stakeholders and help create a new sustainable community.'

John Thompson & Partners, *2007.*

FURTHER INFORMATION

 www.communityplanning.net/casestudies/casestudy009.php

Hudswell Community Pub, UK

Theme
Community enterprise

Location
Hudswell, Swaledale, Yorkshire, UK

Project leader:
Hudswell Community Pub Ltd (HCP)

The George & Dragon was the only pub in an isolated village which had no shop or other community facilities apart from a village hall. Its closure was a major blow to the village. Yet, thanks to the imagination and innovation of villagers, it was reopened as a community enterprise, also incorporating a mini-library, a small village shop and allotments. The business model is fairly risk free and can be applied to many different kinds of community facilities.

Seeking investors
Launching the Prospectus outside the pub, 28 December 2009.

Process

Year	Month	Event
2008	Aug	Last orders at the bar
	Sep	
	Oct	
	Nov	
	Dec	
2009	Jan	Local stirrings
	Feb	
	Mar	
	Apr	Training
	May	Steering Group
	Jun	
	Jul	Public meeting
	Aug	Development work
	Sep	
	Oct	
	Nov	
	Dec	Prospectus launched
2010	Jan	Fundraising
	Feb	Building purchased
	Mar	Refurbishment
	Apr	
	May	
	Jun	Pub reopens
	Jul	
	Aug	
	Sep	
	Oct	
	Nov	
	Dec	Shop opens

Launch
Foreign Secretary, local MP and HCP member, William Hague declares the pub open for business by cutting a George & Dragon cake, 2010.

Outcomes

Successes

- The community run George & Dragon pub has become a real success, with sales figures 50% higher than predicted in the first year.

- The pub has become a vibrant hub for the local community and also for the many tourists and walkers that visit. It hosts a wide range of community events: live music, a book club, a folk club, a Halloween scarecrow competition and much more.

- The pub has 10 allotments, rented to local people. It also hosts a small library, with books provided by North Yorkshire Library Service, free internet access for customers and laptops to hire for a small fee.

- A 'Little Shop' has been created in a small room in the pub but with its own street access. It is thought to be the smallest community shop in the country and sells bread, milk, eggs, vegetables and other groceries.

- Future plans include creating a Bed & Breakfast facility and developing unused land on the site.

- HCP's Annual Report 2011 states: "With the shop, allotments, library and internet access we feel that we have created a hub of services that make the George & Dragon a real centre of village activity and we have helped to create a more cohesive and friendly community in the village. It is clear that there are now far more people involved in village life and we all feel part of a caring and supportive community."

Lessons

- A co-operative is a good model for funding and running local services.

- Communities can do a lot if they have access to fairly minimal but crucial professional advice and assistance at the right time.

Quotes

"We have shown what a community can achieve when its spirit and effort is harnessed and thanks goes out to all of you who have helped in any way to make our community pub the success it is today."

Paul Cullen, Chair, HCP Ltd., *2011.*

"The pub was a casualty of the credit crunch. The last landlord bought it when property prices were at their highest. When business declined as a result of the recession they couldn't make the mortgage repayments. The co-op won't have that problem because we haven't borrowed any money."

Martin Booth, a director of HCP Ltd, *2010.*

"It is fantastic to know the pub is now open and so far, business has been good. The risk in this buy-to-let model is fairly minimal, with the community organisation receiving a fixed income every month from the tenants, and ensuring local repeat clientele from the proud owners of the pub. The directors also have further plans to diversify their income streams, and attract more visitors to their pub, which should ensure its sustainability."

Sophie Michelena, Development Officer for Locality in Yorkshire & Humber, *2011.*

FURTHER INFORMATION

 http://www.communityplanning.net/casestudies/casestudy012.php

Youth Space Pilot, West Midlands, UK

Theme
Youth facilities

Location
West Midlands, UK.
Six locations: Coleshill,
Warwickshire; Hunderton,
Hereford; Romsley,
Bromsgrove; Stechford,
Birmingham; Warndon,
Worcester; Penn Island,
Wolverhampton.

Project leader:
Midlands Architecture and the
Designed Environment (MADE)

A collaborative design project between young people, architects and artists, for the design and construction of six custom-made youth shelters. An innovative pilot programme, which demonstrates the potential of effective and creative community consultation and collaboration processes in improving both the environment and people's lives.

Process

Year	Month	Activity
2003	Jun	National Youth Spaces Seminar
	Jul	Project planning
	Aug	
	Sep	
	Oct	
	Nov	
	Dec	
2004	Jan	Expressions of interest
	Feb	Local client teams selected in six locations
	Mar	
	Apr	Shelter design
	May	
	Jun	
	Jul	
	Aug	
	Sep	
	Oct	Detailed design
	Nov	
	Dec	
2005	Jan	
	Feb	Fabrication starts
	Mar	Construction starts
	Apr	Completions and launch events start
	May	
	Jun	
	Jul	
	Aug	
	Sep	Publicity and good practice dissemination

Note: All shelters were completed by September 2006

Coleshill Shelter completed

Coleshill Shelter in use

Outcomes

- Six pilot projects resulting in six very different new youth shelters, of high design quality.

- Creative involvement of many young people: A core group of 100 and a wider group of 500-1000.

- Collaboration of many professionals and organisations: Total number of artists and architect practices: 14. Total number of partners: 45.

- Anecdotal and statistical evidence of reduced crime and antisocial behaviour.

- Dramatic and positive change in the young people taking part.

Shortcomings

- Unrealistic foresight into the design process and construction costs of the shelters resulting in 2 shelters being delayed and requiring further fundraising.

Quotes

"You feel like you can do a lot more than you ever thought you could, more self esteem. Young people would feel offended if a shelter was just placed there, there would be no respect. Everybody has a right to feel comfortable in their place that they use everyday"

Young person, Coleshill Design Team, *2005.*

"Outside recreation facilities, or as they would put it 'somewhere to chill out', are a very common need raised by the young people I work with. When I'm proposing projects like this to adults I usually get them to imagine what they would do with their free time if they had little or no disposable income, could not go to the pub, or be welcomed in a café. If they did not have their own cars, homes or gardens to relax in, where would they go? Young people are just adults without the same benefits of adulthood."

Sarah Melia, South Hereford Patch Youth Worker, Herefordshire Council, *2005.*

Romsley design image

Stechford completed

FURTHER INFORMATION

http://www.communityplanning.net/casestudies/casestudy004.php

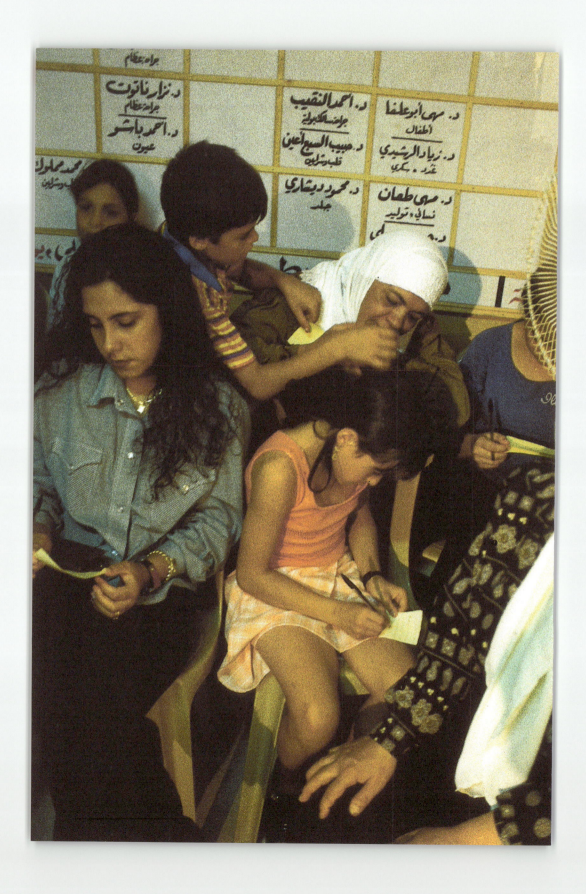

Appendices

Download editable templates for the forms and checklists from the Toolbox at
www.communityplanning.net/useful/toolbox.php

Community planning workshop,
Sidon, Lebanon, 1997

Useful formats

Action planner

For use at workshops or meetings.

Workshop title/theme   Getting around
Date and time   4 October 2001, 4pm
Convenor   Mary

Topic	Action needed	By whom	When	Help needed	Priority (1–5)
Traffic	Pedestrian plan	Environment forum	July	Traffic engineers	2
Cycle racks	Install	Traders	May	Welding	4
Bus timetable	Display at all stops	Bus company	June	-	3
Bins	Obtain more green ones	Local authority	Sept	Councillors	4
etc	etc	etc	etc	etc	etc

Community planning event planner

To help start shaping any kind of community planning event (or thinking through whether one would be useful at all). Can be used in a workshop session after a presentation, or as part of a training exercise (see page 127 for sample format).

AIMS

1. What do you want to **achieve** from a community planning event?

....

2. What are the **main issues** to be addressed?

....

3. What geographical **area** should it cover?

....

NATURE OF EVENT

4. How **long** should the event (or events) be?

....

5. **When** should the event be? (dates)

....

6. What **specific activities** should take place, and in what order?

....

7. Who are the **key people** to invite?

....

8. Should there be an **independent team** of facilitators from outside the area? YES/NO
9. If YES what **expertise** do you want on the team?

....

10. Any ideas for names of **team members** or the **team chairperson**?

....

ORGANISATION

11. Which organisation/s should **host** the event?

....

12. Who else should **help** and how?

....

13. Who will do the **administration**?

....

14. **Where** should the event be held?
    Workshops? ....
    Presentations? ....

Meals? ....

Hotels? ....

15. What **briefing material** should be made available or prepared?

....

16. Who will make sure that the results of the event are used and built on **afterwards**?

....

MONEY

17. How much will it **cost** (roughly)?

		18. Who might **sponsor** it (or do things free)?
Admin	$......	....
Venues	$......	....
Publicity	$......	....
Catering	$......	....
Equipment	$......	....
Photography	$......	....
Travel	$......	....
Accommodation	$......	....
Report printing	$......	....
Follow-up activity	$......	....
Other	$......	....
Total	$......	

IMMEDIATE NEXT STEPS

19. **Who** does **what** now?

....

....

....

OTHER THOUGHTS AND IDEAS

20..

....

....

....

Name and contact details (optional)

....

....

....

Date.............

Consultation statement

For recording and reporting the results of consulting on a draft plan or proposal

Example used: Neighbourhood or community plan

Who consulted	How and when consulted	Issues and concerns raised	How issues considered and addressed	Reasons and notes
Key stakeholder 1 Anywhere Council	Presentation with Q & A 14 Feb	Integrated transport iissues	Detailed comments invited and incoporated	
Key stakeholder 2 Environment Agency	Draft sent for comment 30 Mar	Flooding risk on site B	Amended site B boundaries	
etc				
Local residents 1 Anyplace	Have your say day dropin for anyplace, 5 April	1. Better pedestrian access at anystreet needed 2 Loss of views from anyterrace 3 Traffic on any mews	1 Access requirements improved 2 Not relevant but comments passed to architects 3 Survey commissioned	2 Views not a planning issue 3 Survey results Ok. Posted on website 7 June
Local residents 2 Townwide	Citizens panel questionnaire	1 Traffic generation 2 Consultation with traders needed 3 -	1 Reviewed figures 2 See below 3 -	
etc				
Local businesses 1 Market street traders	Street stall, 12 April	Delivery hours too short	Amended hours	
Local businesses 2 Business park tenants	Letter and survey form, 20 April	None	N/A	
etc				
etc				

Evaluation form

For evaluating most kinds of community planning activity. Can provide insights on impacts, participants' perceptions and improvements needed. Customise to suit. Circulate to a range of participants or use as a basis for an interview or workshop agenda. Repeating the exercise at intervals may be worthwhile as the impact of activity will often not become clear for many years.

Name _____ Organisation (if any) _____
Address _____ Position (if any) _____

Title of activity _____ Date/s of activity _____
Nature of activity _____ Date of evaluation _____

1 Your role in activity _____

2 How did you become involved? _____

3 What do you think are/were the aims? _____

4 What do you think motivated people and organisations to get involved? _____

5 What effect if any has your personal contribution in the activity made? _____

6 What effect has the activity had on the physical environment? _____

7 What effect has the activity had on the local economy? _____

8 What effect has the activity had on local organisations? _____
   (eg changed roles, new partnerships, etc)

9 What effect has the activity had on individuals? _____
   (eg locals, visitors, investors etc)

10 Was the activity worthwhile? _____ If so, why? _____

11 What improvements would you make if it was being done again? _____

12 What would be your advice to others organising a similar activity? _____

13 What additional information sources would be helpful? _____

14 Any other comments? _____

Thank you for your time.
Please return this form to: info@anyevaluators.com

Progress monitor

For summarising the outcome of community planning activity and planning the next steps.

Compile and circulate for comment to a range of participants to get a full picture.

Example used: Developing a community plan

Topic	Action taken	By whom	Outcome	Next step	By whom
Controlled parking	Input into design of questionnaire	Forum	New zones in place.	-	-
Waste recycling	Schools promotion	Forum	Higher recycling rates noted	Resident promotion	Residents associations
Cycle routes	Working party set up	Cycle club	Cycleway plan being developed	Publicise for comment	Radio Libraries
District plan	Consultation	All voluntary organisations	Revisions made	Repeat next year	Planners
Station	Owner contacted.	Planning officer	Nothing	Invite to design workshop	Jenny
etc	etc	etc	etc	etc	etc

Strategy planner

For planning an overall community planning strategy incorporating a variety of methods (see p8).

Example used: Improving a largely residential urban neighbourhood

Method	Who involved?	Timescale (from start)	Purpose	Responsibility
Initial meeting	Resident groups Agency reps	1 month	Discuss process	Agency officer
Process planning session	Resident groups Agency reps Speaker/facilitator	2 months	Decide process	Area Forum
Youth project	Local schools Youth clubs	4 months	Gain children's ideas and support	Youth leaders
Press release	General public	5 months	Launch event. Public awareness and involvement	Co-ordinator
Community planning event	All stakeholders	7 months	Develop strategy options	Area Forum/ Technical College
Interactive exhibition	General public	8 months	Feedback on options	Area Forum/ Housing officers
Local plan revision draft	Local authority	12 months	Improve policy. Formalise action plan	Planning officers
Local planning centre	General public Urban designers	18 months	Implement action plan. Improve agency coordination	Area Forum Housing agency Planning officers
Local plan formal consultation	General public	20 months	Statutory obligation	Local authority
Planning day	All stakeholders	24 months	Review progress	Area Forum
etc	etc	etc	etc	etc

Workshop planner

To help plan a workshop. Suitable for most types of workshop.

Example used: | Afternoon workshop session as part of a conference |

Time	Activity	Format	Minutes	Responsibility	Equipment
10.00	Briefing. Explain roles to facilitators	Meeting	15	John	Workshop sheets
12.25	Announcement. Explain aims & procedure	Conference plenary	5	Sue	None
13.00	Preparation. Setting up of workshop spaces	Lunch break	20	Workshop facilitators	Flipcharts, pads, Blu-tack, pens, banners, labels
14.00	Workshop intros	Workshop groups (4)	10	Workshop facilitators	Attendance sheets
14.10	First exercise. 3 initiatives needed (on separate post-its)	Workshop groups (4)	10	Workshop facilitators	Post its (separate colour for each group)
14.20	Prioritising on large sheets	Workshop groups (4)	15	Workshop facilitators	Large sheets of paper, felt-tips
14.35	Report back	Plenary	20	Sue	Flipchart, masking tape
....	....	....	...	....	....
	....	....		....	....
etc	etc	etc	etc	etc	etc

Useful checklists

Community plan content

A checklist of items that might be considered in a community plan or masterplan. Customise and structure your own list.

- ☐ Accessibility
- ☐ Action plans – for various time periods
- ☐ Advice services
- ☐ Air quality
- ☐ Alcohol abuse
- ☐ Allotments
- ☐ Animals and birds
- ☐ Anti-social behaviour
- ☐ Archaeology
- ☐ Architecture
- ☐ Arts – visual and performing
- ☐ Bad neighbour uses
- ☐ Boating facilities
- ☐ Broadband
- ☐ Building scale and character
- ☐ Building skills
- ☐ Building use
- ☐ Burial sites
- ☐ Buses
- ☐ Cafes
- ☐ Carnivals and celebrations
- ☐ Character of the area
- ☐ Childcare facilities
- ☐ Churches
- ☐ Cinemas
- ☐ Clubs and societies
- ☐ Colour – of buildings and townscape
- ☐ Community care facilities
- ☐ Community centres
- ☐ Community participation strategies
- ☐ Community trusts
- ☐ Conservation of buildings
- ☐ Conservation of landscape
- ☐ Crafts
- ☐ Crime – causes and deterrents
- ☐ Culture
- ☐ Cycle facilities
- ☐ Dance venues
- ☐ Densities of development

- ☐ Development opportunities
- ☐ Disability facilities
- ☐ Disabled access
- ☐ Disaster management
- ☐ Dogs and other pets
- ☐ Drainage
- ☐ Drug abuse
- ☐ Economic generators
- ☐ Education facilities
- ☐ Electricity supplies
- ☐ Employment
- ☐ Energy saving and generation
- ☐ Enterprise
- ☐ Entertainment facilities
- ☐ Environmental art
- ☐ Erosion
- ☐ Events
- ☐ Farming
- ☐ Flooding
- ☐ Fly-posting
- ☐ Fly-tipping
- ☐ Friendliness
- ☐ Fumes
- ☐ Fund-raising
- ☐ Gardens
- ☐ Gas supplies
- ☐ Graffiti
- ☐ Health
- ☐ Historic connections
- ☐ Homework clubs
- ☐ Housing (market, rental, affordable)
- ☐ Human resources
- ☐ Image
- ☐ Implementation mechanisms
- ☐ Indoor sports
- ☐ Infill sites
- ☐ Information availability
- ☐ Information technology
- ☐ Innovation
- ☐ Internet access
- ☐ Lakes and ponds
- ☐ Land and property use
- ☐ Land and property values
- ☐ Landmarks
- ☐ Libraries and other learning facilities
- ☐ Licensing

226

- ☐ Lighting – streets and buildings
- ☐ Links and alleyways
- ☐ Litter
- ☐ Litter bins
- ☐ Leisure facilities
- ☐ Local authorities
- ☐ Local exchange trading
- ☐ Local organisations and institutions
- ☐ Local produce
- ☐ Local shops
- ☐ Low income support systems
- ☐ Maintenance and management systems
- ☐ Market gardens
- ☐ Markets – indoor and outdoor
- ☐ Men's facilities
- ☐ Minority groups
- ☐ Mixed uses
- ☐ Music venues
- ☐ Noise
- ☐ Older people facilities
- ☐ Open spaces
- ☐ Parks and public gardens
- ☐ Paths
- ☐ Pedestrians
- ☐ Planning procedures
- ☐ Play facilities
- ☐ Policing
- ☐ Pollution
- ☐ Poverty and wealth
- ☐ Power supplies
- ☐ Principles of development
- ☐ Public art
- ☐ Public squares
- ☐ Pubs
- ☐ Quality of design
- ☐ Quality of life
- ☐ Quality of local services
- ☐ Railings
- ☐ Railways and station locations
- ☐ Recycling waste materials
- ☐ Refuse collection
- ☐ Religions
- ☐ Resource centres
- ☐ Restaurants
- ☐ Rivers and streams
- ☐ Road building and maintenance

- ☐ Safety
- ☐ Schools
- ☐ School use out of hours
- ☐ Sense of identity
- ☐ Sense of place
- ☐ Sense of safety
- ☐ Sewage disposal
- ☐ Shopping facilities
- ☐ Smell
- ☐ Social inclusion and mix
- ☐ Social services
- ☐ Special needs facilities
- ☐ Sports facilities – pitches, courts
- ☐ Sports opportunities
- ☐ Street cleaning
- ☐ Street lighting
- ☐ Street signs and numbering
- ☐ Street trees
- ☐ Streetscape
- ☐ Sustainability
- ☐ Targets for action
- ☐ Temporary uses
- ☐ Timescales
- ☐ Tourism
- ☐ Townscape
- ☐ Traffic
- ☐ Traffic calming
- ☐ Traffic routes
- ☐ Transport options
- ☐ Vacant buildings
- ☐ Vacant land
- ☐ Vernacular architecture
- ☐ Views
- ☐ Visitors
- ☐ Voluntary organisations
- ☐ Voluntary services
- ☐ Water features
- ☐ Water supplies
- ☐ Women's facilities
- ☐ Youth clubs
- ☐ Youth services
- ☐ ....
- ☐ ....
- ☐ ....
- ☐ ....
- ☐ ....

Equipment and supplies

An overall checklist of items which may be helpful for those planning activities in compiling their own lists. Checklists for some specific methods are provided on the methods pages.

Having the right equipment and supplies can make the difference between success and failure. Different events and activities obviously require different equipment and supplies. Some require very little, if anything.

- [ ] Aerial photographs
- [ ] Banners and directional signs with fixings
- [ ] Base maps and plans of the area at different scales (1:200 and 1:400 most commonly used)
- [ ] Base model with movable parts
- [ ] Bell or whistle (for announcements)
- [ ] Blackboard and chalk
- [ ] Blackout curtains
- [ ] Blu-tack
- [ ] Box files
- [ ] Cameras:
  35mm or digital with wide-angle, telephoto, flash and close-up facility
  Polaroid (for last minute prints needed)
- [ ] Camera accessories (for digital):
  memory cards, battery charger, spare battery, connection cable, card reader, download cable.
- [ ] Cardboard or polystyrene (for modelmaking)
- [ ] Catering gear (cups, plates, cutlery, napkins, urn, kettle)
- [ ] Chairs (stackable?) and stools
- [ ] Chalk (different colours)
- [ ] Clipboards
- [ ] Clock with alarm (for timing speakers)
- [ ] Cocktail sticks (for use with model)
- [ ] Compasses
- [ ] Computer equipment:
  laptop
  laser printer and toner
  scanner if possible
  DTP and word processing software
  disks

- [ ] Correction fluid
- [ ] Cutting knives, mats, metal edge and spare blades
- [ ] Data projector and screen, spare fuses and bulbs, extension cord, remote handset
- [ ] Desks
- [ ] Dictating and transcribing equipment
- [ ] Drawing boards or drawing tables
- [ ] Drinks facility and fridge
- [ ] Easels and pads (24"x 30")
- [ ] Erasers
- [ ] Exhibition facilities
- [ ] Extension cables
- [ ] Filing trays
- [ ] Film projector and screen
- [ ] Flat-bed photo-stand with colour corrected lamps (for shooting drawings and plans) and spare bulbs
- [ ] Flipcharts (with non-squeaky pens)
- [ ] Food and drink
- [ ] Glue-sticks
- [ ] Hole punches
- [ ] Lighting, including desk lighting
- [ ] Lock-up for valuable equipment
- [ ] Name badges (or blank sticky labels)
- [ ] Overhead or opaque projectors with transparency film and markers (handy for sketching and for presentations)
- [ ] Paper:
  A4 & A2 sketch pads
  A4 writing pads (lined)
  tracing (white and yellow)
  A5 note pads
  flipchart pads
  butcher paper (long strips)
- [ ] Paperclips
- [ ] Paper trimmer or guillotine
- [ ] Pencils: normal; coloured
- [ ] Pens:
  felt-tips in bright colours and grey tones (different sizes)
  fibre-tipped with medium and fine tips
  ball points (black and red)
  technical drawing
  highlighters

- ☐ Photocopier with enlarging/reducing facility (and rapid repair service)
- ☐ Photocopier paper, toner etc
- ☐ Pin board or pin-up wall
- ☐ Pins – different colours:
  drawing pins
  stick pins
- ☐ Plan storage system
- ☐ Pocket notebooks (for shirt pockets)
- ☐ Pointer stick/laser for presentations
- ☐ Post-its (different sizes and colours)
- ☐ Power outlets
- ☐ Projector stand
- ☐ Public address system with microphones on stands and roving
- ☐ Ring binders (A4)
- ☐ Rubber bands
- ☐ Rubber cement
- ☐ Rulers and scale rulers
- ☐ Scissors
- ☐ Screen for copying photographs
- ☐ Shelving and filing space
- ☐ Spraymount adhesive
- ☐ Staples and staple extractors
- ☐ Sticky dots (many colours)
- ☐ Tables
- ☐ Tape:
  brown packaging tape
  double sided
  heavy duty gaffer tape (for outside use)
  magic tape
  masking tape
- ☐ Tape recorder and cassettes
- ☐ Telephones and fax machines
- ☐ Toilet paper
- ☐ T-squares, triangles and circle templates
- ☐ USB stick
- ☐ Velcro pads (sticky hook and loop pads)
- ☐ Video camera and accessories
- ☐ Video play-back equipment (if relevant)
- ☐ Waste bins and garbage bags
- ☐ Zip up bags (for Post-its)
- ☐ ....
- ☐ ....
- ☐ ....
- ☐ ....

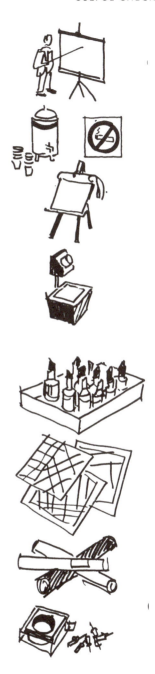

Initiatives needed

A checklist of general policy initiatives that may help make community planning more effective. Customise to suit your country, place and circumstances.

☐ **Build locally**
Locally-based building activity should be encouraged so that the economic benefits of development stay within the community. Provision for the employment of local labour and training of local people in building skills should be considered for inclusion in any building contract.

☐ **Career incentives**
Community planning expertise should be recognised and encouraged with more effective and systematic training programmes and career opportunities.

☐ **Centres of activity and information**
New centres, or networks of centres, on community planning should be established at national and regional level to disseminate good practice, provide advice, and evaluate and follow up on events and activities.

☐ **Community development briefs**
Development briefs should be produced with communities for all major sites and should preferably become mandatory as a basis for land valuation and acquisition.

☐ **Culture of participation**
A general culture of participation should be encouraged so that participation in planning becomes natural and inevitable.

☐ **Delegated planning powers**
Planning powers should be delegated to the lowest possible tiers of government, with regional government retaining powers to intervene only in the event of local corruption or for major strategic issues.

☐ **Derelict land and buildings**
Derelict land and buildings (both public and private) should be made available for community-led initiatives and be made the subject of punitive taxes to encourage their productive use.

☐ **Educating enablers**
The curricula of architecture and planning schools should include relevant training for professional enablers. Live project units – urban design studios – should be set up at all schools, to undertake community projects.

☐ **Environmental education**
Environmental education programmes for the public should be expanded so that people learn how the built environment works and how they can take part in improving it. Environmental education should form part of primary and secondary school curricula, and comprehensive networks of urban and rural studies centres should be established. There should be special emphasis on local vernacular architecture and building techniques.

☐ **Freedom of information**
Land ownership should be public information and always kept up to date. When property in public or social ownership is sold, there should be public debate on its use beforehand, and it should not automatically be sold to the highest bidder.

☐ **Good practice information**
More good practice guidance needs to be produced, made available and kept up to date. Specific items include:

☐ Catalogues of information already available;
☐ Detailed how-to-do-it information on methods;
☐ Toolkits of sample documents and formats;

☐ Contact data for people and
organisations with relevant experience.

☐ Well presented case studies in
print and on film.

☐ Training packs and programmes.

Gradual development
Planning policies should generally
encourage incremental, evolutionary
development with large development sites
broken down into smaller packages.

Information
Information systems should be established
to make data about successful examples
of community planning and development
widely available. Programmes should be
established to encourage more exchange
of experience between the various groups
involved in the process – public, private,
professional and voluntary. Methods
should be devised for exchanging
information internationally so that
relevant lessons may be learned in the
shortest possible space of time.

Lobbying for resources
Multi-agency co-ordination, resources and
leadership are needed to lobby for
increased resources for participatory
planning activity at local level and
supporting services at national or regional
level.

Marketing
The importance and effectiveness of
community planning should be more
forcefully marketed.

Percentage for participation
All significant developments should
include in their budgets a specific amount
of funding for effective participation at all
stages.

Planners out in the community
More professional planners should be
physically located in multidisciplinary
offices in the communities they serve. In

urban areas no one should be more than
a few minutes' walk from such an office.
Architecture centres, community design
centres and neighbourhood planning
offices should all be promoted.

Planning applications
Proposals by property owners for
development should be encouraged or
required to include visual details and
policy statements. It should also be
possible to view proposals nearby, ie in a
local shop or cafe, rather than having to
travel to remote government offices.
Ideally, proposals should be displayed
visually at the site in question.

Planning decisions
All relevant social and environmental
issues should be considered in planning
appeals, public inquiries and local
planning decisions. The recommendations
of public inquiry inspectors should not be
overturned by central government except
for overriding reasons, such as national
security. Community groups should be
given access to the necessary resources to
present their case effectively.

Practitioner listing service
Registers of experienced community
planning and community architecture
practitioners should be established to help
local authorities, developers and
community groups obtain the best
expertise available.

Professional payment
Recommended professional fee scales
should be adjusted to take account of the
extra time needed to involve end-users.

Public funding
Accountability procedures for the receipt
of public funds should be redefined to
encourage community initiatives and
provide voluntary organisations with
consistent, long-term funding, to facilitate
forward planning.

☐ **Public sector enablers**
Central and local government should learn to trust community organisations and actively assist them in their formation and growth. There should be a fundamental policy shift from 'providing' to 'enabling'.

☐ **Public participation statements**
Developers of significant projects should be required to produce a 'public participation statement' identifying those affected and setting out how they will be involved in the development process. This should be an integral part of planning application procedures.

☐ **Quantify benefits**
Funding needs to be allocated to systematic analysis and quantifying of the benefits of community planning approaches.

☐ **Research**
Far more resources should be devoted to research on the built environment by government and the development industry to avoid making the same mistakes over and over again. Research and development programmes should be undertaken on the long-term cost effectiveness of different approaches and the results widely disseminated. Special attention should be directed towards the development of techniques in participatory planning and design.

☐ **Review statutory procedures**
Planning, development and management procedures need to be constantly reviewed to ensure they incorporate the best participatory practice available. This might cover:

☐ Preparing local plans;
☐ Preparing development briefs;
☐ Planning application procedures;
☐ Public inquiry procedures;
☐ Urban management procedures.

☐ **Simplify language**
Planning legislation should be re-written in straightforward language.

☐ **Technical aid**
Networks of community-controlled, publicly-funded multidisciplinary technical aid facilities should be established and maintained.

☐ **Voluntary sector empowered**
Voluntary organisations – representing geographical communities and communities of interest – should willingly demand and accept more responsibility for the creation and management of the environment and should strengthen and restructure themselves in order to become more effective as developers and property managers. Special emphasis should be put on encouraging the formation of housing cooperatives, special project groups, development trusts, neighbourhood forums and development partnerships.

☐ ....
....
....
....

☐ ....
....
....
....

Neighbourhood skills survey

A checklist of skills for finding out what talent exists in a community. Use it to compile your own survey form. Illustrate it if you want. Then distribute it round the neighbourhood or, better still, knock on doors and help people fill it in.

Keen beginner
Experienced

- ☐☐ Acting
- ☐☐ Artwork
- ☐☐ Babysitting
- ☐☐ Bicycle repairs
- ☐☐ Book keeping
- ☐☐ Building
- ☐☐ Campaigning
- ☐☐ Car mechanics
- ☐☐ Catering
- ☐☐ Chatting
- ☐☐ Child minding
- ☐☐ Community planning
- ☐☐ Computer operating
- ☐☐ Computer repairs
- ☐☐ Decorating
- ☐☐ Disc jockey
- ☐☐ Drawing
- ☐☐ Dress making
- ☐☐ Driving a bus
- ☐☐ Driving a car
- ☐☐ Driving a truck
- ☐☐ Electrical work
- ☐☐ Embroidery
- ☐☐ Energy knowledge
- ☐☐ Facilitating workshops
- ☐☐ First aid
- ☐☐ Fundraising
- ☐☐ Gardening
- ☐☐ Graphic design
- ☐☐ Hut erection
- ☐☐ Journalism
- ☐☐ Keeping people informed
- ☐☐ Knitting
- ☐☐ Landscaping
- ☐☐ Letter writing
- ☐☐ Managing

- ☐☐ Motorbike repairs
- ☐☐ Negotiation
- ☐☐ Nursing
- ☐☐ Organising events
- ☐☐ Photography
- ☐☐ Playing music
- ☐☐ Plumbing
- ☐☐ Pottery
- ☐☐ Public speaking
- ☐☐ Publicity
- ☐☐ Recycling
- ☐☐ Roofing
- ☐☐ Running a bar
- ☐☐ Running a cafe
- ☐☐ Social networking
- ☐☐ Sports (please specify)
- ☐☐ Sculpting
- ☐☐ Site clearing
- ☐☐ Teaching
- ☐☐ Translating (specify languages)
- ☐☐ Typing
- ☐☐ Video work
- ☐☐ Website construction
- ☐☐ Woodwork
- ☐☐ Writing and editing
- ☐☐ Youth work
- ☐☐ ....
- ☐☐ ....
- ☐☐ ....
- ☐☐ ....

Who to involve

A checklist of people and organisations who might need to be involved in any community planning initiative. Customise your own list.

☐ Allotment holders
☐ Archaeological groups
☐ Archaeologists
☐ Architects
☐ Builders
☐ Businesses
☐ Chambers of commerce
☐ Charities
☐ Children
☐ Churches
☐ Civic societies and groups
☐ Colleges
☐ Community associations
☐ Community-based organisations (CBOs)
☐ Community leaders
☐ Community woodland groups
☐ Companies
☐ Conservation groups
☐ Countryside management officers
☐ Craftspeople
☐ Cycle groups
☐ Data processors
☐ Designers
☐ Developers
☐ Disability groups
☐ Ecologists
☐ Economists
☐ Energy providers
☐ Engineers
☐ Environmental groups
☐ Ethnic groups
☐ Estate agents
☐ Farmers
☐ Financial institutions
☐ Footpath and access groups
☐ Funding agencies
☐ Health workers
☐ Homeless people
☐ Industrialists
☐ Journalists
☐ Land managers
☐ Landowners
☐ Landscape architects
☐ Lawyers
☐ Local authorities

☐ Local history groups
☐ Media groups and organisations
☐ Migrants
☐ Minority groups
☐ Mothers' unions
☐ Museums (especially local history)
☐ Non-governmental organisations (NGOs)
☐ Parent–teacher organisations
☐ Parish councils
☐ Photographers
☐ Planners
☐ Playgroups
☐ Police
☐ Postmen and women
☐ Professional institutions and groups
☐ Property owners
☐ Public works departments
☐ Publicans
☐ Ramblers
☐ Religious groups
☐ Residents groups and associations
☐ Rural community councils
☐ Schools
☐ Senior citizens
☐ Shopkeepers
☐ Sports groups
☐ Statutory agencies
☐ Street cleaners
☐ Student groups
☐ Surveyors
☐ Teachers
☐ Tenant groups and associations
☐ Town managers
☐ Traders
☐ Transport groups
☐ Transport operators
☐ Transport planners
☐ Unions
☐ Universities
☐ Urban designers
☐ Utility providers
☐ Village hall committees
☐ Wildlife groups
☐ Women's groups
☐ Women's institutes
☐ Workforces
☐ Young people
☐ Youth clubs, guides and scouts
☐ ....
☐ ....

Glossary A–Z

Common and not-so-common terms and concepts used in community planning simply explained.

Focuses on process and includes some methods not covered elsewhere in the book, with cross-references to sources of further information.

➡ Refer to glossary item with similar meaning.

☞ See also *glossary item* or *page reference*.

A-Z Item covered more fully in the Methods A–Z.

๏ Publication with further information (p260).

✉ Contact with further information (p266).

▣ Website with further information (p274).

The online glossary is more extensive and also includes terms and concepts from the worlds of planning, regeneration, project management and environmental sustainability:
www.communityplanning.
net/glossary/glossary.php

Editorial note
In compiling this book I have had to make many decisions on terminology. Different people have used the same term to mean different things and different terms to mean the same thing. I have tried to use the simplest and most explanatory term wherever possible and avoid jargon.

21st century town meeting
Method involving very large numbers of community, industry and government representatives (100 to 5000 or more) in a forum of one or two days.

Action group
Informal organisation set up to get something achieved, usually through visible and public protest.

Action minutes
Record of a meeting in the form of a list of steps required, who should take them and when.

Action plan
Proposals for action. Usually in the form of a list of steps required, who should take them and when. ☞ *p222*.

Action planning
Developing an action plan. Term also used in the 1990s to describe *community planning events*. ☞ *Action plan* ☞ **A-Z** *Community planning event*

Action planning event
Similar meaning to *community planning event*. Term popular in the 1990s. ☞ **A-Z** *Community planning event*

Activity mapping
Plotting on a map or plan how people use places as an aid to understanding how best to improve them. ☞ *Mapping*.

Activity week
Week of activities designed to promote interest in, and debate on, a chosen theme: eg Architecture week; Urban design week; Environment week. ☞ **A-Z** *p28*.

Activity year
Year of activities designed to promote interest in, and debate on, a chosen theme: eg Glasgow 1999; UK City of Architecture and Design.

Adaptable model
Flexible model of an area or building which allows people to test out alternative design options. ☞ *Models*.

Adventure playground
Playground that encourages children to construct and manage their own environment.

Advocacy planning
Professional planners working on behalf of the disadvantaged. Term popular in the United States in the early 1970s.

Agenda
Plan for a meeting. List of items to be discussed.

Alternative plan
Plan for a site or neighbourhood putting forward a different approach to the prevailing plan. ☞ *Community plan*.

Amenity trust
Charitable organisation established to manage a public amenity. ☞ *Development trust*.

Animateur
Person with good communication skills employed to assist in organising and enlivening a community process, such as children's participatory design activities. Often a community artist.

Appraisal
➡ *Community appraisal*.

Appreciative inquiry
Group working process which builds on potentials, solutions and benefits to create change. ➔ *The Thin Book of Appreciative Inquiry.*

Appropriate technology
Construction materials and techniques geared to local social and economic needs, possibilities and sources of materials. Sometimes referred to as *user-friendly technology.*

Archetype
Place with certain easily identifiable qualities. Concept sometimes used in briefing and design workshops to get people to describe the kind of place they aspire to; for instance, a certain part of a certain city or a certain building.

Architects in schools
Environmental education programme involving architects working with children in schools.

Architecture centre
Place aimed at helping people understand, and engage in, the design of the local built environment. ☞ **A-Z** *p30.*

Architecture week
Week of activities designed to promote interest in, and debate on, architecture. Usually includes opening interesting buildings to the public. ☞ *Activity week.*

Architecture workshop
Workshop session on architecture. Term also sometimes used to describe an architecture or community design centre. ☞ *Architecture centre. Community design centre.*

Art centre
Place providing a focus for the arts and local artists.

Art house
Building used as a base for local artists producing and exhibiting work with and about the local community. Used as a regeneration technique for developing local pride and talent. ☞ *Art centre.*

Art workshop
Session where local residents work with artists designing and making artworks to improve their environment. ☞ **A-Z** *p32.*

Asset base
Capital assets of property or cash which underpin the operations of an organisation, for instance by generating revenue from rents.

Asset based development
Strategy to secure the future of community organisations and charities through possession of tangible assets such as land, buildings or a dedicated income. Ensures self-sufficiency, independence and sustainability.

Assistance team
➡ *Design assistance team.*

Award scheme
Programme set up to promote good practice by presenting awards for excellence or effort. ☞ **A-Z** *p34.*

Awareness raising day
Day of activities designed to promote interest in a community planning issue, normally held prior to a planning day or other intensive activity.

Awareness walk
➡ *Reconnaissance trip.*

Balanced incremental development
Development process undertaken in stages that lead on from one another. Allows schemes to evolve organically.

Barefoot architect
Architect who works in villages helping people construct their homes. Term used in Asia. ☞ *Community architect.*

Baseline data
Information about the starting point of any project or initiative against which improvement can be measured later.

Before and after
Photos, drawings or computer simulations showing a place before and after development has taken place from the same viewpoint. One of the most effective ways of helping people understand proposals. ☞ *example p24.*

Best fit slide rule
A visual discussion tool designed to examine alternative street infill solutions and their consequences. An elevation of a street is drawn or assembled with photos and alternative designs inserted. ➔ *Participatory design.*

Block models
Physical models where buildings are made out of wooden blocks. ☞ *Models.*

Blu-tack®
Registered brand name for re-usable adhesive 'gum' for fastening paper to a surface.

bottom up
Term used to refer to initiatives led by the community, as opposed to 'top down' initiatives led by the authorities.

Brainstorming
Vigorous discussion to generate ideas in which all possibilities are considered. Widely used first step in generating solutions to problems.

Brainwriting
Workshop process where group members respond in silence with four written suggestions to a given problem. Papers are then exchanged and members add suggestions to a 'new' paper. All papers are then compared and discussed by the group.

Briefing workshop
Working participatory sessions held at an early stage in a project or community planning event to establish a project agenda or brief. ☞ **A-Z** *p36.*

Building cooperative
Cooperative building contractor. All members usually receive equal rates and decisions are made collectively.

Business planning
Testing the viability of a project or organisation by predicting income and expenditure over a period of time.

Business planning for real
Computer-based simulation which helps new or existing organisations 'play through' the choices they will face in developing a business plan. Groups assemble a list of projects they would like to undertake. These are fed into a computer and the cost implications printed out.
⊘ *Good practice guide to community planning and development.*

Business planning workshop
Session where participants work in small groups to determine project priorities and programme targets. Normally a draft business plan is prepared as a basis for discussion which is then amended until an agreed cash flow is arrived at.

Buzz group
Small group of people who work through an issue. Similar to a *focus group* or *workshop*.

Capability
The quality of being capable; the ability to do something.

Capacity and vulnerability analysis (CVA)
➡*Vulnerability and capacity analysis.*

Capacity building
The development of awareness, knowledge, skills and operational capability by certain actors, normally the community, to achieve their purpose.
☞ *Empowerment.*

Capacity building workshop
Event organised primarily to establish partnerships between the public, private and voluntary sectors on development issues.

Case study
Description of a project. Used for helping others understand how it worked, or failed to work.

Chairperson
Individual who controls a meeting, deciding who can speak when. ☞ *Facilitator.*

Champion
Individual who believes in an idea and will promote it through thick and thin. Important ingredient for most projects. ☞ *Moving spirits.*

Charity
Organisation which acts in the interests of society rather than in pursuit of profit. May receive tax breaks and other benefits.

Charrette
➡ *Design charrette.*

Chart
Large sheet of paper used for writing or drawing on, usually attached to walls or placed on an easel. Essential tool of participative working.
☞ *Flipchart.*

Charter
Prospectus containing a set of principles to guide development of a place. Best created using a collaborative process with key stakeholders. Three steps: Looking and Learning together; Setting standards for excellence; Committing resources to longer term priorities.

Choice catalogue
Menu of items, usually visually illustrated, showing a range of design choices available.
☞ **A-Z** *p38.*

Choices method
Visioning process based on four steps:
1. Meetings throughout the community to brainstorm ideas for making life better.
2. Consolidation of ideas into goals and vision statements.
3. A 'vision fair' where people vote on which visions they would like to pursue and make personal commitment pledges.
4. Setting up of action groups to carry out chosen ideas.
⊘ *Participation Works!*

Citizens advisory group
Group made up of members of the public (usually between 10 and 30) which informs and advises decision makers. Can take many forms.

Citizens jury
Informal inquiry method where a group of around 16 people, selected to be representative of the community, spend a few days examining an issue, listening to witnesses and producing a report.
◌ *Participation Works!*

Citizens panel
A large, demographically representative group of citizens used regularly to assess public preferences and opinions.

Citizens summit
Large-scale deliberative public meeting (typically involving between 500 to 5,000 people) that uses advanced communications technology to facilitate discussions.

City farm
Working farm in an urban area, normally run by a voluntary committee of local people. Primary role is educational rather than food production.

Civic forum
➡ *Forum.*

Civil renewal
Individuals and groups becoming more actively involved in the well-being of their community, identifying and tackling problems to bring about change and improve the quality of life.

Civil society
The arena of organised citizen activity outside of the state and market sectors. People coming together to define, articulate, and act on their concerns through various forms of organisation and expression.

Client
Individual or organisation that commissions buildings or other projects. ☞ *User-client.*

Cohousing
Housing with shared living components. Ranges from sharing of gardens to sharing of workshops, laundry rooms and even kitchens.
◌ *Cohousing.*

Collaborative planning
Planning undertaken by two or more parties working together. A key concept in community planning.

Committee
Group of people elected or delegated to make decisions, usually in meetings.
☞ *Workshop.*

Community
Used in many ways. Usually refers to those living within a small, loosely defined geographical area. Yet any group of individuals who share interests may also be described as a community. Also sometimes used to describe a physical area rather than a group of people.
☞ *following entries on community.*

Community action
A process by which the deprived define for themselves their needs, and determine forms of action to meet them, usually outside the prevailing political framework.

Community action planning
➡ *Microplanning workshop.*
☞ *Action planning.*

Community anchor
Independent community-run and led organisation, rooted in a sense of place (whether an inner city neighbourhood or a rural district), and with a mission to improve things for the whole community. Likely to own or manage assets and use income from these to provide services.

Community appraisal
Survey of the community by the community to identify needs and opportunities. Usually based on a self-completion questionnaire devised by the community and delivered to every household.
☞ *Community profiling.*

Community architect
Architect who practises *community architecture.* Will often live and work in the neighbourhood he or she is designing for.
☞ *Community architecture.*

Community architecture
Architecture carried out with the active participation of the end users. Similarly *community design, community planning* and so on.

Community art
Visual and performance art addressed to the needs of a local community. Often related to environmental issues.
☞ *Art workshop.*

Community based organisation (CBO)
Voluntary organisation operating at a local level to represent a local community or interest group. Term used at international level. Similar in meaning to *community group.*
☞ *Community group. Non-governmental organisation.*

Community based regeneration

Programmes focused on people that usually involve some form of capacity building. Improves the ability of local people to influence decision making within their own community.

Community build

Building construction carried out by members of the local community, often voluntarily or as part of a training course. ☞ *Self-build*.

Community building

Building conceived, managed and sometimes built, by the local community for community use. Phrase also used to describe the activity of building a community; physically, socially and economically.

Community business

Trading organisation owned and controlled by the local community which aims to create self-supporting and viable jobs for local people and to use profits to create more employment, provide local services or support local charitable work.

Community car scheme

Provides a pool of cars across a district, for use by local people. Alternative to individual or family ownership of vehicles.

Community champion

Natural leader within a community who enjoys a great deal of respect from other residents. Has a strong concern for the community and other residents and is able to motivate others.

Community cohesion

Where diverse backgrounds and cultures are valued and where there is a common vision and sense of belonging.

Community consultation

Finding out what local people want. ☞ *Consultation*.

Community design

Design carried out with the active participation of the end users. Similarly *community architecture*, *community planning* and so on.

Community design centre

Place providing free or subsidised architectural, planning and design services to people who cannot afford to pay for them. Also known as a *community technical aid centre*. ☞ **A-Z** *p40*.
☞ *Community technical aid centre*.

Community design house

Local office used by a *community designer* or *community architect*. Term used in Japan. ☞ *Community design centre*.

Community designer

Practitioner of *community design*. Person who designs places *with* people rather than *for* people.

Community development

Promotion of self-managed, non-profit-orientated projects to serve community needs.

Community development corporation

Non-profit-orientated company undertaking development for community benefit. American concept similar to the UK's *development trust*.
☞ *Development trust*.

Community development trust

➥ *Development trust*.

Community driven

Term used to reflect key role of the community in an initiative.

Community energy

Renewable energy development involving local residents and community groups.

Community enterprise

Enterprise for the benefit of the community rather than private profit by people within the community.

Community forest

Woodland area developed and managed by and for the communities living in and around it.

Community garden

Publicly accessible garden or small park created and managed by a voluntary group.

Community group

Voluntary organisation operating at local level.
☞ *Community based organisation*.

Community indicators

Measures devised and used by communities for understanding and drawing attention to important issues and trends. Useful for building an agenda for education and action.
๑ *Communities Count!*

Community land trust

Independent non-profit trust which owns or controls land and facilities in perpetuity for the benefit of the community.

Community landscaping

Landscape design carried out with the active participation of the end users.

Community learning and education centre
Focal point for information and education at community level.

Community led plan
Plan founded on community involvement and led by voluntary groups.

Community mapping
Making maps as a communal activity. ☞ *Mapping*.

Community memory
Collective sense of local identity and experience (eg of past participatory activity).

Community newspaper
Information source controlled by the local community. Also *community newsletter*; similar on a smaller scale.

Community plan
Plan for the future of a community devised by the local community. Sets out proposals for the way in which a community wants to develop and respond to changes in the future. No set format. Will usually contain statements of principle, physical design proposals and targets.
☞ *checklist p230*.

Community planning
Planning carried out with the active participation of the end users. Similarly *community architecture, community design* and so on.

Community planning council
Neighbourhood level organisation with powers to deal with planning matters. Concept recommended by the UK's Royal Town Planning Institute in 1982. Councils would comprise representatives from various sectional voluntary interests. ☞ *Forum*.

Community planning day
➡ *Planning day*.

Community planning event
Carefully structured collaborative event at which all stakeholders, including the local community, work closely with specialists from all relevant disciplines to make plans for the future of that community or some aspects of it.
☞ **A-Z** *p42*

Community planning forum
Multipurpose session lasting several hours designed to secure information, generate ideas and create interaction between interest groups.
☞ **A-Z** *p44*.

Community planning weekend
➡ *Planning weekend*.

Community politics
Style of political action through which people are enabled to control their own destinies. Identified with an on-going political movement which seeks to create a participatory democracy.

Community profiling
Way of reaching an understanding of the needs and resources of a community with the active involvement of the community. Similar approach as *participatory appraisal*. ☞ **A-Z** *p46*.

Community project
Facility for the local community, created and managed by a voluntary committee, elected or unelected, from that community.

Community projects fund
➡ *Feasibility fund*.

Community resilience
The ability of a community to withstand shocks and to bounce back from them.

Community safety plan
Plan drawn up by the local community to reduce crime and disorder.

Community technical aid
multidisciplinary expert assistance to community groups enabling them to play an active role in the development of land and buildings. The term 'technical aid' is used to cover the diverse range of skills likely to be needed including architecture, planning, landscaping, engineering, surveying, ecology, environmental education, financial planning, management, administration and graphics.

Community technical aid centre
Place staffed by multidisciplinary group of experts who work for voluntary groups, helping them to undertake any project involving the development of buildings and land. Will provide whatever assistance is needed – design, planning, organisation, decision making, management – from start to finish. Similar to a *community design centre*.
☞ *Community design centre*.

Community trust
Independent fundraising and grant-making charity which funds initiatives in the local community.

Community visioning
Thinking collectively about what the future could be. Term used to describe group working processes which help a community to develop

imaginative shared visions for the future of a site, area or organisation.
✉ *New Economics Foundation*.
☞ *Future search conference*.

Community woodland
➡ *Community forest*.

Consensus building
Procedure for helping people with different views to come together interactively on a dispute, project, plan or issue, to work towards agreeing a sensible solution or way forward which is mutually satisfactory.

Consultation
Seeking people's views (usually, but not necessarily, involving them in decision making).

Consultation day
One-day event designed to consult key stakeholders or the general public on a particular issue.
➡ *Stakeholder participation day.*

Consultation fatigue
Lack of public interest in consultation initiatives. Usually caused by an excess of consultations (due to lack of coordination by agencies) and/or a perceived lack of any results from past consultations.

Co-operative
An enterprise conducted for the mutual benefit of its members. This might be a business that is democratic, each member having one vote irrespective of capital or labour input. Any economic surplus belongs to the members – after providing for reserves for the development of the business.
☞ *Housing co-operative*.

Co-ownership
Tenure arrangement in which property is partly owned by the occupier, the remaining portion being gradually purchased during the period of occupation.

Coproduction
Shared responsibility between citizens and public officials for producing services and managing development processes. Term used widely in Europe to mean community engagement.

Core costs
Expenditure essential to keep an organisation going. As opposed to project costs. Includes such things as staff wages, rent, heating.

Countryside design summary
Simple description of the design relationship between the landscape, settlement patterns and buildings. Usually produced by the planning authority for a region, often combined with the production of local design statements for neighbourhoods within the region.
☞ *Local design statement*.

Critical friend
Someone who will point out what you are getting wrong, as well as right, constructively.

Critical mass event
Umbrella term for organisation development techniques involving large-scale events often lasting several days and often involving hundreds of people. Mostly used for organisational change but may also be appropriate for community planning. Labels given to specific types of event – structured in different ways and promoted by different

people – include *future search conference*, *large-scale interactive process, conference model, real-time strategic change, participative work redesign* and *Open Space workshops*.
☞ *Future search conference*. *Open Space workshop*.

Crowdsourcing
Obtaining services, ideas or content by soliciting contributions from a large group of people, often an online community.

Crowdwise
Participative method for taking shared decisions that uses a combination of consensus voting and constructive dialogue in order to overcome differences, find common ground and reach more productive outcomes.
✉ *New Economics Foundation*.

Daily routine chart
Diagram showing people's daily activities and time taken to accomplish each of them. Usually produced by groups of women, men and children separately. Useful to deepen the analysis on seasonal calendars and highlight divisions of labour and responsibilities.
☞*Community profiling*. *Seasonal calendars*.

Design assistance team (DAT)
Multidisciplinary team which visits an area and produces recommendations for action, usually after facilitating a community planning event. Similar terms in use include *Urban design assistance team (UDAT)* and *Housing assistance team (HAT)* (where only housing involved). ☞ **A-Z** *p48*.

Design charrette
Intensive design session, often including 'all-nighter', originally just for architecture students but more recently including the public and professionals. Term originated at the Paris Ecole des Beaux-Arts at the turn of the century. Projects were collected at designated times on a cart ('charrette') where students would be found putting finishing touches to their schemes. Term now widely used in the USA to describe any intensive, group brainstorming effort. *Charrette* often used without the *'Design'* in front. Similar to *design workshop*.
☞ *Design workshop.*

Design day
Day when architects and local people brainstorm for design solutions to particular building problems, usually in teams. Term also used to describe day when local residents can drop in and talk through design ideas with professionals.
⊚ *Building Homes People Want.*
☞ *Drop-in office.*

Design fest
Community planning event where multidisciplinary design teams develop and present their ideas in public. ☞ **A-Z** *p50*

Design game
Method for devising building and landscape layouts with residents using coloured cut-outs of possible design features on plans. ☞ **A-Z** *p52.*

Design guide
Document setting out general urban design principles which should be adopted by any development in an area.
☞ *Local design statement.*

Design meeting
Meeting for developing designs. Usually organised on a regular basis during the design stage of a project. Users and professionals will be present. The users, or clients, set the agenda but the meeting is normally conducted by the professionals. Various techniques will be used to present information and make decisions: showing photos, models, drawings, catalogues. Normal arrangement is for participants to sit round a table.

Design simulation
Playing at designing to get people used to the various roles in the design process.

Design surgery
Where architects, planners or other professionals work through design issues with individuals, for instance occupants in a new housing scheme.

Design workshop
Hands-on session allowing groups to work creatively developing planning and design options.
☞ **A-Z** *p54.*
☞ *Design charrette.*

Designing for real
Term used to describe the use of adaptable models to develop detailed design proposals for a building or site. Participants explore options by moving parts of the model around: ie, parts of a building or whole buildings. Similar concept to *Planning for Real* but on a smaller scale.
☞ *Planning for Real p120*

Development officer
Individual who gets a project or organisation up and running.

Development partnership
Arrangement for collaboration by two or more parties to facilitate development, usually between the public and private sectors. ☞ *Partnership.*

Development planning for real
Adaptation of *Planning for Real* specially devised for developing countries. ☞ *Planning for Real.*

Development trust
Independent, not-for-profit organisation controlled by local people which facilitates and undertakes physical development in an area. It will have significant community involvement or control, will bring together a wide range of skills and interests, and will aim to sustain its operations at least in part by generating revenue. ☞ **A-Z** *p56.* ☞ *Community development corporation.*

Diagramming
Creating diagrams in groups.
☞ *Diagrams.*

Diagrams
Visual representations of information which help explain current issues or future proposals. ☞ **A-Z** *p58.*

Direct action
Exertion of political pressure by tactics other than voting at elections. Usually used to refer to strikes, squatting or occupations.

Direct observation
Noting of events, objects, processes and relationships; particularly useful for issues hard to verbalise.

Disabling
Non-participatory form of service which renders the user unable to have a say in the process.

Disaster
Serious disruption of the functioning of society, causing widespread human, material, or environmental losses which exceed the ability of the affected society to cope using its own resources (UNDP 91).

Disaster management
All aspects of planning for, and responding to, disasters.

Disaster mitigation
Reducing the impact of disasters on society by reducing the hazards and/or society's vulnerability to them.
☞ *Mitigation. Risk assessment.*

Disaster preparedness
The ability to predict, respond and cope with the effects of a disaster.

Disaster relief
Extraordinary measures for coping with a disaster.

Discussion group
Method of social research involving a group of people who are brought together to discuss their views or experiences surrounding a particular topic.

Discussion method
Structure for effective communication which allows everyone in a group to participate.
☞ *Technology of participation.*

Door knocking
Basic engagement method of knocking on front doors and speaking to the people who open the door. ☞ **A-Z** *p60.*

Draft
Document or plan which is not finalised and may be consulted on and revised before being so.
☞ *Draft plan consultation.*

Draft plan consultation
Seeking views on a draft plan or proposal. ☞ **A-Z** *p62.*

Drop-in office
Working office open to the public. Set up by architects or urban designers working in a neighbourhood to encourage local involvement in the design process. May be permanent or temporary (on an *open day* for instance).

E-government
Delivery of government services and information through electronic means such as the internet, digital television and other digital technologies.

E-petition
Online version of traditional petition. Way of demonstrating support for a particular viewpoint. See for example: epetitions.direct.gov.uk

E-planning
Provision of planning services online, accessible via the internet and email.

E-voting
Voting electronically, normally using instant polling or audience response systems.
☞ **A-Z** *p70*

Eco-town
Exemplar green development which meets the highest standards of sustainability, including low and zero carbon technologies and quality public transport systems. It will make use of brownfield land and surplus public sector land where practical and lead the way in design, facilities, services and community involvement.

Economic audit
Audit of local economy, usually undertaken by independent professional economist.

Elevation montage
Display technique for helping people to understand and make changes to streetscapes.
☞ **A-Z** *p66.*

Empowerment
Development of confidence and skills in individuals or communities leading to their being able to take more control over their own destinies.
☞ *Capacity building.*

Enabler
Professional or other person with technical expertise or in a position of authority who uses it to help people to do things for themselves. The term can also be used for organisations which behave likewise.

Enabling
Professional and other services that consciously encourage or allow users to participate.
☞ *Enabler.*

Energy fair
Event which allows residents to engage with suppliers and installers of energy saving equipment. ☞ **A-Z** *p68.*

Enquiry by design
Intensive community planning workshop process involving urban designers and local stakeholders. Devised for developing plans for new urban villages.
✉ The Prince's Foundation.

Enspirited envisioning
Way of developing individual and shared visions of the future through personal and group development.
⊘ *Participation Works!*

Enterprise agency
Non-profit-making company whose prime objective is to respond through practical action to the economic and training needs of its local community. A principal activity is providing free advice and counselling to support the setting up and development of viable small businesses. Mostly public sector-led in partnership with the private sector but there are many exceptions.

Enterprise trust
➡ *Enterprise agency*

Environment forum
Non-statutory body for discussing and co-ordinating environmental issues in an area. ☞ *Forum.*

Environment shop
Shop selling items and providing information which helps people improve their environment. Similarly *architecture shop, conservation shop.*
☞ **A-Z** *p72.*

Environment week
Week of activities designed to promote interest in, and debate on, the environment.
☞ *Activity week.*

Environmental education
Programmes aimed at making people more aware of their environment and the forces which shape it.

Environmental impact assessment
Process whereby all impacts of a development are identified and their significance assessed. Increasingly a statutory requirement before planning permission is granted by a local authority.

Envisioning
➡ *Visioning.*

Equity sharing
➡ *Co-ownership.*

Evidence scanning
Evaluating vital evidence without having to plough through reams of statistics by actions such as: checking a few key statistics; using other people's analysis; testing statistics against your own knowledge; doing a small survey; finding an expert from amongst your group.

Exhibition
Displays of information. May be simply for presenting information or for getting feedback too.
☞ *Interactive exhibition.*

Facilitation
The art and science of managing meetings and group processes. Bringing people together to decide what they wish to do, and to work together to decide how to do it.

Facilitator
Person who steers a process, meeting or workshop. Less dominant role than a 'chairperson'. Also known as a *moderator*.

Farmers market
Market exclusively for local food producers and countryside products.

Feasibility fund
Revolving fund providing grants to community groups for paying professional fees for the preparation of feasibility studies for community projects. Also known as a *community projects fund.* ☞ **A-Z** *p74.*

Feasibility study
Examination of the viability of an idea, usually resulting in a report. ☞ *example p75.*

Fence method
Prioritising procedure using a line with a fence in the middle to establish people's views on conflicting alternatives.
☞ *example p125.*

Festival market
Market for bric-a-brac and crafts.

Field workshop
Workshop programme on location. Term used to describe events lasting several days involving a range of *community profiling, risk assessment* and plan-making activities. ☞ **A-Z** *p76.*

Fish bowl
Workshop technique where participants sit around, and observe, a planning team working on a problem without taking part themselves.
➋ *Community Participation in Practice.*

Five Ws plus H
What, When, Why, Who, Where and How. Useful checklist in planning any activity.

Flipchart
Large pad of paper on an easel. Standard equipment for participatory workshops as it allows notetaking to be visible.

Flipcharter
Person who records points made at a workshop or plenary session on a flipchart or large sheet of paper pinned on a wall in full view of the participants. ☞ *Flipchart.*

Fly-posting
Pasting up posters in public places, usually without permission from building owners or authorities.

Focus group
Small group of people who work through an issue in workshop sessions. Membership may be carefully selected or entirely random.

Forum
Non-statutory body for discussing and coordinating activity and acting as a pressure group for change. ☞ *Environment forum. Neighbourhood forum.* Term also used to describe a one-off open meeting aiming to create interaction. ☞ *Community planning forum. Public forum.*

Full-scale simulation
Acting out a scenario to test a design idea using full-scale mock-ups. Particularly useful for helping people design new building forms. ☞ *Design simulation. Mock-up.*

Future search conference
Highly structured two and a half day process allowing a community or organisation to create a shared vision for its future. Ideally 64 people take part; eight tables of eight. ☞ **A-Z** *p78.*

Futures workshop
Term used for a workshop devised to discuss options for the future. Various formats are possible. ☞ *Briefing workshop. Design workshop.*

Gallery walk
Report back process where workshop flipchart sheets are pinned up at a plenary session and the reporter 'walks' past the sheets, using them as a prompt to summarise what took place.

Gaming
The use of games to simulate real situations. ☞ **A-Z** *p80.* ☞ *Role play. Simulation.*

Giving evidence
Formal presentation of information, for instance to a public inquiry or local authority committee.

Goal-oriented project planning (GOPP)
Tool for project management in which interactive workshops involving all stakeholders in a project, and an external moderator, are held at different points in the project lifecycle. Uses logical framework analysis. 🖳 GOPP Moderators Assoc.

Group interview
Pre-arranged discussion with an invited group to analyse topics or issues against a checklist of points or local concerns. ☞ *Interview.*

Group modelling
Use of physical models as a basis for working in groups to learn, explore and make decisions about the environment. ☞ *Models.*

Guided visualisation
Group process using mental visualisation techniques for establishing a community's aspirations. ᗟ *Participation Works!*

Habitat
The social and economic, as well as physical, shelter essential for well-being.

Hands-on exhibition.
➡ *Interactive exhibition.*

Hands-on planning
Method of community involvement in planning where small groups make plans for the future using table top plans or flexible cardboard models. Often referred to as *Planning for real* but this term has been registered by the Neighbourhood Initiatives Foundation to apply to its own method only.

Have your say drop-in
Drop-in workshop set up to enable people to make their views known in an informal setting. ☞ **A-Z** *p82.*

Hazard
Phenomenon that poses a threat to people, structures or economic assets and which may cause a disaster. It could be either human-made or naturally occurring.

Hazard analysis
Identification of types of hazard faced by a community, their intensity, frequency and location.

Healthcheck
Tool based on worksheets and community consultation to help identify the strengths and weaknesses of a town as a basis for producing plans of action. ✉ *Action for Market Towns.*

Heritage centre
Place aimed at helping people understand, and engage in, the historic local built environment. Key elements: old photos, old artefacts, leaflets, books, information sheets, maps, postcards, models, trails. ☞ *Architecture centre. Local heritage initiative.*

Historic buildings trust
Charitable organisation set up to preserve historic buildings.

Historical profile
Key events and trends in a community's development, usually displayed visually.
☞ *Community profiling.*

Historical profiling
Construction of historical profile in groups. Information about past events is gathered to explain the present and predict possible future scenarios. One approach involves people describing and explaining their life history with respect to particular issues. Information is marked up on maps or charts to build a comprehensive time-line of events and issues that mould and affect a community.

Homeowners file
File of book-keeping schedules designed to help families to control the construction and management of their homes.

Homesteading
Programme in which property owners (usually local authorities) offer substandard property for sale at low cost to householders who will work on them in their own time, doing basic repairs and renovation to standards monitored by the original owners.

House manual
Record of useful information and tips from previous occupants on how to manage and look after a house.

Housing association
Association run by an elected management committee which uses government money to provide housing in areas and

for people which the government believes to be a high priority. Building society money is also increasingly used to fund housing associations.

Housing co-operative
Organisation which owns or manages housing and which is owned and managed by the occupants of that housing. Often referred to as a *housing co-op.* ☞ *Co-operative. Secondary co-operative.*

Hub space
Place which inspires and engenders collaboration, enterprise and /or innovation.

Human capital
Ability of individuals to do productive work; includes physical and mental health, strength, stamina, knowledge, skills, motivation and a constructive and co-operative attitude.
☞ *Social capital.*

Icebreaker
Group activity aimed at making people feel comfortable with each other. Often held at the start of community planning events.

Ideas competition
Competition for generating options for improving a neighbourhood, building or site aimed at stimulating creative thinking and generating interest.
☞ **A-Z** *p84.*

Illustrated questionnaire
Questionnaire with pictures to find out people's design preferences.
☞ *Choice catalogue. Questionnaire survey.*

Imagine
Method for establishing positive initiatives based on a structured approach to imagining the future.
⊘ *Participation Works!*

Imaging day
Day when people visualise the future with the assistance of a skilled artist.

Immediate report writing
Writing reports in the field or at an event rather doing it later in the office.

Informal walk
Walking in a group without a definite route, stopping to chat and discuss issues as they arise.
☞ *Community profiling.*

Interactive display
Visual display which allows people to participate by making additions or alterations. Also known as a *hands-on display.* ☞ **A-Z** *p86.*

Interactive exhibition
Exhibition which allows people to participate by making additions or alterations. Also known as a *hands-on exhibition.* ☞ *Interactive display. Open house event.*

Interview
Recorded conversation, usually with prepared questions, with individuals or groups. Useful for information gathering. More flexible and interactive than a questionnaire.
☞ *Group interview. Key informant interview. Semi-structured interview.*

Jigsaw display
Exhibit where groups prepare different parts which are then assembled as a whole.

Ketso kit
A hands-on toolkit for creative engagement invented in Southern Africa and developed at the University of Manchester, UK. Ketso means *action* in Lesotho. ☞ **A-Z** *p90*.

Key informant
Person with special knowledge.

Key informant interview
Informal discussion based on a pre-determined set of questions with people who have special knowledge. ☞ *Interview*.

KISS
Stands for 'Keep It Simple, Stupid'. Useful reminder in a complex field.

Ladder of participation
Useful and popular analogy for likening the degree of citizen participation in any activity to a series of rungs on a ladder. First put forward in 1969 (by Sherry Arnstein) with 8 rungs:
1. Citizen control.
2. Delegated power.
3. Partnership.
4. Placation.
5. Consultation.
6. Informing.
7. Therapy.
8. Manipulation.
This has been modified in many different ways by many people since. ☞ *page 12*. ⊘ *The Guide to Effective Participation*.

Landscape character assessment
Process for describing an area's sense of place, features and attributes. Useful foundation for making planning decisions for an area. ☞ *Local character workshop*.

Large group interventions
Similar meaning to *Critical mass event*. ➡ *Critical mass event*.

Launch
Event to promote the start of an initiative or project. Useful for generating interest and involvement.

Leaflet
Sheet of paper providing information, usually produced in large quantities. Standard publicity technique. Also known as a *flyer*.

Linkage diagram
Shows flows, connections and causality. ☞ *Diagrams*.

Listener
Facilitator at an issue stall in a *SpeakOut*. ☞ *SpeakOut*.

Livability
Somewhat loose measure of the quality of life where needs that are justifiable according to natural justice are met.

Living over the shop scheme
Programme to encourage people to occupy vacant premises over shops, usually by offering grant aid. Town centre regeneration method.

Lobbying
Influencing decision-makers through individual and group face-to-face persuasion or letter writing.

Local
Pertaining to a particular rural or urban place or area.

Local agenda 21
Comprehensive action strategy prepared by local authorities to help achieve sustainable development.

Local authority
Organisation governing local area. For instance; borough council, county council, town council, village council.

Local character workshop
Workshop designed to help people identify what makes an area special. Usually undertaken as part of preparing a local design statement or landscape character assessment. Involves mapping and photo surveys. ☞ *Landscape character assessment. Local design statement.*

Local design statement
Published statement produced by a community identifying the distinctive character of the place. The aim is for it to be used by planning authorities to ensure that future development and change is sympathetic and has community support. ☞ **A-Z** *p92*.

Local environmental resource centre
Resource centre focusing on local environmental issues. ☞ *Resource centre*.

Local heritage initiative
Process for helping people record and care for their local landscape, landmarks and traditions.

Local people
People who live in a particular rural or urban place or area.

Local plan
Plan that sets out detailed policies and specific proposals for the development and use of land in a district and guides most day-to-day planning decisions.

Local regeneration agency
Organisation set up to undertake regeneration work in an area.

Local resource centre
Place providing information and support for people at a community level.
☞ *Resource centre.*

Local support team
Locally-based team providing expertise for an activity or event.

Local sustainability model
Process allowing a community to assess its present position and test the likely effect of projects.
⊘ *Participation Works!*

Localism
Drive to devolve power from central government to the local level. Signals a move away from centralisation towards strengthened local bodies.

Logical framework analysis
Method for thoroughly testing the effectiveness of any project proposal. Assesses objectives, purposes, inputs, assumptions, outputs, effects and inputs. Much used by international funding agencies.

Low-cost housing
Housing affordable by people on low incomes.

Maintenance manual
Instructions on how to maintain a building or open space. Important for helping users to keep places in good order.

Managed workspace
Communally managed building for individual, and independent, enterprises sharing common support facilities and services. Sometimes known as a *working community.*

Management committee
Governing body of a project or organisation. Similar to board of directors in a company.

Mapping
Physical plotting of various characteristics of an area in two dimensions. May be done individually or communally.
☞ *Activity mapping. Community mapping. Mental mapping. Mind map. Parish mapping.* ☞ **A-Z** *p94.*

Market
Place for buying and selling goods and services. An important regeneration tool. Types of market include: street market, covered market, farmers market, festival market.

Masterplan
Overall planning framework for the future of a settlement. May be highly detailed or schematic. Used to provide a vision and structure to guide development.

Matrix
Diagram in the form of a grid allowing comparison of two variables. Used for assessing options. ☞ *Diagrams.*

Mediation
Voluntary process of helping people resolve their differences with the assistance of a neutral person.

Meeting
Event where people come together to discuss and decide. May be formal or informal, public or private.

Mental mapping
Production of maps by individuals or communities showing how they perceive their neighbourhood (as opposed to geographically accurate maps). ☞ *Mapping.*

Micro-finance
Banking system which provides small loans to poor people without collateral.

Microplanning workshop
Intensive planning procedure developed specifically for upgrading settlements in developing countries involving a minimum of preparation, materials and training. Also referred to as *community action planning.* ☞ **A-Z** *p96.*

Mind map
Diagram showing people's perceptions of trends and linkages. Not a geographical map. Used in future search conferences. ☞ *Diagrams. Future search conference.*

Mini visioning
Basic and succinct visioning workshops. ☞ *Visioning.*

Mission statement
Written explanation of the purpose of a project, event or organisation. Usually brief and to the point. Useful for avoiding misunderstanding, particularly in partnerships.

Mitigation
Measures taken to minimise the impact of a disaster by modifying the hazard itself or by reducing vulnerability to it. Ranges from physical measures such as flood defences, to raising living standards so people no longer need to inhabit areas at risk. Mitigation can take place before, during and after a disaster. ☞ *Risk assessment.*

Mobile unit
Caravan or mobile home converted into an office/studio as a base for undertaking community planning activity on location. ☞ **A-Z** *p98.*

Mock-up
Full-size representation of a change or development, usually on its proposed site, prior to finalising the design.

Modelling
Making models. Usually refers to making models as a group process. Similar to mapping but in three dimensions instead of two. ☞ *Mapping. Models.*

Models
Physical three-dimensional constructions simulating a building or neighbourhood. ☞ **A-Z** *p100*.

Moderated planning workshop
Structured meeting in which partners in a project can discuss and agree objectives, goals and responsibilities to create a plan for further action. Run by a neutral facilitator. Increasingly used in multi-partner, transnational projects in Europe.

Moderator
➡ *Facilitator*.

Moving spirits
People in a community who want to improve things for the better and who are prepared to give time and thought to something they think might help. Also referred to as *movers and shakers* or *social entrepreneurs*. ☞ *Champion*.

Mutual aid
Where people help each other without formal organisation.

Neighbourhood
A district within a town, city or rural area, often seen as providing the physical location of a community or providing a sense of identity. ☞ *Community*

Neighbourhood branding
Establishing an identity for an area.

Neighbourhood council
Elected body at neighbourhood level with certain statutory powers. Urban equivalent of a parish council and effectively a mini local authority.

Neighbourhood forum
Non-statutory body for discussing a neighbourhood's affairs and acting as a pressure group for improvements. Members may be publicly elected – usually in categories (eg residents, traders, churches, etc.) – or be nominated by organisations entitled to be represented under the constitution. May be effectively a non-statutory *neighbourhood council* although procedural practice varies considerably.

Neighbourhood plan
Plan for a neighbourhood. Term often used loosely to describe any plan for a local area. Also used formally in England to describe the lowest tier of statutory plans introduced by the Localism Act 2011. Full title is *neighbourhood development plan*.

Neighbourhood planning
The process by which a plan to guide and shape the development or regeneration of a neighbourhood is created. Good practice requires the active and influential involvement of local residents and businesses.

Neighbourhood planning office
Local office established to co-ordinate community planning activity. ☞ **A-Z** *p102*.

Neighbourhood renewal
Programme to narrow the gap between rich and poor communities involving physical, economic and social recovery of deprived areas. Also used to refer to neighbourhood improvement.

Neighbourhood skills survey
Survey to establish what skills and abilities people have in a neighbourhood. Used to find out what a community can do for itself and to generate interest. Sometimes referred to as a neighbourhood *talent* survey. ☞ *Useful checklists p229*. ☞ *Resource survey*.

Neighbourhood talent survey
➡ *Neighbourhood skills survey*.

Neighbourhood warden
Semi-official presence in a local area to prevent anti-social behaviour, maintain the local environment, reduce crime and fear of crime. Provides a complementary service alongside the police and environmental services.

Networking
Exchanging experience with people engaged in similar activities. Usually in an informal manner.

Newsletter
Means of communication using print or email.

Newspaper supplement
Special insert or section of a newspaper. Can be used to cover local design issues. ☞ **A-Z** *p104*.

Non-governmental organisation (NGO)
Voluntary and non-profit-distributing organisation. The difference between an NGO and a CBO (community-based organisation) is that an NGO is normally organised and funded from outside the local community in which it operates.
☞ Community-based organisation.

Notetaker
Person who records points made at a workshop with a view to writing up a record and/or making a presentation of the results.

Off-setting biases
Being self-critically aware of biases in behaviour and learning, and deliberately countering them.

One stop shop
Single multi-purpose facility that enables local residents to access a wide range of services.

Open design competition
Competition open to everyone. Contrasts with limited or closed competitions to which entry is restricted. ☞ Ideas competition.

Open day
Day when a project or organisation encourages people to come and find out what it is doing and how it works. Often used to generate interest and momentum.

Open house event
Event designed to allow those promoting development initiatives to present them to a wider public and secure reactions in an informal manner. Halfway between an exhibition and a workshop.
☞ A-Z p108.

Open Space technology
Framework within which open Space workshops are held.
☞ Open Space workshop.

Open Space workshop
Workshop process for generating commitment to action in communities or organisations. Features include starting without an agenda.
☞ A-Z p110.

Opinion survey
Survey to find out what people think about an issue. ☞Survey.

Outcomes
Results of projects or programmes, usually unmeasurable (eg, people are happier). ☞ Outputs.

Outputs
Measurable results of projects or programmes (eg, number of trees planted). ☞ Outcomes.

Outreach
Taking consultation to the people rather than expecting them to come to you.

Outsiders
Non-local people. Usually refers to professionals and facilitators.

Ownership
Term often used to refer to a sense of responsibility for an initiative or project. eg, 'People will have ownership of an idea or a project if they have been involved in creating it'.

Pair-wise ranking
Rapid and simple way of selecting the most important issues or problems facing a community. Brainstorming generates a preliminary list. A group of people then vote on the significance of every item against each other item using a matrix.

Paradigm
A coherent and mutually supporting pattern of concepts, values, methods and action, amenable or claiming to be amenable, to wide application.

Parish mapping
Arts based way in which a community can explore and express what they value in their place through the creation of maps out of a wide variety of materials. ☞ Mapping.
🖥 Common Ground.

Participation
Act of being involved in something.

Participationitis
When everything has to be checked by everyone. Too much participation.

Participation matrix
A simple illustration of how different levels of participation are appropriate at different stages of a project. ☞ p12

Participation training
Short courses or workshop sessions on participation approaches. May be aimed at professionals or community activists.

Participatory 3D Modelling (P3DM)
Merges conventional spatial information (contours) with people's mental maps; makes information tangible and meaningful-to-all, and visualizes scaled and geo-coded indigenous spatial knowledge.
🖥 Participatory Avenues.

Participatory appraisal

An approach to gaining a rapid in-depth understanding of a community, or certain aspects of a community, based on the participation of that community and a range of visual techniques. Allows people to share and record aspects of their own situation, conditions of life, knowledge, perceptions, aspirations, preferences and develop plans for action. Not restricted to planning issues. Many terms used to imply similar concept including participatory learning and action.
☞ *Community profiling.*
⊘ *Whose Reality Counts?*

Participatory budgeting

Mechanism which brings local communities closer to the decision making process regarding the allocation of public funds.
⌨ *Participatory Budgeting UK.*

Participatory building evaluation

Method for users and providers to jointly assess the effectiveness of buildings after they have been built.
⊘ *User Participation in Building Design and Management.*

Participatory democracy

Process which involves people directly in decision making which affects them, rather than through formally elected representatives such as councillors or MPs as in representative democracy.

Participatory design

Design processes which involve the users of the item or places being designed.

Participatory editing

Method of involving large numbers of people in producing reports and other material. ☞ **A-Z** *p112.*

Participatory monitoring and evaluation (PME)

Monitoring and evaluation undertaken with the participation of those who took part in the activity being monitored and evaluated.

Participatory rapid appraisal (PRA)

➡ *Participatory appraisal.*

Participatory theatre

The use of physical movement and creativity to explore people's experience and develop a common vision.
⊘ *Participation Works!*

Partnership

Agreement between two or more individuals or organisations to work together to achieve common aims.
⊘ *Managing Partnerships.*

Partnership agreement

Formal document setting out the terms and conditions of a partnership arrangement.
☞ *Partnership.*

Pattern language

Method devised to enable untrained people to design their own buildings and cities in accordance with well-tried principles of good design.
⊘ *A Pattern Language.*

People's organisation

➡ *Community-based organisation.*

People's wall

Wall covered with large sheets of paper where visitors to a design fest or workshop can write and draw. ☞ *Public wall.*

Percent for participation

Campaign to get a percentage of total development costs spent on participation. Started by the Royal Institute of British Architects' Community Architecture Group.
✉ *Royal Institute of British Architects.*

Permaculture

Approach to designing sustainable environments based on ecological principles of co-operation with nature.

Permaculture design course

Courses aimed at making groups self-reliant and sustainable and helping them to take initiatives.
✉ *Permaculture Association.*
⊘ *Permaculture Teachers Handbook.*

Photo survey

Survey of locality using cameras. ☞ **A-Z** *p114.*

Pile sorting

Method of categorising by sorting cards or other items into piles. Used in group sessions.

Place-shaping

The ways in which local players collectively use their influence, powers, creativity and abilities to create attractive, prosperous and safe communities, places where people want to live, work and do business.

Placecheck

A way of assessing the qualities of a place, showing what improvements are needed, and focusing people on working together to achieve them.
⌨ *Placecheck*

Placemaking
The art of making places.

Planning aid scheme
The provision of free and independent information and advice on town planning to groups and individuals who cannot afford consultancy fees. ☞ **A-Z** *p116*.

Planning assistance kit
Series of worksheets designed to assist community organisations in physical planning, implementation and management of their environment.

Planning assistance team
Similar to a *design assistance team*.
☞ *Design assistance team.*

Planning day
Day when interested parties work intensively together developing urban design options for a site or neighbourhood. ☞ **A-Z** *p118*.

Planning department
Section of local authority dealing with planning issues.

Planning for Real ®
Registered brand name for a method for community involvement in planning and development focusing on the construction and use of flexible cardboard models and priority cards. ☞ **A-Z** *p120*.

Planning weekend
Sophisticated and highly structured community planning procedure in which professionals work with local people over a long weekend to produce proposals for action. The term *community planning weekend* is also used (often with the word 'community'

being added during the process). Terms *planning week* and *community planning week* have also been used for slightly longer events. ☞ **A-Z** *p122*.

Plenary session
Meeting of all participants at an event (for instance after a number of separate workshop groups).

Popular planning
Planning from the bottom up. Term used by the Greater London Council in the 1980s.

Post-it note ®
Or simply 'Post-it'. Registered brand name for a sheet of paper with a sticky edge. Come in pads. Great technical aid to collective working as, unlike cards, they can be stuck on vertical surfaces and moved around to create groups.

Prioritising
Deciding what needs doing when. Ranking of problems to be dealt with or projects to be undertaken. Term usually used to refer to group prioritising processes. ☞ **A-Z** *p124*.

Priority Estates Project
Experimental UK government programme to give council tenants a chance to exercise more control over their homes and neighbourhoods by establishing estate-based management systems. Set up in 1979. ✉ PEP.

Priority search
Survey technique based on a computerised questionnaire package which analyses responses to structured questions.

Problem tree
Visual way of analysing the inter-relationships among community issues and problems. A process of asking why is used to arrive at consensus about root causes and related effects. A symbolic tree is drawn with the trunk representing problems, the roots representing causes and branches representing the effects. ☞ *example page 47*.

Process design
Activity of designing the process to be followed.

Process planning session
Event organised to allow people to determine the most appropriate process for their particular purposes. ☞ **A-Z** *p126*.

Public forum
Public meeting with an emphasis on debate and discussion rather than speeches and a question and answer session. Participants will normally sit in a circle or a horseshoe arrangement. ☞ *Forum. Public meeting.*

Public meeting
Advertised, open access event at which issues are presented and commented on and at which decisions may be made. Term normally used to refer to fairly formal events with the audience sitting in rows facing a speaker or panel of speakers with a chairperson who controls the proceedings. ☞ *Public forum. Workshop.*

Public wall
Area of wall space or display boards where members of the public can make their views known by putting up drawings or text and making comments on material already there.
☞ *People's wall*.

Publicity
Raising awareness of a situation through use of posters, leaflets, websites and so on.

Questionnaire survey
Survey which involves collection of information in the form of written responses to a standard set of questions. Often a starting point for participation processes. Frequently used with other methods. ☞ *Survey*.

Rapporteur
➡ *Reporter*.
French term often used even at English speaking events.

Reconnaissance trip
Direct inspection of area under consideration by mixed team of locals and technical experts.
☞ **A-Z** *p128*.

Recycling
The reprocessing of waste, either into the same product or a different one.

Referendum
Public vote on an issue of special importance. May be used for strategic planning issues (for instance in the Netherlands).

Regeneration
To bring new and more vigorous life to an area or institution; to be reborn; to grow; to improve an area's social, physical and economic environment.

Regional/urban design assistance team (R/UDAT)
Name originally given to the planning weekend programme started by the American Institute of Architects in 1967. A *generic R/UDAT* uses the same process to look at problems common to many communities. A *mini R/UDAT* uses a similar process with a student team.
☞ *Design assistance team*.
☞ *Planning weekend*.

Reinvigorate
Event usually lasting one day where 'outsiders' and 'insiders' undertake a workshop process to identify solutions to an area's problems. Process developed by the British Urban Regeneration Agency (BURA) which spells it Re:Invigorate.

Renewable energy
Energy flows that occur naturally, for example from the wind, water flow, tides or the sun. It is renewable as it never runs out.

Reporter
Person who reports to a plenary session on the outcome of a workshop.

Residents' choice catalogue
➡ *Choice catalogue*.

Residents' tool loan service
Service lending out tools and equipment to make it easier for residents to carry out building work on their environment.

Resource assessment
Identification of resources and capacities within a community.
☞ *Resource survey*.

Resource centre
Place designed to provide community groups with the facilities they need to make the most of their energies and enthusiasm. No two centres are exactly alike but will provide some or all of the following: information, office equipment, professional advice and support, meeting facilities, equipment for meetings and fund raising, training courses and opportunities for groups to meet and share ideas.
☞ *Neighbourhood planning office*.

Resource survey
Survey to identify local resources which may be mobilised. Will include people, organisations, finance, equipment and so on.
☞ *Neighbourhood skills survey*.

Risk assessment
Examination of risks from disasters existing in any community. The basis for risk reduction. Comprises three components: hazard analysis; vulnerability analysis; resource assessment. ☞ **A-Z** *p132*.

Roadshow
Series of linked public workshops, exhibitions and public forums to explore the potential for improving the built environment and provide a catalyst for action.
☞ **A-Z** *p134*.

Role play
Adopting the role of others and acting out scenarios. Used to help people understand the views and aspirations of others.
☞ *Gaming*.

Round table workshop
Workshop process for engaging the main stakeholders in generating a vision and strategy for an area. Often used for consensus building between previously antagonistic parties.
⌐ *Participation Works!*
✉ Urbed.

Rural rapid appraisal (RRA)
➡ *Participatory appraisal.* Similar approach in rural areas.

Scoping
Preliminary exploration of a subject or project.

Search conference
Conference or workshop for key interested parties organised as a first stage in a consultation process on a project. May include briefings, role play, reconnaissance, interactive displays, workshops and plenary sessions. Term much used in Australia. Similar to *planning day* or *community planning forum.*
⌐ *Community Participation in Practice.*

Seasonal calendar
Chart showing a community's work and social activities month by month to highlight problems or concerns about such things as livelihood, health and community relations.
☞ *Community profiling.*

Secondary co-operative
Organisation which provides services, such as technical aid, to a co-operative which is also owned and managed by that co-operative.
☞ *Co-operative. Housing co-operative.*

Secondary data
Indirect information sources; files, reports, maps, photos, books and so on.

Secondary data review
Collection and analysis of published and unpublished material such as maps, reports, census statistics and newspaper clippings. Normally done prior to field work.

Self-build
Construction (or repair) work physically undertaken directly by future (or present) occupiers on an individual or collective basis.

Self-help
Where people take responsibility, individually or collectively, for solving their problems.

Self-management
Where a facility is managed by the people who use it.

Self-sufficiency
Reduction of dependence on others, making devolution of control easier and encouraging self-reliance.

Seminar
Meeting or workshop with educational slant.

Semi-structured interview
Conversational open discussion with local inhabitants to understand their needs, problems and aspirations. Uses a checklist of questions as a flexible guide in contrast to a formal questionnaire. Different types include individual, group, focus group and key informant. ☞ *Interview.*

Serendipity
Making happy discoveries by accident.

Shared presentation
Presentation by a group or several individuals.

Shell housing
Construction system where only floors, walls, roofs and services are provided, leaving occupiers free to build their own interiors.

Short-life housing
Use of empty property on a temporary basis, usually by a voluntary organisation.

Simulation
Acting out an event or activity as a way of gaining information and insights prior to formulating plans.
☞ **A-Z** *p136.*

Site and services
Provision of a serviced site for self-builders. Usually by government, but increasingly also by the private sector.

Skills survey
Assessment of skills and talent. Often done in a neighbourhood to establish what the community can do for itself and what extra help is needed. Also known as a *skills audit* or *skills inventory.*
☞ *Neighbourhood skills survey.*

Slide show
Presentation originally based on projecting images from transparencies but now done on a computer. Widely used in workshops as they can be prepared and presented by participants (more easily than video) and enable people to present visual information to groups (if the projector doesn't break down!).

Small group discussion
➡ *Small group work*

Small group work
People working together in small groups of 8 – 15. Term used to cover a range of similar methods such as workshops and focus groups which enable people to discuss, evaluate, learn and plan together. Group work can be formal or informal, one-off or regular, topic related or wide-ranging.

Social architecture
Similar concept to *community architecture*. Term commonly used in the United States. ☞ *Community architecture.*

Social audit
Tool to help an organisation understand, measure and report upon its social performance through the eyes of its stakeholders. Over time, the approach can be used to help an organisation improve its social performance. ✉ *New Economics Foundation.*

Social capital
Ability of social structures and institutions to provide a supportive framework for individuals; includes firms, trade unions, families, communities, voluntary organisations, legal/political systems, educational institutions, health services, financial institutions and systems of property rights. ☞ *Human capital.*

Social entrepreneur
Person who makes things happen by taking initiative in the interests of his or her community rather than for private or personal gain.

Social exclusion
Exclusion from accepted norms through unemployment, poor skills, low incomes, poor housing, high crime environments, bad health and family breakdown.

Social survey
Survey to find out about the nature of a community. May cover aspects like age, gender, wealth, health and so on. ☞ *Survey.*

SpeakOut
Interactive event intensively staffed with facilitators (or *listeners*) and *recorders* where participants drop in and visit a number of issue stalls set up with interpretative material about the community or the planning issues under consideration. Provides an informal environment where a wide range of people have a chance to participate. Encourages casual, 'drop-in' participation at people's convenience. People find issues about which they wish to 'speak out' and have their say, with comments clearly recorded. Similar to *Have your say drop-in*. ☞ **A-Z** *p82.* ⊘ *SpeakOut.*

Special interest group
Group championing a particular cause or interest. May be topic or geographically based. May be formally or informally constituted.

Special projects group
Non-statutory group formed to undertake a particular project. ☞ *User group.*

Squatting
Unlawful occupation of land or housing.

Staffed exhibition
Exhibition where organisers are present to engage in discussion. ☞ *Interactive exhibition. Open house event.*

Stakeholder
Person or organisation with an interest because they will be affected or may have some influence.

Stakeholder analysis
Gaining an understanding about who is affected by any proposal and therefore who should be involved in any participation process. Useful first step in most participation processes.

Stakeholder participation day
One-day event to involve key stakeholders. Often held at the start of a planning process. Sometimes called a *consultation day.*

Statement of community involvement (SCI)
Document produced by local authorities to highlight how they intend to engage the community in their activity.

Statement of consultation
Report issued by a local planning authority explaining how it has complied with its *statement of community involvement* during consultation on local development documents. ☞ *Useful checklists p221.*

Steering group
Informal group set up to pursue a project or goal. ☞ *User group.*

Stick
Metaphor for control. 'Handing over the stick' is a much used term to mean the experts or facilitator handing over the chalk, pen or microphone to enable local people to become the analysts, planners and facilitators of their own situation.

Sticky wall
Rectangular sheet of parachute silk sprayed with repositional adhesive. Useful for workshops because notes can be moved around and do not require adhesive backing.

Storefront studio
Community design office located in a prominent shop, often temporarily for a community planning event or 'charrette'. Term used in the USA.

Story-telling
Verbal recounting of tales which may be actual or mythical. Used to understand local values, standards, practices and relationships. Particularly valuable with children and people who are illiterate. Also the singing of local songs and reciting of poetry. Performance sets off discussion to explain local knowledge and beliefs.

Strategic planning
Organised effort to produce decisions and actions that shape and guide what a community is, what it does, and why it does it.

Street party
Party for the whole community held in the street. Often organised to galvanise regeneration initiatives.

Street stall
Way of securing public comment on planning issues by setting up an interactive exhibition in a public street or square. ☞ **A-Z** *p138.*

Street survey
Survey carried out by stopping people in a street or shopping centre. Used for securing views of people using a place (rather than necessarily living or working there). ☞ *Survey.*

Study day
Day spent examining a particular issue. Similar to a *planning day* but less structured. Useful for simple issues. ☞ *Planning day.*

Subsidiarity
Maximum local autonomy.

Suggestions box
Box in which people place their written suggestions or comments on a place or proposals. Useful device in consultation allowing participants to remain anonymous if they wish.

Supports and infill
Concept of design, management and construction which aims to distinguish between individual and collective areas of responsibility. Developed at the Stichting Architecten Research in the Netherlands.

Surgery
➡ *Design surgery.*

Survey
Systematic gathering of information. ☞ *Opinion survey. Questionnaire survey. Resource survey. Social survey. Street survey.*

Sustainable community
Community that lives in harmony with its local environment and does not cause damage to distant environments or other communities – now or in the future. Quality of life and the interest of future generations are valued above immediate material consumption and economic growth.

Sustainable development
Development that meets the needs of the present without compromising the ability of future generations to meet their own needs (Brundtland Report definition).

Sustainable travel
Travel creating minimal damage to the environment. Mostly assumed to mean walking, cycling, use of public transport and car sharing.

Sweat equity
Where an individual or community acquires an asset by expending labour rather than money.

SWOT analysis
Determination of the Strengths, Weaknesses, Opportunities and Threats relating to an organisation or activity.

Table group
Group of six to ten people at a workshop who work under the guidance of a Facilitator and are assisted by a Recorder. They usually work through a structured agenda and report back to all participants at plenary sessions.
➛ *SpeakOut.*

Table scheme display
Simple way of securing comment on design proposals by taping drawings on a table top and requesting people to vote with sticky dots.
☞ **A-Z** *p140*.

Talent survey
➥ *Skills survey*.

Task force
Multidisciplinary team of students and professionals who produce in-depth proposals for a site or neighbourhood based on an intensive programme of site studies, lectures, participatory exercises and studio working, normally lasting several weeks.
☞ **A-Z** *p142*.

Team-building
Learning to work together as a group by getting to know each other and developing shared aims, values and working practices.

Technology of participation
A framework of practical methods that help facilitators working with groups. Term used by the Institute of Cultural Affairs. Includes Discussion method, Workshop method and Action Planning method.
✉ *Institute of Cultural Affairs*.

Temporal snapshot
Finding out how spaces are used at different times of day and night.

Tenant management organisation (TMO)
Organisation set up to allow housing tenants to participate in the management of their homes.

Think tank
Brainstorming group. Often used by governments and city authorities. Often for 'experts' only. May use a community planning format. Sometimes called an *expert panel* or *symposium*.

Third wave
Revolution currently transforming society based on growth of high technology and information systems. The first wave was the agricultural revolution, the second the industrial revolution.

Timeline
Line calibrated to show a historical sequence of events or activities. ☞ *Diagrams. Historical profiling*.

Time money
Alternative currency which credits the time people spend helping each other. Participants earn credit for doing jobs – an hour of your time entitles you to an hour of someone else's time. Credits are deposited centrally in a 'time bank' and withdrawn when the participant needs help themselves. ✉ *New Economics Foundation*.

Time-use analysis
Assessment of time spent on various activities, on a daily or seasonal basis.

Top down
Term used to refer to initiatives led by the authorities as opposed to 'bottom up' initiatives led by the community.

Topic workshop
Workshop session on a particular topic.
☞ **A-Z** *Briefing Workshop*.
☞ *Workshop*.

Town centre manager
Person employed to improve town centres by working with all interested parties and taking initiatives.

Town development trust
Organisation created by a local urban community to revitalise that community's physical surroundings.
☞ *Development trust*.

Town team
Group of people who work within their community to identify and shape projects designed to improve it. Term used in Yorkshire, UK.

Town workshop
Workshop organised on the future of a town.

Trail
Carefully planned walk through an area designed to help people understand the problems and opportunities. Designed to be walked unaccompanied.
☞ *Reconnaissance trip*.

Transect walk
Systematic walk along a pre-determined route through an area to gather information about such things as land-use, social and economic resources or the state of the environment. Usually done by community members with facilitators or technical experts. Information is subsequently recorded on maps and as text.
☞ *Reconnaissance trip*.

Treasure hunt
Trail designed with the added incentive of prizes for the correct answers to questions about things seen on route. Useful warm up to a community planning event, generating interest and getting people to look closely at the physical nature of an area. ☞ *Trail.*

Trust
Term used in the name of an organisation, usually implying that it has charitable objectives. Also used to mean 'have confidence in'.

Urban community assistance team
➡ *Design assistance team.*

Urban design
Discipline concerned with three-dimensional built form and the ecology of streets, neighbourhoods and cities.

Urban design action team
➡ *Design assistance team.*

Urban design assistance team
➡ *Design assistance team.*

Urban design game
Role-play game designed to help people to understand the planning process and the views of others by simulating future scenarios. ☞ *Gaming.*

Urban design studio
Unit attached to an architecture or planning school which focuses on involving local communities in live project work. ☞ **A-Z** *p144.*

Urban design workshop
➡ *Design workshop.*

Urban farm
➡ *City farm.*

Urban laboratory
➡ *Urban design studio.*

Urban resource centre
Local or regional centres aiming to co-ordinate training in cross-professional skills and disseminate best practice and innovation in regeneration and community planning.

Urban studies centre
Centre of environmental education, usually focusing on the immediate surroundings. ☞ *Architecture centre. Environmental education.*

Urban village
Mixed use development. Term used successfully to promote the idea that urban areas are more popular when they are diverse and lively rather than dominated by single uses as mostly preferred by conventional developers and planners.

User
Actual or future occupier of a building or neighbourhood or beneficiary of a service. ☞ *User-client.*

User-client
People who are the end-users of buildings and are treated as the client, even if they are not technically responsible for paying the bills.

User group
Group of actual or future occupiers of a building or neighbourhood or beneficiary of a service. ☞ **A-Z** *p146.*

Venn diagram
Diagram using circles of different sizes to indicate roles of different organisations and the relationships between them. For analysing institutional and social networks. ☞ *Diagrams.*

Vernacular architecture
Architecture of and by the people and rooted in a particular locality.

Video box
Use of video to help people express and communicate ideas and opinions. Used for presentation or as a discussion tool. Particularly useful for young people. ☞ *Video soapbox.*

Video soapbox
Use of large screens in public locations to project people expressing ideas and opinions. ☞ **A-Z** *p148.* ☞ *Video box.*

Village appraisal
➡ *Community appraisal.*

Village design day
Day when people work intensively developing ideas for their village. ☞ *Planning day.*

Village design statement
Local design statement produced by a village community. ☞ *Local design statement.*

Vision
An image of how things might be in the future. May be in words or pictures. Provide useful guide for developing project and programme priorities. 'Having vision' implies being imaginative. ☞ *Visioning.*

Vision fair
Event where people vote on their favourite visions. Vision statements or images, usually from a previous workshop or brainstorm, are exhibited. People use sticky dots to indicate which visions they would like to pursue. They may also make personal pledges to take action. ☞ *Choices method. Vision.*

Visioning
Thinking about what the future could be and creating a vision. ☞ *Community visioning. Vision.*

Visioning conference
➡ *Future search conference.*

Visit
Trip by a group of people planning an initiative to a community that has recently undertaken a similar initiative, to learn from their experience. May be highly structured with formal notetaking, interviews and feedback sessions, or informal. ☞ *photos p19.*

Visual minutes
Recording a meeting, conference or workshop visually with cartoon illustrations rather than by producing traditional minutes using text. p200

Visual simulation
Showing how buildings or townscape will look when constructed using photomontages.

Voluntary sector
Organizations controlled by people who are unpaid, and usually elected, but do not form part of statutory government. Range from national to local organizations. Increasingly the divisions between the public, private and voluntary sectors are becoming blurred.

Vulnerability
Extent to which a community, structure or service is likely to be damaged or disrupted by a disaster. ☞ *Disaster.*

Vulnerability analysis
Identification of what and who is vulnerable to disaster and the extent of that vulnerability. ☞ *Disaster.*

Vulnerability and capacity analysis
Method based on a matrix chart for organising information about a community's vulnerability to, and capacity to withstand, the effects of extreme events such as natural disasters. ☞ **A-Z** Risk assessment *p132–133.*

Walkabout
Direct inspection of area under consideration on foot ☞ *Reconnaissance trip.*

Wealth ranking
➡ *Well-being ranking.*

Website
Space on the internet. Immense potential for providing sites with information, discussion groups and interactive material on community planning projects. ☞ **A-Z** The internet *p88.*

Well-being ranking
Assessment of well-being of different households, usually using pile-sorting technique. Also known as *wealth ranking*. ☞ *Community profiling.*

Wheel of fortune
Graphic way for people to collectively rank competing priorities. ☞ *p125.*

Wish poem
Poem made up by combining wishes of participants at a workshop.

Working community
➡ *Managed workspace.*

Working group
Small number of individuals with a specific task to complete.

Working party
➡ *Working group.*

Workshop
Session at which people, aided by a facilitator, explore issues, develop ideas and make decisions. A less formal and more creative alternative to a public meeting or committee. ☞ *Briefing workshop. Design workshop. Public meeting. Seminar. Topic workshop.*

World café
A non-confrontational and creative structured process to help large numbers of people engage in interactive conversations and build mutual understanding and collective learning about important issues by working in small groups.

Youth forum
Way for young people to meet to discuss issues that concern them in whatever way best suits them.

Youth planning day
Day of activities designed specifically to involve young people in the planning process. ☞ *Planning day.*

Zero-carbon home
Energy-efficient dwelling where the net carbon emissions from all energy uses over a year are zero. This includes energy use from cooking, washing and electronic entertainment appliances as well as space heating, cooling, ventilation, lighting and hot water.

Publications A–Z

An annotated selection of useful publications. Focus on classic and generic works by mainstream publishers. In alphabetical order by title.

A bigger selection, including reports, toolkits and film, many downloadable, at:
www.communityplanning.
net/pub-film/pubfilm.php

Information listed

- *Title*
- *Subtitle*
- Author/editor/director
- Publisher
- Date of first edition
- ISBN number
- (details of recent editions)
- Annotation
- Languages available other than English
- (Where to obtain if non-standard publisher and not listed in Contacts A–Z p266)

New material

If you know of material which should be listed on the website and in future editions, please complete the online submission form or send details to the address on page 290.

If you have difficulties getting hold of material, let us know.

Action Planning for Cities
A guide to community practice, Nabeel Hamdi and Reinhard Goethert, John Wiley & Sons, 1997, 0-471-96928-1.
Well illustrated textbook on the theory and practice of community planning in developing countries.

After the Planners
Robert Goodman, Pelican Books, 1972, 0 14 02.1568 9
Stimulating and controversial indictment of prevailing planning and architectural practices which provoked the development of alternative ways of doing things. Introduction by John Palmer relates the US based analysis to concerns in the UK.

Architecture and Participation
Peter Blundell Jones, Doina Petrescu and Jeremy Till (eds), Spon Press, 2005, 0-415-31746-0
Collection of essays by practitioners and theorists, divided into three sections: politics, histories and practices.

Architecture, Participation and Society
Paul Jenkins and Leslie Forsyth (eds), Routledge, 2010, 978-0-415-54724-6
Thorough academic review of participatory architectural practice based on a research project by architecture schools in Scotland.

The Art of Consultation
Public dialogues in a noisy world, Rhion Jones and Elizabeth Gammell, Biteback Publishing Ltd, 2009, 978-1-84954-002-5
Tells the story of the emergence of the consultation culture and unravels some misconceptions and myths that have grown up around it.

At Risk
Natural hazards, people's vulnerability and disasters, Piers Blaikie, Terry Cannon, Ian Davis and Ben Wisner, Routledge, 1994, 0-415-08477-2. Comprehensive explanation of why a people-first approach is essential and how to initiate it.

Beyond Public Meetings
Connecting Community Engagement with decision making, Vivien Twyford et al, Twyford Consulting, 2007, 0-646-46720-4
Useful mapping of the wider landscape of community engagement by a leading Australian practitioner.

Building Democracy
Community architecture in the inner cities, Graham Towers, UCL Press, 1995, 1-85728-089-X.
Detailed account of the development of community architecture with some UK case studies.

Building Homes People Want
A guide to tenant involvement in the design and development of housing association homes, Pete Duncan and Bill Halsall, National Housing Federation, 1994, 0-86297-272-8NHF
Useful guide by and for practitioners. Includes case study of a community planning weekend in Hull, UK.

The Change Handbook
Group methods for shaping the future, Peggy Holman and Tom Devane, Berrett-Koehler, 1999, 1-57675-058-2.
Guide to 18 change strategies for tapping human potential in organisations and communities.

Changing Places
Children's participation in environmental planning, Eileen Adams & Sue Ingham, The Children's Society, 1998, 1-899783-00-8.
Practical guide for practitioners and teachers wishing to involve children in planning and design.

The Charrette Handbook
The Essential Guide for Accelerated, Collaborative Community Planning, National Charrette Institute, American Planning Association, 2006, 978-1-932364-21-7
Excellent detailed guide for organisers of charrettes.

Children's participation in sustainable development
The theory and practice of involving young citizens in community development and environmental care, Roger Hart, Earthscan, 1997, 1853833223
Excellent guide to both the theory and practice of children's participation. Explains how children can be given constructive and important roles in contributing to sustainability. Includes detailed case studies as well as a range of pratical resources.

Co-design
A process of design participation, Stanley King et al, Van Nostrand Reinhold, 1989, 0-442-23333-7.
Lovely, well illustrated guide to conducting design workshops, based on 197 case studies in the USA.

Cohousing
A contemporary approach to housing ourselves, Kathryn McCamant & Charles Durrett, Habitat Press/Ten Speed Press, Berkeley, 1994, 0-89815-306-9.
How to develop housing schemes with a strong shared element as pioneered in Denmark.

Communities Count!
A step by step guide to community sustainability indicators, Alex MacGillivray, Candy Weston & Catherine Unsworth, New Economics Foundation, 1998. 1-899407-20-0.
Handy guide to using indicators to measure trends that really matter and build an agenda for education and action.

Community & Sustainable Development
Participation in the future, Diane Warburton (ed), Earthscan, 1998. 1-85383-531-5.
Inspiring collection of writings on the current state of the art.

Community Architecture
How people are creating their own environment, Nick Wates & Charles Knevitt, Penguin, 1987, 0-14-010428-3 (Routledge, 2013, 978-0-415-70853-1).
Overview of movement for community participation in architecture and planning. Also in Chinese and Japanese.

Community Design Primer
Randolph T. Hester, Ridge Times Press, 1990, 0934203067.
Good introduction to community design USA style with do-it-yourself training exercises for the would-be community designer.

Community Involvement in Planning and Development Processes
Department of the Environment, HMSO, 1994, 0-11-753007-7.
Results of a planning research study which demonstrates the value of community participation.

Community Led Planning Toolkit
Philip Vincent (ed), Action with Communities in Rural England (ACRE), 2012, 978-1-871157-94-9
Step-by-step guidance for communities who want to produce a local plan which can deliver a range of actions with social, economic and environmental benefits.

Community Participation in Practice
Wendy Sarkissian, Andrea Cook and Kelvin Walsh, Institute for Science and Technology Policy, Murdoch University.
Excellent series of publications and film designed to assist community planning and design work.
Comprises:
• *A Practical Guide,* 1997, 0-86905-556-9.
Covers a range of useful methods, some pioneered in Australia.
• *The Workshop Checklist,* 1994, 0-869053027.
How-to for workshop organisers.
• *Casebook,* 1994, 0-86905-363-9.
Describes and illustrates 12 case studies from Australia.
• *The Community Participation Handbook; Resources for public involvement in the planning process,* 1986, revised 1994, 0-86905-359-0.
Practical and theoretical essays by a number of authors.

Community Participation Methods in Design and Planning
Henry Sanoff, Wiley, 2000, 0-471-35545-3.
Detailed, well-illustrated guide for professionals and students. Combines theoretical analysis with practical design games and international case study material for a broad range of applications.

The Community Planning Event Manual
How to use Collaborative Planning and Urban Design events to improve your environment, Nick Wates, Earthscan, 2008, 978-1-84407-492-1
Explains why and how to organise community planning events. With lots of illustrations, sample documents and checklists to help save you time.

Consensus Design
Socially inclusive process, Christopher Day with Rosie Parnell, Architectural Press, 2003, 0 7506 5605 0
Practitioners' step by step guide to codesign illustrated by case studies. Foreword by HRH The Prince of Wales.

Consult your community
A guide to using citizens juries, Dr Lyn Carson, Department of Planning, New South Wales, 2003, 0-7347-0414-3
Comprehensive handbook on citizens juries with Australian case studies.

Creating a Design Assistance Team for Your Community
American Institute of Architects (AIA), 1996.
Guidebook on the AIA's Assistance Team Programme. Particularly useful for organisations wanting to set up their own support systems.

Creative Community Planning
Transformative engagement methods for working at the edge, Wendy Sarkissian and Dianna Hurford with Christine Wenman, Earthscan, 2010, 9781844077038
Theory, principles, case studies and discussion exploring the boundaries of community planning and engagement within a sustainability framework.

Disaster Mitigation
A community-based approach. Andrew Maskrey, Oxfam, Oxford 1989. 0-85598123-7.
Seminal polemic.

Effective working with rural communities
James Derounian, Packard Publishing, 1998, 1-85341-106-X.
Includes a useful chapter on community appraisals.

Engaging the Community in Decision Making
Case studies tracking participation, voice and influence, Roz Diane Lasker, John A. Guidry, McFarland, 2009, 978-0-7864-4312-3
Summarises how five community partnerships in the US, working with a team of researchers, explored how effective engagement processes are in promoting the influence of people traditionally marginalised.

Freedom to Build
Dweller control of the housing process, John F.C.Turner and Robert Fichter (eds), Collier-Macmillan, 1972. Classic work showing that where dwellers are in control, their homes are better and cheaper than those built through government programmes or large corporations.

From Place to Place
Maps and parish maps, Sue Clifford and Angela King (eds), Common Ground, 1996. 1-870-364-163.
The background and experience of parish mapping with contributions from several authors.

Future Search
An action guide to finding common ground in organisations and communities, Marvin R Weisboard and Sandra Janoff, Berrett-Koehler, 1995,1-881052-12-5.
Good step-by-step guide to running future search conferences.

Good Practice Guide to Community Planning and Development
Michael Parkes, London Planning Advisory Committee, 1995.
Detailed guide with case studies by a seasoned practitioner.

The Good, the Bad and the Ugly
Cities in crisis, Rod Hackney, Frederick Muller, 1990. 0-09-173939-X.
Inspiring personal account of a crusade to help people shape their own environments by a pioneering community architect.

The Guide to Development Trusts and Partnerships
David Wilcox, Development Trusts Association, 1998. 0-9531469-0-3.
Handbook aimed particularly at those setting up trusts. (Full text also on www.partnerships.org.uk.)

The Guide to Effective Participation
David Wilcox, Partnership Books, 1994, 1-870298-00-4.
Overview of general participation methods.

Housing by people
Towards autonomy in building environments, John F. C. Turner, Marion Boyars, 1976, 0-7145-2569-3.
Seminal work on housing, drawing on experience in developing countries to illustrate the universal necessity for dweller control.

Involving communities in urban and rural regeneration
A guide for practitioners, Pieda plc, Department of the Environment, 1995, 1-85112201-X.
Useful overview to general approaches with handy checklists and summaries.

Kitchen Table Sustainability
Practical Recipes for Community Engagement with Sustainability, Wendy Sarkissian with Nancy Hofer, Yollana Shore, Steph Vajda and Cathy Wilkinson, Earthscan, 2008, 9781844076147
A powerful, reflective contribution on the vital importance of community engagement for achieving local and global sustainability.

Large Group Interventions
Engaging the entire organisation for rapid change, Barbara Benedict Bunker and Billie T. Alban, Jossey-Bass, 1997, 0-7879-0324-8. Practical guide to some of the many ways of involving everybody in improving whole systems.

The Linz Cafe
Christopher Alexander, Oxford University Press, 1981. 0-19520-263-5. Beautiful account of the design and construction of an Austrian cafe based on user participation.

Making Planning Work
A guide to approaches and skills, Cliff Hague, Patrick Wakely, Julie Crespin and Chris Jasko, ITDG Publications, 2006, 1-85339-648-6, 978-1-85339-648-9 Prepared for the UN to focus attention on the urgent need to increase global understanding of sustainable urban development processes and pro-poor planning practices. Explores approaches that work and skills needed to implement them.

Managing Partnerships
Tools for mobilising the public sector, business and civil society as partners in development, Ros Tennyson, Prince of Wales Business Leaders Forum, 1998. 1-899159-84-3. Excellent how-to on partnerships crammed with useful checklists, tips and sample documents.

Open Space Technology
A user's guide, Harrison Owen, Berrett-Koehler, 2008, 978-1-57675-476-4. Step-by-step guide to setting up and facilitating an Open Space event. Third edition.

The Oregon Experiment
Christopher Alexander et al., Oxford University University Press, 1975. 0-19-501824-9. Classic account of the planning process for the University of Oregon where the entire community of 15,000 were involved in the planning and design.

The Paris-Lexington Road
Community-based planning and context sensitive highway design, Krista L. Schneider, Island Press, 2003, 1-55963-110-4. Critical review of this project which has come to be regarded as a model for context-sensitive highway design in the USA.

Participation Works!
Twenty-one techniques of community participation for the twenty-first century, Julie Lewis, Catherine Unsworth and Perry Walker (eds), New Economics Foundation, 1998, 1-899407-17-0. Useful standard summary profiles on a varied range of general participation methods.

Participatory Design
Theory and techniques, Henry Sanoff (ed), North Carolina State University, 1990, 0-9622107-3-0. Rich compendium of interesting theoretical and practical material, particularly from USA experience.

Participatory Learning and Action
A trainer's guide, Jules Pretty, Irene Guijt, John Thompson and Ian Scoones, International Institute for Environment and Development, 1995, 1-899825-00-2. Excellent handbook for trainers involved in using participatory methods.

Participatory Planning for Sustainable Communities
International experience in mediation, negotiation and engagement in making plans, C Hague, M Higgins, P Jenkins, K Kirk, A Prior, H Smith, S Elwood, E Hague, A Papadopoulos, W Grimes, C Platt, London: Office of the Deputy Prime Minister, 2003. Radical and extensive research study based on international case studies which heralded the change from thinking about public participation to participatory planning.

Participatory Workshops
A sourcebook of 21 sets of ideas & activities, Robert Chambers, Earthscan, 2002, 978-1-85383-863-7 A wealth of practical tips from a highly experienced practitioner and academic.

A Pattern Language
Christopher Alexander et al., Oxford University Press, 1977, 0-19501-919-9. Influential book describing working method enabling untrained people to design any part of the environment themselves; homes, streets, neighbourhoods.

Permaculture Teachers' Guide
Andrew Goldring (ed), WWF-UK, 2000, 9781858501680. Explains how to run permaculture design courses.

Placemakers Guide to Building Community
Nabeel Hamdi, Earthscan, 2010, 9781844078035. Handbook for urban development worldwide.

Plan, Design and Build
21st Century Halls for England, Alan Wilkinson, Action with Communities in Rural England (ACRE) 1997, 1-871157-48-X. Excellent how-to-do-it on creating community centres including community involvement.

Planning your Community's Future
A guide to the Regional/Urban Design Assistance Team Program, American Institute of Architects, 2004. Updated manual for this pioneering programme which has been running since 1967.

The Power in our Hands
Neighbourhood-based world-shaking, Tony Gibson, Jon Carpenter Publishing, 1996, 1-897766-28-9. Powerful account of ordinary people doing extraordinary things all over the world by the inventor of Planning for Real.

Projects with People
The practice of participation in rural development, Peter Oakley et al., ILO (IT Publications), 1991. 922-107-2827.
Comprehensive analysis based on international experience over several decades. Especially good on rationale, benefits and practical problems and how to overcome them. Excellent summaries and tables.

Real Time Strategic Change
Robert Jacobs, Berrett-Kohler, 1994, 1-881052-45-1.
How-to on this participatory approach to enterprise management.

Reducing Risk
Participatory learning activities for disaster mitigation in southern Africa, Astrid von Kotze and Ailsa Holloway, University of Natal, South Africa and International Federation of Red Cross, Geneva, 1997. 0-85598-347-7.
Reference material and ideas for participatory training/learning exercises for field workers involved in community-based disaster mitigation.

The Resilience Imperative
Co-operative transitions to a steady-state economy, Michael Lewis and Pat Conaty, New Society Publishers, 2012, 9780865717077
Important book which argues for a major SEE (Social, Ecological, Economic) change as a prerequisite for replacing the paradigm of limitless economic growth with a more decentralised, cooperative, steady-state economy.

Revolutions in Development Inquiry
Robert Chambers, Earthscan, 2008, 978-1-84407-624-6.
Review of the participatory approaches that are transforming the world of development.

Rising from the Ashes
Development strategies in times of disaster, Mary B Anderson and Peter J Woodrow. Intermediate Technology Publications, 1998 (reissue), 1-85339-439-4.
Explains capacities and vulnerabilities analysis and how to apply it to projects.

Rules for Radicals
A Pragmatic Primer for Realistic Radicals, Saul Alinsky, Random House, 1971, 0-394-44341-1
Classic work on community and neighbourhood organising.

The Scope of Social Architecture
Richard Hatch, Van Nostrand Reinhold, 1984. 0-442-26153-5.
Fascinating and detailed case studies of community architecture and planning projects from twelve countries, mostly in the developed world. Range from housing projects to replanning entire cities.

The Self-Build Book
How to enjoy designing and building your own home, Jon Broome and Brian Richardson, Green Books,1995, 1-900322-00-5.
Clear explanation of a variety of self-build techniques including the timber frame method evolved by the architect Walter Segal.

Small is Bankable
Community reinvestment in the UK, Ed Mayo et al., New Economics Foundation, 1998, 1-85935-047-X.
Guide to a range of community finance initiatives which can help build financially sustainable regeneration.

Social Sustainability
Process, place, people, JTP Cities, JTP Press, 2013, 978-0-9573093-0-2
An evaluation of the community engagement approaches developed by John Thompson & Partners. Focuses on a case study of Caterham Barracks (see p210) to reflect on the relationship between social sustainability and the design of new neighbourhoods. Obtain via www.jtp.co.uk

SpeakOut
The Step-by-Step Guide to SpeakOuts and Community Workshops, Wendy Sarkissian and Wiwik Bunjamin-Mau with Andrea Cook, Kelvin Walsh and Steph Vajda, Earthscan, 2009, 978-1-84407-704-5
Detailed how-to manual for organisers and promotors of community workshops and especially SpeakOuts; a style of interactive workshop pioneered in Australia.

Successful Transport Decision Making
A project management and stakeholder engagement handbook, anon., Guidemaps, 2004
Many useful hints on the management of projects related to sustainable transport. Includes many examples of stakeholder involvement with descriptions of useful stakeholder engagement tools. Theoretical background is supported with different examples from cities.

Supports
An alternative to mass housing, John Habraken, Architectural Press, 1972, 0 85139 225 3
Classic work on the need for new adaptable housing systems. First English language edition of a book first published in Dutch in 1961.

Sustainable Community
Learning from the cohousing model, Graham Meltzer, Trafford Publishing, 2005, 1-4120-4994-6
Explores the link between sustainability and community based on a ten year study of cohousing.

Sustainable Urban Extensions: Planned through Design
A collaborative approach to developing sustainable town extensions through Enquiry by Design, Various authors, The Prince's Foundation, 2000, 978-1-898465-26-3
Useful account of early UK experience using Enquiry by Design (from The Prince's Foundation)

Taking Power
An agenda for community economic renewal, Ed Mayo, Stephen Thake and Tony Gibson, New Economics Foundation, 1998, 1-899407-14-6.
Provocative paper on how to build on the work of people at community level to rebuild society neighbourhood by neighbourhood.

The Thin Book of Appreciative Inquiry
Sue Annis Hammond, Kodiak Consulting, 1998, 0-9665373-1-9.
Handy introduction to this technique.

Tenant Participation in Housing Design
A guide for action, Royal Institute of British Architects and the Institute of Housing, RIBA Publications, 1988. 0-947877-02-9.
Simple, practical advice aimed mainly at development professionals and housing managers.

Unleashing the Potential
Bringing residents to the centre of regeneration, Marilyn Taylor, Joseph Rowntree Foundation, 1995. 1-85935-014-3.
Draws lessons from 33 studies from the Foundation's Action on Estates programme. Covers many different aspects of community involvement and ways of developing a more central role for residents in the regeneration of estates. Useful for principles and examples.

Urban Design in Action
The history, theory and development of the American Institute of Architects' Regional/Urban Design Assistance Teams Program (R/UDAT), Peter Batchelor and David Lewis, North Carolina State University School of Design and the American Institute of Architects, 1985. 0-913962-80-5.
Classic work on the development of community planning in the USA.

Urban Projects Manual
A guide to preparing upgrading and new development projects accessible to low income groups, Forbes Davidson and Geoff Payne (eds), Liverpool University Press, 1986, revised 1999, 0-85323-484-1.
Well-illustrated guide based on field experience, mainly in Egypt.

User Participation in Building Design and Management
David Kernohan, John Gray, John Daish, Butterworth-Heinneman, 1996, 0-7506-2888-X.
Useful how-to-do-it on participatory evaluations of buildings after they have been erected. Well-thought through process. Good drawings.

A Vision of Britain
A personal view of architecture, HRH The Prince of Wales, Doubleday, 1989. 0-385-26903-X.
Inspiring statement of the Prince's influential approach to architecture including Ten Principles for creating humane environments.

Visioning as Participatory Planning Tool
Learning from Kosovo practices, Frank Dhondt, UN Habitat, 2012, 978-92-1-132498-3
Explores how community visioning can be used to improve the quality of life, based on the experience of 10 workshops organised by UN-Habitat and partners.

Viterbo; Santa Maria in Gradi
Brian Hanson and Liam O'Connor (eds), Union Printing Edizioni, Viterbo, 1994. 1-898465-09-6.
Fully illustrated account of an urban design task force in Italy. Also in Italian. (The Prince's Foundation.)

The Weller Way
The story of the Weller Streets housing cooperative, Alan McDonald for the Weller Streets, Faber and Faber, 1986, 0-571-13963-9.
Lively blow-by-blow narrative of how 61 working-class families battled tirelessly to build Liverpool's first new-build housing co-operative.

When We Build Again
Let's have housing that works, Colin Ward, Pluto Press, 1985. 0-74530-022-7.
Very readable summary on how paternalistic government housing policies should be transformed to enable people to house themselves.

Whose Reality Counts?
Putting the first last, Robert Chambers, Intermediate Technology Publications, 1997, 1-85339-386-X.
State of the art treatise on Participatory Rapid Appraisal (PRA).

Contacts A–Z

An annotated selection of contacts for further information and support on community planning. Emphasis on organisations able to:

- supply publications or film;
- supply local, national or international contacts;
- provide more info on methods in this handbook.

UK and USA covered more fully than elsewhere.

Information listed

- **Name of organisation** or **individual**
- address
- tel (**t**)
- fax (**f**) (minus code if same)
- email (**e**)
- website (**w**)
- contact name (if any)
- annotation

Bigger selection at:
www.communityplanning.net/contacts/contacts.php
and
www.communityplanning.net/consultants/consultants.php

New material
If you know of contacts which should be listed on the website and in future editions, please complete the online submission form or send details to the address on page 290. Contacts from places not already covered particularly welcome.

If you find any contacts listed unhelpful, please let us know.

Academy of Urbanism
70 Cowcross Street, London
EC1M 6EJ, UK
t +44 (0)20 7251 8777 **f** 7251 8777
e info@academyofurbanism.org.uk
w www.academyofurbanism.org.uk
High level, cross-sector group of individuals from a wide range of disciplines, brought together to champion the cause of good quality urbanism throughout Great Britain and Ireland.

Action for Market Towns
5 Baxter Court, Higher Baxter Street, Bury St Edmunds, Suffolk, IP33 1ES, UK
t +44 (0)1284 756567 **f** 761816
e info@towns.org.uk
w www.towns.org.uk
National membership group that provides small towns, local authorities and others with information and advice, examples of best practice and national representation. Provides support on neighbourhood planning with publications, training and facilitation.

Action with Communities in Rural England
First Floor, Northway House West, The Forum, Cirencester, Gloucestershire, GL7 2QY, UK
t +44 (0)1285 653477 **f** 653477
e acre@acre.org.uk
w www.acre.org.uk
National English umbrella of the Rural Community Action Network (RCAN), which operates at national, regional and local level in support of rural communities across the country. Promotes community led planning including parish plans.

America Speaks
1050 17th Street NW, Suite 250, Washington, DC 20036, USA
t 202-775-3939 **f** 202-775-0404
e info@americaspeaks.org
w www.americaspeaks.org
Engages citizens in the public decisions that impact their lives. Developing national infrastructure for democratic deliberation that institutionalises the links between decision-makers and citizens in determining public policy. Organisers of '21st Century Town Meeting' programme.

American Institute of Architects
1735 New York Avenue, NW
Washington DC 20006, USA
t +1 202 626 7300 **f** 626 7365
e infocentral@aia.org or rudat@aia.org
w www.aia.org
The Institute's Centre for Communities by Design promotes design assistance team (DAT) programmes. Has films, tapes, brochures and reports from US events. Supplies addresses of experienced team members and local and state support programmes.

American Planning Association
122 S. Michigan Ave, Suite 1600, Chicago, Illinois, 60603, USA
t :+1-312-431-9100 **f** 431-9985
e WebsiteFeedback@planning.org
w www.planning.org
Professional association organised to advance the art and science of planning and to foster the activity of planning. Good range of publications related to community planning.

Article 25
One Canada Square, Canary Wharf, London, E14 5AB, UK
t +44 (0)20 3197 9800
e info@article-25.org
w www.article-25.org
UK registered charity that designs and delivers architectural solutions for those in greatest need worldwide. Strong emphasis on community participation and participatory design.

Association for Community Design
e info@communitydesign.org
w www.communitydesign.org
International network of individuals, organisations and institutions committed to increasing the capacity of design and planning professionals to better serve communities. Based on US community design centres.

Ball State University
Community-Based Projects, Architecture Building Room 332, Muncie, Indiana 47306, USA
t +1 765 285 1350 f 285 2607
e cbp@bsu.edu
w www.bsu.edu/cbp
Contacts: Scott Truex.
Urban design studio within a university setting. Experience of running charrettes, using mobile studios and producing newspaper supplements. Good website.

Building and Social Housing Foundation (BSHF)
Memorial Square, Coalville, Leicestershire, LE67 3TU, UK
t +44 (0)1530 510444 f 510332
e bshf@bshf.org
w www.bshf.org
Independent research organisation that promotes sustainable development and innovation in housing through collaborative research and knowledge transfer. Good website with case studies from all over the world.

Business in the Community
137 Shepherdess Walk, London N1 7RQ, UK
t +44 (0)20 7566 8650
e info@bitc.org.uk
w www.bitc.org.uk
Inspires, engages, supports and challenges companies to continually improve the impact they have on society and the environment through Corporate Social Responsibility (CSR). Its ProHelp group is a national UK network of over 800 professional firms committed to making a difference in their local community by providing free advice and support.

Centre for Development and Emergency Practice
Oxford Brookes University, Gypsy Lane Campus, Headington, Oxford OX3 0BP, UK
t +44 (0)1865 482844 f 483298
w www.architecture.brookes.ac.uk/research/cendep/
Contact: Jeni Burnell
Postgraduate Masters programme. Expertise on community planning, in UK and in developing countries. Research.

Centre for Disaster Preparedness
CSWCD Bldg., Ramon Magsaysay Avenue, University of the Philippines Diliman Campus, Quezon City, Philippines
t +63 2 9240386 f 9240836
e cdp@info.com.ph
w www.cdp.org.ph
Training courses on community-based urban and rural planning focusing on disaster prevention. Publications and consultancy.

Centre for Environment and Human Settlements
School of the Built Environment, Heriot-Watt University, Edinburgh E14 4AS, UK
t +44 (131) 451 4616
e h.c.smith@hw.ac.uk
w www.sbe.hw.ac.uk/research/ibud/centre-environment-human-settlements.htm
Teaching, training, research in planning and housing issues related to developing world. Main focus on best practice in conditions of rapid urbanisation.

Centre for Sustainable Energy
3 St Peters Court, Bedminster Parade, Bristol, BS3 4AQ, UK
t 0117 934 1400 f 934 1410
e info@cse.org.uk
w www.cse.org.uk
Independent charity that shares knowledge and experience to help people change the way they think and act on energy. Runs PlanLoCal website (see Websites A-Z). Hires out physical model demonstrating low carbon community elements.

Chinese University of Hong Kong
School of Architecture, Room 106, AIT Building, Shatin, New Territories, Hong Kong SAR, China
t +852 394-36583 f 394-20982
e architecture@cuhk.edu.hk
Contact: Mee Kam NG.
Expertise in collaborative design.

Civic Practices Network
Center for Human Resources, Heller School, Brandeis University, 60 Turner Street, Waltham, MA 02154, USA
t +1 617 736 4890 f 736 4891
e cpn@cpn.org w www.cpn.org
Collaborative and nonpartisan project dedicated to bringing practical tools for public problem solving into community and institutional settings across America.

Civic Voice
60 Duke Street, Liverpool, L1 5AA,
t +44 (0)151 707 4319
e info@civicvoice.org.uk
w www.civicvoice.org.uk
National charity for the civic movement in England. Makes places more attractive, enjoyable and distinctive. Promotes civic pride. Created after the demise of the Civic Trust.

Community Matters
12-20 Baron Street, London, N1 9LL, UK
t +44 (0)20 7837 7887 f 7278 9253
e info@community matters.org.uk
w www.communitymatters.org.uk
Stands for the collective action of ordinary people within their neighbourhood through inclusive, locally rooted and accountable community organisations. Represents the largest network of grassroots community organisations (1,200) in the UK. Provides comprehensive expert advice and legal services on all aspects of running a community organisation.

CONCERN, Inc
P.O.Box 5892, Washington, DC
20016, USA
t +1 (202) 328 8160 **f** 387 3378
e concern@sustainable.org
w www.sustainable.org
Nonprofit US environmental
education organisation focusing on
building sustainable communities.
Aims to build public understanding
of, and support for, programmes,
policies and practices that are
environmentally, economically and
socially sound. Manages
Sustainable Communities Online.

**Confederation of Co-operative
Housing**
19 Devonshire Road, Liverpool,
L8 3TX, UK
t +44 (0)151 726 2228
e info@cch.coop
w www.cch.coop
UK organisation for housing cooperatives, tenant-controlled
housing organisations and regional
federations of housing co-ops.

Congress for the New Urbanism
The Marquette Building, 140 S.
Dearborn Street, Suite 404,
Chicago, Illinois, IL 60603, USA
t +1 312 551 7300 **f** 346 3323
e cnuinfo@cnu.org **w** www.cnu.org
Influential movement for humanising
the built environment based on the
organisation of charrettes,
congresses and task forces.

Consense
42C Barrack Square, Martlesham
Heath, Ipswich, Suffolk, IP5 3RF, UK
t +44 (0)1473 627100 **f** 622515
e info@consense.co.uk
w www.consense.co.uk
Specialists in online consultations.
Developed award winning Open
Debate method to engage the
community and stakeholders in
planning. Has run online
consultations for major
infrastructure projects including
renewable energy schemes.

The Conservation Volunteers
Sedum House, Mallard Way,
Doncaster, DN4 8DB, UK
t +44 (0)1302 388 883 **f** 311 531
e information@tcv.org.uk
w www.tcv.org.uk
Helps people reclaim local green
places. Runs training programmes
on participatory approaches.

Consultation Institute
Baystrait House, Station Road,
Biggleswade, Bedfordshire, SG18
8AL, UK
t +44 (0)1767 318 350 **f** 622 515
e info@consultationinstitute.org
w www.consultationinstitute.org
Training and information resource
in fields of consultation and public
engagement. Promotes high
standards of practice.

**Deicke Richards Architecture
and Design**
58 Baxter Street, PO Box 507,
Fortitude Valley, Queensland, 4006,
Australia
t +61 7 3852 8700 **f** 3852 8701
e peter@deickerichards.com.au
w www.deickerichards.com.au
Multidisciplinary practice with
collaborative culture and experience
in community design.

**Department for Communities
and Local Government**
Eland House, Bressenden Place,
London, SW1E 5DU, UK
t +44 (0)303 444 0000
e Contactus@communities.gsi.gov.uk
w www.communities.gov.uk
UK government department
responsible for housing, local
government, regeneration, planning
and urban and regional issues.

**Department for International
Development**
22 Whitehall, London, SW1A 2EG, UK
t +44 (0)1355 84 3132 **f** 843632
e enquiry@dfid.gov.uk
w www.dfid.gov.uk
UK government department
focusing on helping developing
countries eliminate poverty.

Design Council
Angel Building, 407 St John Street,
London , EC1V 4AB, UK
t +44(0)20 7420 5200 **f** 7420 5300
e info@designcouncil.org.uk
w www.designcouncil.org.uk
Contacts: Nicola Mathers, Graham
Fernandez.
Mission is to bring the
transformative power of design to
things that matter. Provides support
for neighbourhood planning.
Merged with CABE in 2011.
Enterprising charity.

Deutsche Institut fur Urbanistik
Zimmerstraße 15, Berlin, 10969,
Germany
t +49 (0)30 39001 0 **f** 39001 100
e difu@difu.de
w www.difu.de/en/institute
German Institute of Urban Affairs.
Expertise in community planning in
Germany. Offices in Berlin and
Cologne.

Development Alternatives Group
B-32 Tara Crescent, Qutab Institutional
Area, New Delhi 110016, India
t +91 (11) 2656 4444 **f** 2685 1158
e tara@devalt.org
w www.devalt.org
Training, consultancy and
publications on participatory urban
and rural development.

Development Planning Unit
34 Tavistock Square, London,
WC1H 9EZ, UK   **t**
+44 (0)20 7679 1111 **f** 7679 1112
e dpu@ucl.ac.uk
w www.bartlett.ucl.ac.uk/dpu
International centre for research,
teaching, training and consultancy
focusing on Asia, Africa and Latin
America.

Directory of Social Change
24 Stephenson Way, London NW1
2DP, UK
t +44 (0)20 7391 4800 **f** 7391 4808
e enquiries@dsc.org.uk
w www.dsc.org.uk
Publishes a range of useful
fundraising and other directories,
aimed at the voluntary sector.

Empowerment Zone and Enterprise Community Program
t +1 (202) 512-4325
e contact@gao.gov
w www.gao.gov/products/GAO-06-727
US Presidential initiative to empower local communities.

Energy Saving Trust
21 Dartmouth Street, London, SW1H 9BP, UK
t +44 (0)300 123 1234
e energy-advice@est.org.uk
w www.energysavingtrust.org.uk
Non-profit organisation that provides free and impartial advice on how to stop wasting energy. Useful website for anyone interested in saving money and reducing energy consumption. Comprehensive and clear information on insulation and heating, renewable energy, recommended products and funding from grants. EST is a non-profit organisation, funded both by Government and the private sector.

Environmental Design Research Association
1760 Old Meadow Road, Suite 500, McLean, Vermont, VA 22102, USA
t +1 703 506 2895 **f** 506 3266
e headquarters@edra.org
w www.edra.org
International association promoting advancement and dissemination of environmental design research.

Environmental Partnership for Central Europe
Nadaci Partnerství, Údolní 33, 602 00 Brno, Czech Republic
t +420 515 903 111
e partnerstvi@nap.cz
w www.nadacepartnerstvi.cz
Supports NGOs, municipalities and other partners in their environmental care, promotion of sustainable development, inter-sector cooperation and participation of citizens in public affairs.

Essex Sustainability Institute
University of Essex, Wivenhoe Park, Colchester CO4 3SQ, UK
t +44 (0)1206 873333 **f** 873416
e enquiries@essex.ac.uk
w www.essex.ac.uk/esi/
Contact: Jules Pretty.
Information on deliberative democracy and participatory governance methods.

European Environmental Bureau
4, Bd. de Waterloo, Brussels, B-1000, Belgium
t +32 2 289 10 90 **f** 289 10 99
e eeb@eeb.org
w www.eeb.org
Federation of environmental citizens organisations with over 140 members. Campaigns for environmental justice, sustainable development and participatory democracy.

European LEADER Gateway
ENRD Contact Point, Rue du Marteau 81, Bruxelles, B-1000, Belgium
t +32 2 235 20 20 **f** 280 04 38
e info@enrd.eu
w http://enrd.ec.europa.eu
Information on rural community-led local development in the European Union.

Federal Emergency Management Agency
PO Box 10055, Hyattsville, MD 20782-8, USA
t +1 800-621-3362
e info@fema.gov **w** www.fema.gov
Independent US disaster agency. Mission is to ensure that people work together to build, sustain and improve the ability to prepare for, protect against, respond to, recover from and mitigate all hazards.

Forum for the Future
Overseas House, 19-23 Ironmonger Row, London, EC1V 3QN, UK
t +44 (0)20 7324 3630
e info@forumforthefuture.org
w www.forumforthefuture.org
Partnership of independent experts committed to building a sustainable way of life. Has directory of over 500 sustainable rural initiatives.

Future Search Network
4700 Wissahickon Ave, Suite 126, Philadelphia, PA 19144, USA
t +1 800 951 6333 **f** 215 849 7360
e fsn@futuresearch.net
w www.futuresearch.net
Contacts: Sandra Janoff, Marvin Weisbord, Sally Theilacker. Network of future search practitioners. Supplies publications, videos, local practitioner contacts.

The Glass-House Community Led Design
Third Floor, 47–49 Pitfield Street, London, N1 6DA, UK
t +44 (0)20 7490 4583 **f** 7490 4584
e info@theglasshouse.org.uk
w www.theglasshouse.org.uk
Contact: Sophia de Sousa, CEO. Independent UK national charity supporting and promoting public participation and leadership in the design of the built environment. Offers advice, training and hands-on support to community groups and organisations, housing associations, developers, local authorities and other stakeholders, to help them work more effectively together to create better quality places and spaces.

Groundwork
Lockside, 5 Scotland Street, Birmingham, B1 2RR, UK
t +44 (0)121 236 8565 **f** 236 7356
e info@groundwork.org.uk
w www.groundwork.org.uk
UK network of local trusts working through partnership to improve the quality of life in deprived areas. Sister organisations in Japan and USA. Useful publications and videos.

Habitat International Coalition
General Secretariat, 12 Tiba St., 2nd Floor, Muhandisin, Giza, Egypt
t +20-2-37486379 **f** 37486379
w www.hic-net.org
Contact: Alvaro Puertas
Global forum for NGOs concerned with human settlements.Secretariat revolves so check website for latest information.

Halsall Lloyd Partnership (HLP)
98 Duke Street, Liverpool,
Merseyside, L1 5AG, UK
t +44 (0)151 708 8944 f 709 1737
e liverpool@hlpdesign.com
w www.hlpdesign.com
Contact: Bill Halsall.
multidisciplinary architecture and
design practice with a track record
of involving communities in housing
design.

**Homes and Communities
Agency**
Maple House, 149 Tottenham
Court Road, London, W1T 7BN, UK
t + 44 (0)300 1234 500
e mail@homesandcommunities.co.uk
w www.homesandcommunities.co.uk
National housing and regeneration
delivery agency for England, whose
role is to create thriving
communities and affordable homes.

HUD USER
P.O. Box 23268, Washington DC,
20026-3268, USA
t +1 800 245 2691 f 301 519 5767
e helpdesk@huduser.org
w www.huduser.org
Government department for
housing and urban development,
USA. Information and publications.

Imagine Chicago
910 W Castlewood Terrace,
Chicago, Illinois 60640, USA
t +1 312 330 1015
e bliss@imaginechicago.org
w www.imaginechicago.org
Contact: Bliss Brown, President.
Innovative project helping people
develop their imagination as city
creators, based on future search
and appreciative inquiry methods.
Resource materials available.

**Institute of Architecture and
Town Planning**
Technical University of Lodz,
Al.Politechniki 6A, 90-240 Lodz,
Poland
e mhanzl@mojemiasto.org.pl
w www.p.lodz.pl
Contacts Małgorzata Hanzl
Expertise in public participation in
urban planning.

Institute of Cultural Affairs
International Secretariat, % ICA
Canada, 655 Queen Street East,
Toronto, Ontario, M4M 1G4, Canada
t +1.416.691.2316 f 691.2491
e icai@ica-international.org
w www.ica-international.org
Global network of private, non-
profit organisations concerned with
the human factor in world
development. Runs courses based
on its Technology of Participation
(ToP) methodology.

**Institute of Development
Studies, Brighton**
Library Road, Brighton, BN1 9RE, UK
t +44 (0)1273 606261 f 621202
e ids@ids.ac.uk
w www.ids.ac.uk
Global charity for international
development research, teaching
and communications. Hosts
research teams, postgraduate
courses and a family of knowledge
services.

**International Association for
Public Participation (IAP2)**
13762 Colorado Blvd, Suite 124
PMB 54, Thornton, Colorado,
80602, USA
e iap2hq@iap2.org
w www.iap2.org
Helps organizations and communities
around the world improve their
decisions by involving those people
who are affected by those decisions.
Many resources on website.

**International Centre for
Participation Studies**
Department of Peace Studies,
University of Bradford, Bradford,
West Yorkshire, BD7 1DP, UK
t +44 (0)1274 232323
e ssis-professional-services@bradford.ac.uk
w www.bradford.ac.uk/ssis/icps/
Academic and applied research unit
in the field of participatory politics.

**International Institute for
Environment and Development**
3 Endsleigh Street, London
WC1H ODD, UK
t +44 (0)20 7388 2117 f 7388 2826
e mailbox@iied.org
w www.iied.org
Independent organisation
promoting sustainable world
development. Its Resource Centre
for Participatory Learning and
Action has over 2000 documents
covering most participatory
approaches, focusing primarily on
Africa, Asia and South America.

Involve
33 Corsham Street, London, N1
6DR, UK
t +44 (0)20 7336 9444
e info@involve.org.uk
w www.involve.org.uk
Exists to put people at the heart of
decision making. Believes public
participation can help solve some of
our most pressing challenges and
lead to the genuine empowerment
of people. Core activities include:
influencing decision makers, new
thinking, better practice and
networking.

John Thompson & Partners
23–25 Great Sutton Street, London,
EC1 0DN, UK
t +44 (0)20 7017 1780 f 7017 1781
e info@jtp.co.uk
w www.jtp.co.uk
Contacts: John Thompson. Charles
Campion.
Architects, urbanists and
placemakers with much experience
of participatory community
planning methods in the UK and
internationally. Community
planning weekends and charrettes
a speciality.

Kansara Hackney Ltd
St Peters House, Windmill Street,
Macclesfield, Cheshire, SK11 7HS,
UK
t +44 (0)1625 431792
e kansarahackney@gmail.com
w www.kansarahackney.com
Experienced community
architecture and planning practice.

Kevin Murray Associates
Fergus House, 127 Fergus Drive,
Glasgow, Scotland, G20 6BY, UK
t +44 (0)141 945 3651
e info@kevinmurrayassociates.com
w www.kevinmurrayassociates.com
Consultancy operating across the
spectrum of spatial planning,
regeneration, urban design and
community consultation.

Living Streets
Universal House, 88–94 Wentworth
Street, London, E1 7SA, UK
t +44 (0)20 7377 4900
e info@livingstreets.org.uk
w www.livingstreets.org.uk
UK charity that stands up for
pedestrians. Campaigns to create
safe, attractive and enjoyable
streets where people want to walk.

The Local Futures Group
2nd floor, 43 Eagle Street, London,
WC1R 4AT, UK
t +44 (0)20 7440 7360 f 7440 7370
e info@localfutures.com
w www.localfutures.com
Specialises in regeneration based on
joined up policies and private-public
partnerships. Relationship marketing
for companies through focus
groups, workshops and use of local
knowledge databases.

Locality
33 Corsham Street, London, N1
6DR, UK
t +44 (0)845 458 8336 f 458 8337
e info@locality.org.uk
w www.locality.org.uk
The UK's leading network for
settlements, development trusts,
social action centres and
community enterprises. Useful
publications, training and
information exchange.

Massachusetts Institute of Technology
Department of Architecture and
Planning, 77 Massachusetts Ave., 7-
231, Cambridge, Mass 02130, USA
t +1 617 253 4401 f 253 9417
e sap-info@mit.edu
w www.sap.mit.edu
Contact: Professor Jan Wampler.
Academic and practical expertise in
many countries. Useful publications.

National Coalition for Dialogue and Deliberation (NCDD)
114 W. Springville Road, Boiling
Springs, PA 17007, USA
t +1 (717) 243 5144
e info@ncdd.org w www.ncdd.org
Contact: Sandy Heierbacher, Director
Brings together and supports
people, organizations, and
resources in ways that expand the
power of discussion to benefit
society. .

New Economics Foundation
3 Jonathan Street, London, SE11
5NH, UK
t +44 (0)20 7820 6300 f 7820 6301
e info@neweconomics.org
w www.neweconomics.org
Think tank promoting social,
economic and environmental
justice. Promotes community
visioning, indicators, community
finance and social audit.
Coordinates UK Participation
Network.

Nick Wates Associates
Creative Media Centre,
45 Robertson Street, Hastings
TN34 1HL, UK
t +44 (0)1424 712612 f 205401
e info@nickwates.co.uk
w www.nickwates.co.uk
Community planning consultants.
Publishers of communityplanning.net.

North Carolina State University
School of Architecture, College of
Design, Raleigh, North Carolina,
27695-7701, USA
t +1 919 515 2205
e henry_sanoff@ncsu.edu
w www4.ncsu.edu/unity/users/s/
sanoff/www/henry.html
Contact: Henry Sanoff.
Expertise in participatory design.
Great publications available.

The Partnering Initiative
3rd Floor, 20-22 Bedford Row,
Holborn, London, W1X 4EB, UK
t +44 (0) 20 3397 9060
e info@thepartneringinitiative.org
w www.thepartneringinitiative.org
Dedicated to driving widespread,
systematic and effective
collaboration between civil society,

government and companies
towards a sustainable future.
Provides organisational
development services and training
and capacity building.

Permaculture Association
BCM Permaculture Association,
London WC1N 3XX, UK
t +44 (0)845 458 1805
e office@permaculture.org.uk
w www.permaculture.org.uk
Can provide details of Permaculture
design courses and local contacts.

Planning for Real Unit
Neighbourhood Resource Centre
for Central England, Innovation
Works@Rubery Owen, Booth
Street, Darlaston, West Midlands,
WS10 8JB, UK
t +44 (0)121 568 7070
e info@planningforreal.org.uk
w www.planningforreal.org.uk
Provides support and training for
those wanting to use Planning for
Real. Part of the Accord Group.

Post-war Reconstruction and Development Unit
University of York, The King's
Manor, York YO1 2EP, UK
t +44 (0)1904 433959 f 433949
e iaas1@york.ac.uk
w www.york.ac.uk/depts/prdu
Contact: Sultan Barakat.
Community planning expertise in
post-war situations.

Practical Action
The Schumacher Centre, Bourton
on Dunsmore, Rugby,
Warwickshire, CV23 9QZ, UK
t +44 (0)1926 634501 f 634502
e practicalaction@practicalaction.org.uk
w www.practicalaction.org
Works alongside communities to
find practical solutions to poverty.
Publishes material on all aspects of
development and appropriate
technology including community
participation.

The Prince's Foundation
19–22 Charlotte Road, Shoreditch, London EC2A, UK
t +44 (0)20 7613 8500 f 7613 8599
e enquiries@princes-foundation.org
w www.princes-foundation.org
Unites and extends HRH The Prince of Wales's initiatives in architecture, building and urban regeneration. Encourages a more holistic and humane approach to the planning and design of communities.

Priority Estates Project
Dominique House, 1 Church Road, Netherton, Dudley, West Midlands, DY2 0LY, UK
t +44 (0)1793 737294
e admin@pep.org.uk
w www.pep.org.uk
Non-profit consultancy and training on locally-based housing services and resident involvement. Useful publications and information sheets.

Project for Public Spaces
419 Lafayette Street, Seventh Floor, New York, NY 10003, USA
t +1(212) 620-5660 f 620-3821
e info@pps.org
w www.pps.org
A nonprofit organization dedicated to creating and sustaining public places that build stronger communities. Its placemaking approach helps people transform their public spaces into vital places that highlight local assets, spur rejuvenation and serve common needs.

Royal Institute of British Architects
66 Portland Place, London W1B 1AD, UK
t +44 (0)20 7580 5533 f 7225 1541
e info@riba.org
w www.riba.org
Runs Architects in Schools programme. Can supply a Schedule of Services for Community Architecture. Clients Advisory Service provides lists of local community architects. Bookshop and library have useful publications.

Royal Town Planning Institute
41 Botolph Lane, London EC3R 8DL, UK
t +44 (0)20 7929 9494 f 7929 9490
e contact@rtpi.org.uk
w www.rtpi.org.uk
Promotes public participation in planning through education for sustainable development, awards schemes, publications and Planning Aid.

Society for Development Studies
India Habitat Centre, Core 6A, IInd Floor, Lodhi Road, New Delhi, 110003, India
t +91 11 24699368 f 24699368
e info@sdsindia.org
w www.sdsindia.org
Contact: Vinay D. Lall, Director. Research, training and consultancy institution. Useful regional contact point.

Studio Real
Oxford Centre for Innovation, New Road, Oxford, OX1 1BY, UK
t +44 (0)1865 261461
e urbanism@studioreal.co.uk
w www.studioreal.co.uk
Urban design practice with community planning expertise.

Sustrans
Head Office, NCN Centre, 2 Cathedral Square, College Green, Bristol, BS1 5DD, UK
t +44 (0)117 926 8893 f 929 4173
e reception@sustrans.org.uk
w www.sustrans.org.uk
Has some of the UKs foremost experts on non-motorised transport infrastructure. Works on travel behaviour change and research, monitoring and evaluation, community-led street design, transport and its relation to health, education and carbon emissions.

Taipei City Urban Regeneration Office
9th Floor, No. 8, Sec. 1, Roosevelt Road, Taipei City, 10074, Taiwan, ROC
t + 886.2.2321.5696
e uroweb@uro.taipei.gov.tw
w www.uro.taipei.gov.tw
Emphasizes the importance of innovative planning, efficiency in amending regulations and monitoring construction quality. Focuses on cooperation between government and the public, and gathers all the ideas and resources to make infinite possibilities in the city. Hopes to make Taipei a city that is attractive and vibrant while enriching quality of life in the living environment.

Tenants Participatory Advisory Service
Suite 4b Trafford Plaza, 73 Seymour Grove, Manchester, M16 0LD, UK
t +44 (0)161 868 3500 f 877 6256
e info@tpas.org.uk
w www.tpas.org.uk
Provides information, advice, training, consultancy, seminars and conferences on involving tenants in their housing management.

Town & Country Planning Association
17 Carlton House Terrace, London SW1Y 5AS, UK
t +44 (0)20 7930 8903 f 7930 3280
e tcpa@tcpa.org.uk
w www.tcpa.org.uk
Campaign group for reforming the planning system. Useful publications.

United Nations – Habitat
P.O. Box 30030, GPO, Nairobi, 00100, Kenya
t +254 20 7621234 f 7624266
e infohabitat@unhabitat.org
w www.unhabitat.org
The United Nations Human Settlements Programme, UN-HABITAT, is the United Nations agency for human settlements. It is mandated by the UN General Assembly to promote socially and environmentally sustainable towns and cities with the goal of providing adequate shelter for all. Website includes many useful resources and contact details of regional offices.

Urban Design Group
70 Cowcross Street, London
EC1M 6EJ, UK
t +44 (0)20 7250 0872 **f** 7250 0892
e admin@udg.org.uk
w www.udg.org.uk
Contact: Rob Cowan.
National voluntary organisation that
helps set urban design agenda.
Register of experienced
professionals and good practice
guidance on website.

**The Urbanists Collaborative -
Taipei**
4F, No.310, Sec. 4, Zhongxiao E. Rd,
Da-an District, Taipei City, 10694,
Taiwan, ROC
t +886.2.7711.0779
w www.urbancollab.com
Group of urbanists who practice in
urban, architectural, landscape
planning and design. Believes in the
synergy of human beings, urban
events and the man-made
environment. Focuses on social
development. Determined to
improve the environment in
creative, fun and smart ways.

URBED
10 Little Lever Street, Manchester,
M1 1HR, UK
t +44 (0)161 200 5500 **f** 7831 2466
e info@urbed.coop
w www.urbed.coop
Contacts: Nicholas Falk, David Rudlin.
Urban regeneration consultants
with long experience of community
planning. Expertise in round table
workshops. Also has London office.

Vista Consulting
16 Old Birmingham Road, Lickey
End, Broomsgrove B60 1DE, UK
t +44 (0)1527 837930 **f** 837940
e enquiries@vista.uk.com
w www.vista.uk.com
Contact: Ann Brooks.
Information and consultancy on
critical mass events such as real
time strategic change.

Wendy Sarkissian
PO Box 20117, Nimbin, NSW, 2480,
Australia
t +61 2 6689 0432
e wendy@sarkissian.com.au
w www.sarkissian.com.au
Experienced practitioner and
academic. International
presentations. Useful regional
contact.

Wikima
Tyddyn Y Pwll, Carno, Caersws,
Powys, SY17 5JU, UK
t/f +44 (0)7767 370739
e romy.shovelton@gmail.com
w www.wikima.com
Contact: Romy Shovelton.
International design and facilitation
consultancy, specialising in effective
and productive engagement of
large groups of stakeholders. Uses a
wide variety of methods, including
Open Space Technology,
Appreciative Inquiry and Future
Search.

Yale Urban Design Workshop
1203 Chapel Street, New Haven,
Connecticut, 06511, USA
t +1 203 764-5696 **f** 764-5697
e udw@yale.edu
w www.architecture.yale.edu/UDW
Contacts: Alan Plattus, Michael
Haverland.
Well-established urban design
studio at Yale University working
with surrounding communities..

Young Foundation
18 Victoria Park Square, Bethnal
Green, London, E2 9PF, UK
t +44 (0)20 8980 6263 **f** 8981 6719
e reception@youngfoundation.org
w www.youngfoundation.org
Devoted to social innovation and
finding and developing new and
better ways of meeting pressing
unmet needs. Founded in 2005,
formed from the merger of the
Institute of Community Studies and
the Mutual Aid Centre.

Websites A–Z

An annotated selection of the most useful websites for community planning.

Emphasis on sites providing:

• community planning information complementing this handbook;

• gateways to closely related subject areas, regionally and internationally.

Bigger selection at:
www.communityplanning.net/websites/websites.php

See also Contacts A–Z p266

See also Contacts A–Z p266

New material
If you know of websites which should be listed here, please complete the online submission form or send details to the address on page 290. Contacts from countries or regions not already covered particularly welcome.

If you find any websites listed unhelpful, please let us know.

Aarhus Convention
www.unece.org/env/pp/introduction.html
Official site of the Convention for Access to Information, Public Participation in decision making and Access to Justice in Environmental Matters. Hosted by United Nations Economic Commission for Europe which acts as Secretariat.

Active Democracy
www.activedemocracy.net
Provides access to information which individuals, groups or organisations can use to enhance citizens' involvement in the activities of local, state or federal government. Run by Lyn Carson, lecturer in applied politics at the University of Sydney, Australia.

Architecture Centres Network
www.architecturecentre.net
Website of UK architecture centres network.

Big Lunch
www.thebiglunch.com
Website for an initiative to stimulate annual get-togethers for neighbours.

Brainstorming made simple
www.bubbl.us
An internet version of brainstorming with Post-it notes.

Carbon Independent
www.carbonindependent.org
Information on carbon dioxide emissions. Includes a personal carbon calculator.

Carbon Leapfrog
www.carbonleapfrog.org
Supports communities and social entrepeneurs actively engaged in climate change mitigation. Range of useful case studies. Business-led charity.

Change.org
www.change.org
Social change platform. Website which enables anyone anywhere to start a petition.

Cohousing Network UK
www.cohousing.org.uk
Promotes the awareness and development of cohousing and provides support to forming and established cohousing communities. Useful website.

Common Ground
www.commonground.org.uk
Environmental arts charity linking people and place. Expertise on parish mapping and community orchards and campaigning for local distinctiveness. Lovely publications: books, posters, cards.

Community 21
www.community21.org
Social networking and neighbourhood planning tool for sustainable low carbon communities. Includes community led planning toolkit. Created by Action in Rural Sussex and the University of Brighton.

Community Almanac
www.communityalmanac.org
Where people can share stories about the heart & soul of the places in which they live. US based. Created by the Orton Family Foundation and the Open Planning Project.

Community Design Exchange
www.communitydesignexchange.org
Information exchange for community design. Explore what other projects do and learn from their experience. Share stories. Discuss. Site managed by the Open University and Glass-House Community Led Design, London.

Community Land Trusts Network
www.communitylandtrusts.org.uk
Resource to assist people 'develop community land trust solutions for affordable housing, amenity and workspace'. Useful sample documents and publication downloads. Aimed at UK audience.

Community Led Planning
www.acre.org.uk/our-work/community-led-planning
Resource for community led planning based on experience from rural communities in the UK. Includes an online toolkit.

Community Matters
www.communitymatters.org
Online network of leaders, thinkers and doers established by the Orton Family Foundation. (See Contacts A–Z for UK organisation with same name.)

Community Planning Toolkit
www.communityplanningtoolkit.org
Website resource aimed at the community and voluntary sectors in Northern Ireland. Produced prior to legislation being introduced in 2015 by Community Places with support from the Big Lottery Fund.

Community Rights
www.communityrights.communities.gov.uk
UK Government website with information about the Community Rights which enable local communities to take more control over their areas. The Rights to Bid, to Build, to Challenge and to create a Neighbourhood Plan.

Community Tools Software
www.communitytools.info
Free web-based software for managing location-based community activities and communication. Map based.

Crowd Wise
www.crowd-wise.org
Dedicated website for a method for taking shared decisions developed by the New Economics Foundation.

Cyburbia
www.cyburbia.org
Portal and networking site for planners, planning students and others interested in shaping the built environment of their communities. Includes busy message board, image gallery, planning and urbanism-related blog feed aggregator, wiki and feature articles. US based, with international user base.

Design quality indicator (DQI)
www.dqi.org.uk
All about design quality indicators, a process for evaluating design quality of buildings which can be used by everyone involved in the development process.

Digital Democracy
www.digitaldemocracy.org.uk
Website that helps you to start and gain support for campaigns and also to identify the priorities of your local community. Based on UK postcodes.

ELTIS – the urban mobility portal
www.eltis.org
European Local Transport Information Service. Facilitates exchange of information on urban mobility in Europe. Supports the creation of urban transport systems which use less energy and produce less emissions. Tools, case studies, news and more.

Energy Cities
www.energy-cities.eu
European association of local authorities inventing their energy future. Website has proposals for the energy transition of cities and towns.

Energy Saving Trust
www.energysavingtrust.org.uk
A key website for anyone interested in saving money and reducing energy consumption. Comprehensive and clear information on insulation and heating, renewable energy, recommended products and funding from grants and supplier offers.

Energyshare
www.energyshare.com
Brings people together in person and online to source, use and even generate renewable energy. UK oriented.

Engaging Places
www.engagingplaces.org.uk
Online guide to using buildings and places for learning. Aimed at schools and trainers. Includes lesson plans and teaching resources.

European Community Development Network
www.eucdn.org
Website of a non-governmental European umbrella organisation which brings together partners from a dozen countries both inside and outside of the European Union.

Fix My Street
www.fixmystreet.com
Site which sends on your reports of local maintenance problems (eg broken streetlight) to the relevant authorities and monitors whether they get fixed.

Forum for Neighbourhood Planning
www.ourneighbourhoodplanning.org.uk
Supports people and communities using new powers under the Localism Act 2011 to create neighbourhood plans. Contains forums on a range of topics and links to resources. Managed by Planning Aid England, Royal Town Planning Institute.

Green Map System
www.greenmap.org
A global eco-cultural movement, creating local maps that chart the natural and cultural environment. Aims to cultivate citizen participation and community sustainability in hundreds of places around the world.

GreenSpace
www.green-space.org.uk
The importance of green space. Includes a GreenStat visitor survey system, which records users views of their local parks and green spaces and makes the information available to those who manage them (UK only).

I Wish This Was
www.iwishthiswas.com
Neat method for getting people to think about building uses by placing stickers on them.

IdeaScale
www.ideascale.com
Online crowdsourcing and ranking of ideas.

International Association of Facilitators (IAF)
www.iaf-world.org
Dedicated to growing facilitators and encouraging the use of group process methodologies world-wide.

Ketso
www.ketso.com
Online backup for the Ketso kit for creative engagement (p90). Includes workshop plans that can be adapted for different contexts; examples; case studies; analysis templates; training videos.

Kickstarter
www.kickstarter.com
A funding platform for creative projects.

Landshare
www.landshare.net
Connects those who have land to share with those who need land for cultivating food.

Local Development Network
www.ldnet.eu
Informal European network to bring together knowledge and people on Local Development (LD). Website provides a forum for sharing information and knowledge.

Low Carbon Communities Network
www.lowcarboncommunities.org
Encourages the adoption of low carbon and zero carbon technologies and lifestyles at a community level, and helps groups engaged in this to be as effective and efficient as possible.

Mapping for Change
www.mappingforchange.org.uk
Social enterprise that supports the development of sustainable communities by providing participatory mapping services to communities, voluntary sector organisations, local authorities and developers.

Meanwhile Project
www.meanwhile.org.uk
Project promoting and supporting temporary uses of empty property and land. Website has case studies and further info.

mPolls
www.mpolls.org
Mobile phone voting platform.

My Community Space
www.mycommunityspace.org.uk
Specialist premises website for the community and voluntary sector which provides a facility for those either seeking or wanting to advertise a space. FAQ service on community premises and useful links directory.

National Charrette Institute (NCI) (USA)
www.charretteinstitute.org
Contains explanations, toolkits and other resources for planning and running a charrette.

National Coalition for Dialogue & Deliberation (NCDD)
www.ncdd.org
Website for a loose-knit community of practitioners, researchers, activists, artists, students and others who are committed to giving people a voice and making sure that voice counts. US based.

Neighborland
www.neighborland.com
Website aiming to bring more people into the development process by promoting a simple engagement method where people publicly declare – on name badges window stickers and on the website - what they want for their neighbourhood. Based in New Orleans, USA, and spreading.

Neighborhood Planning
www.neighborhoodplanning.org
Great website which provides a universal historical and intellectual context to neighbourhood planning.

Open Space World
www.openspaceworld.org
Portal for Open Space Technology (see Methods A–Z) with links to valuable information, videos, blogs, news, stories, training, online forums and other resources, including a worldwide network of Open Space users.

Participate in Design
www.participateindesign.org
Student led initiative to explore and promote community involvement in design in Singapore.

ParticipateDB
www.participatedb.com
A collaborative catalogue for online tools for participation (often referred to as tools for web-based engagement, online participation, e-participation, e-consultation, online dialogue, online deliberation).

Participation Compass
www.participationcompass.org
Provides practical information for those working to involve people. Includes methods, case studies, news, library, events listing, advice service and a process planner. UK based and oriented. Run by Involve. Based on the website People and Participation.

Participation Works
www.participationworks.org.uk
Online gateway to the world of children and young people's participation. Policy, practice, networks and information from across the UK. Run by the Children and Young People's Participation Partnership (CHYPP).

Participatory Avenues
www.iapad.org
Focal point for sharing lessons and innovation in community mapping and participatory Geographical Information Systems (GIS) as a means to add value and authority to people's spatial knowledge and improve bottom up communication.

Participatory Budgeting UK
www.participatorybudgeting.org.uk
Shares information on participatory budgeting experience within the UK and around the world.

Participatory Design
www.pdcproceedings.org
Portal providing free access to all papers published in Participatory Design Conferences since the first one was held in 1990. Includes link to forthcoming conferences.

Place Matters
www.placematters.org
A living laboratory where a US network of creative practitioners come together to learn, share, inspire and seed innovation in place, collectively elevating the art and science of planning for vibrant and sustainable communities. An initiative of the Orton Foundation.

Placebook
www.placebook.org.uk
Showing how spaces make places. A hub for connecting the placemaking industry. It lets you show people interested in placemaking spaces you have created... it lets you publish anything else you have seen and like.

Placecheck
www.placecheck.info
Online user guide for the Placecheck method for assessing the qualities of a place, showing what improvements are needed, and focusing people on working together to achieve them.

Planetizen
www.planetizen.com
Public-interest information exchange for the urban planning, design, and development community. US oriented.

PlanLoCal
www.planlocal.org.uk
Suite of resources including the website, films and a resource pack to support communities and groups planning for low carbon living. Website includes useful sections on community engagement, the planning system and low carbon communities.

Planners Network
www.plannersnetwork.org
Association of progressive planners. Useful publications, papers, contacts. USA and Canada based.

Planning Tool Exchange
www.planningtoolexchange.org
Online hub for tools, resources and organisations in community planning. USA oriented. Published by the Orton Family Foundation.

Poll Everywhere
www.polleverywhere.com
Mobile phone and web voting platform.

Public Debate, France
www.debatpublic.fr
Website of the Commission for Public Debate (CNDP) in France. Full
details of the initiative. French only.

Public Decisions
www.publicdecisions.com
Interactive online training courses on public involvement and
community engagement.

Public Participation Geographical Information Systems Research
www.ppgis.manchester.ac.uk
Site developing and testing new ideas of participation focused on
Geographical Information Systems (GIS) to enhance public
involvement and participation in environmental planning and
decision making processes. Based at the Department of Planning
and Landscape, University of Manchester, UK.

RUDI - Resource for Urban Design Information
www.rudi.net
Independent web resource on urban design and placemaking.
Contains up-to-date material needed for research, proposal
preparation, commissioning projects, fact-checking and general
reference.

Scottish Sustainable Communities Initiative
www.scotland.gov.uk/Topics/Built-
Environment/AandP/Projects/SSCI/Mainstreaming
Information on the Scottish Government Charrette Mainstreaming
Programme. Includes downloadable event reports and links to
further sources of information.

Shared-ownership.org.uk
www.shared-ownership.org.uk
Resource for people wanting to know about shared ownership
housing schemes whereby you part own and part rent your home.

Shelter Housing Insights for Communities
www.shelter.org.uk/housinginsights
A resource for facilitating targeted engagement with local
communities on housing development in the UK. Based on real data.

Sponsume
www.sponsume.com
Crowdfunding platform for creative projects in Europe.

Strategic Environmental Assessment Information Service
www.sea-info.net
Gateway to the latest information on Strategic Environmental
Assessment (SEA) and Sustainability Appraisal (SA)

Sustainable Communities Online
www.sustainable.org
Website developed by a broad coalition of organisations in the US to pool information on sustainability and make it more accessible to the public.

Sustainable Community Action Wiki
sca21.wikia.com
Collaboratively constructed site which seeks to link up community action for sustainability worldwide.

Sustainable Energy Academy
www.superhomes.org.uk
Promotes education and action to reduce the carbon footprint of buildings and communities.

Talk About Local
www.talkaboutlocal.org.uk
Aims to give people in their communities a powerful online voice so that people can communicate and campaign more effectively to influence events in the places in which they live, work or play.

Toolkit Citizen Participation
www.toolkitparticipation.nl
A database of case studies of participation in local decision making. International. Managed by the Toolkit Participation Partnership, a group of civil society (NGO) and local government organisations from all over the world, working together to promote participatory local governance. French, Spanish.

Transition towns wiki
www.transitiontowns.org
Network set up to support TransitionTowns Initiatives around the world.

Turning Point
www.turningtechnologies.com
Keypad polling provider.

Upgrading Urban Communities
web.mit.edu/urbanupgrading
Resource for communities including tools and resources

Woodland Trust
www.woodlandtrust.org.uk
Woodland conservation charity. Website includes a neighbouhood planning hub focusing on the need to include trees in local planning.

The Workhome
www.theworkhome.com
Resources for designers and legislators promoting the construction of places that can be used for both living and working. Home-based work is a popular, family friendly, environmentally sustainable practice which is good for the enconomy and for cities.

World Cafe
www.theworldcafe.com
Online resource on this method of engaging people.

World Habitat Awards
www.worldhabitatawards.org
Site for international award scheme for practical, innovative and
sustainable solutions to current housing needs and problems.
Includes useful case study database of past winners and finalists.

Credits and thanks

This handbook was initially the product of three related initiatives:

Tools for Community Design Programme
Supported by The Prince's Foundation (and formerly The Prince of Wales's Institute of Architecture), this initiative promotes good practice through the production of high quality, universally applicable, how-to-do-it information using participatory editing techniques.

Urban Design Group Public Participation Programme (UDGPPP)
Funded by the Department of the Environment, Transport and the Regions (DETR) for England, this action research programme assisted and evaluated 12 public participation events and 10 seminars in England during 1996 and 1997 to establish good practice principles.

Action Planning in Developing Countries Research Project
Funded by the UK's Department for International Development (DFID), this project examined practice in countries in many parts of the world during 1998 and 1999 to establish methods most appropriate for developing countries.

The book has benefited from close collaboration with other related initiatives. These include:

Community-based Disaster Mitigation
A research project funded by the European Community and based at London's South Bank University.

Tools for Community Regeneration
A project to develop a database of community regeneration based at Hastings Trust, UK.

Supporting Communities and Neighbourhoods in Planning
UK government programme for launching neighbourhood planning in 2011/12.

An advisory group of individuals from the above initiatives – listed on the imprint page – has been particularly helpful in guiding the book's evolution.

Many **people** have helped with the work. Special thanks are due to all those who sent in material, participated in editing workshops, provided inspiration or commented on drafts. They include:

Jon Aldenton
Alice Aldous
Edna Alexis
Anthea Atha
John Barstow
Debbie Bartlett
Stephen Batey
Roger Bellers
Dianah Bennett
John Billingham
Jennifer Birtill
Jeff Bishop
Peter Blake
Jeremy Brook
Charles Campion
Jeremy Caulton
June Cannon
Emma Collier
Tony Costello
Robert Cowan
Simon Croxton
Robin Deane
Nicki Dennis
James Derounian
Stephanie Donaldson
Roger Evans
Sarah Fish
Jane Freund
Yanaka Gakko
Flora Gathorne-Hardy
Joanna Gent
Mike Gibson
Christine Goldschmidt
Suzanne Gorman
Andrew Goldring
Peter Greenhalf
Virginia Griffin
Felicity Gu
Susan Guy
Rod Hackney
Nick Hall
Nabeel Hamdi
Brian Hanson
Lorraine Hart

Yasuyoshi Hayashi
Michael Hebbert
Mandy Heslop
Michelle Hou
David Hughes
Paul Jenkins
Richard John
Sam Jones-Hill
Ripin Kalra
Joan Kean
Sonia Khan
Sally King
Charles Knevitt
Anne Kramer
Alison Lammas
Birgit Laue
Akan Leander
David Lewis
Julie Lewis
Arnold Linden
Melanie Lombard
Melanie Louise
David Lunts
Caroline Lwin
Frances MacDermott
Lee Mallett
Milena Marega
Tony Meadows
Jo McCaren
Nim Moorthy
Babar Mumtaz
Michael Mutter
Mary Myers
Arthur Orsini
Jenneth Parker
Michael Parkes
Charles Parrack
Geoffrey Payne
Ollie Pendered
Alan Plattus
Jules Pretty
Cathryn Pritchard
Richard Pullen
Debbie Radcliffe

Renate Ruether-Greaves Catherine Tranmer
Peter Richards Susie Turnbull
William Roden John F C Turner
Alex Rook John Twigg
Jon Rowland Phillip Vincent
Rebecca Sanborn Stone Pat Wakely
David Sanderson Perry Walker
Henry Sanoff Diane Warburton
Yoshimitsu Shiozaki Colin Ward
Romy Shovelton Margaret Wilkinson
Jack Sidener Mae Wates
Jonathan Sinclair Wilson Max Wates
Harry Smith Dick Watson
Steve Smith Richard Watson
Miriam Solly Nicholas Wilkinson
Ian Taylor Adele Wilter
Ros Tennyson Julie Witham
Simon Thomas John Worthington
John Thompson Song-Nien Xiao
Stephen Thwaites Charles Zucker
Joanne Tippett

Organisations which assisted include:

Architecture Foundation
Ball State University
Building Design
Centre for Community Visions
Centre for Disaster Preparedness
Civitas Elan
Countryside Commission
CLAWS 2
Chinese University of Hong Kong
Consense
Department for Communities & Local Government
Edinburgh World Heritage Trust
Free Form Arts Trust
Hackney Building Exploratory
Hertfordshire County Council
Neighbourhood Initiatives Foundation
Orton Family Foundation
Planning Aid UK
RUDI
Roger Evans Associates
Scottish Participatory Initiatives
Shoevegas
Taipei City Council Urban Regeneration Office

Apologies for any omissions.

Book evolution

The production of this book has been guided by the belief that participatory editing and testing of good practice guidance is one of the most effective ways of achieving widespread improvement of practice and knowledge transfer.

The process adopted has been as follows:

1 **Title and format**
   Overall concept established by the author, designer and supporting organisations.
2 **Publicity**
   Call for information leaflet distributed widely.
3 **Pilot projects, seminars and research**
   Monitoring and evaluation of pilot projects, participation in seminars and workshops, desk research.
4 **Sample material published**
   Ten methods and four scenarios published in *Urban Design Quarterly*, July 1998. Over 1,000 copies distributed. Also available on Urban Design Group website.
5 **Editing workshops**
   Held at the South Bank University in London, November 1998, and in the Philippines, January 1999.
6 **Consultation draft**
   Circulated to over 60 practitioners. Over 35 responses received.
7 **Final draft**
   Circulated to main supporting organisations and advisors.
8 **Publication of first edition**
   Translations in Chinese and Korean.
9 **Website created**
   Based on book structure and content.
10 **Website development**
   Addition of new content to website.
11 **Publication of second edition**
   Input by over 20 practitioners and academics.

Feedback at each stage has been invaluable, although the editor takes full responsibility for all views expressed.

It is planned to continue the process with further editions, translations and adaptations.

Photocredits

Location, date, and photographer or source of photos and illustrations. Many thanks to all those who have allowed their material to be used.

Photos not credited otherwise are by Nick Wates.

Cover: Lanice Park, Zvolen, Slovakia, 09; Charlotte, Vermont, USA, 03; St Leonards on Sea, UK, 03; Taipei, Taiwan, 13; Ringmer, UK, 13.

ii	Duke Street, Liverpool, UK, 97.
15	Wakefield, UK, 97.
16	Woodberry Down, London, UK, 97.
17	Philippines, 99, Nick Hall. Liverpool, UK, 97.
18	Punjab, Pakistan, 92, Jules Pretty. Hastings, UK, 97.
19	Honduras, 94, Jules Pretty. Runcorn, UK, 79, CDS Liverpool.
21	Aylesham, Kent, UK, 04. Big Local North East Hastings, UK, 13.
23	Pruitt Igoe, USA, unknown; Drummond Street, London, UK, 74.
24	Sri Lanka, 92, Jules Pretty. Wenceslas Square, Prague, Czech Republic, 96, John Thompson & Partners.
25	Trans Nzoia, Kenya, 93, John Thompson. Hastings, UK, 90.
26	Hong Kong, 98, Jack Sidener.
28	Hastings, UK, 90.
30–1	Hackney Building Exploratory, London, UK, 99.
32	Town Quay, Barking, UK, 98, Free Form Arts Trust.
33	Caldmore Green, Walsall, UK, 98, Free Form Arts Trust.
35	*Leeds Evening Post*, 9.8.94 *The Times*, 23.8.94 &

	29.12.94. *West Cumbrian News & Star*, 15.11.94.
36	Blairs College, Aberdeen, UK, 94, John Thompson & Partners. Holy Trinity Brompton, London, UK, 97 (2). Wornington Green, London, UK, 89, John Thompson & Partners.
37	Sidon, Lebanon, 97, John Thompson & Partners. Liverpool, UK, 97.
39	West Cork, Ireland, 87 (6).
41	Setagaya Community Design Centre, Tokyo, Japan, 95.
43	Prague, Czech Republic, 96, John Thompson & Partners.
45	Richmond Virginia, USA, 96.
46	Fiji, 95, Jules Pretty.
48	Duke Street, Liverpool, 97.
51	Hong Kong, 98, Jack Sidener.
52–3	London, UK, Alexandra Rook, CLAWS (2). Tokyo, 98, Henry Sanoff.
54–5	Brixton, London, UK, 93. Duke Street, Liverpool, UK, 97 (2).
58	Kiambu, Kenya, 93, Jules Pretty. Anon.
59	Sri Lanka, 92, John Thompson. Kiambu, Tamil Nadu, India, 91, Irene Guijt. Burkina Faso, Africa, 92, Jules Pretty.
60	Bray, Berkshire, UK.
64	Hastings, 13, Graphic Ideas.
65	Shoreditch, London, 98, ShoeVegas.
66	Birmingham, UK, 94.
67	Kingswood, UK, 96, Roger Evans Associates.
69	Event branding, Communities Matter,13, Ollie Pendered; Playden, East Sussex, UK, 13
71	USA, Orton Family Foundation, 12
73	New Town, Edinburgh, 96, Edinburgh World Heritage Trust.
75	Hastings, UK, 90.
76	Yellamanchilli, Adrapradesh,

	India, 96, Nick Hall. Yellamanchilli, 96, Roger Bellers. Igbalangao, Panay Island, Philippines, 95, Nick Hall. Yellamanchilli, 96, Nick Hall.
78–9	Reproduced from *Future Search*.
80	Tower Hamlets, London, UK, 99, Architecture Foundation.
81	Ball State University, Indiana, USA, 95, Tony Costelllo.
83	Shipley, UK, 12.
85	George Street, Hastings, UK, 89.
86–7	East Street, Farnham, UK, 97 (4). Bath, UK, 97.
90	Gavin Duthie, courtesy Beacon North East; University of Sussex, UK, 11; University of Durham, Ketso Ltd.
93	Kent, UK, 97, Debbie Bartlett.
94	Igbalangao, Panay Island, Philippines, 95, Nick Hall.
95	Easton, Bristol, UK, 93, Vizability Arts. West Bengal, India, 90, Robert Chambers.
96	Bangaladesh, 94, Nabeel Hamdi.
98	London, 70s, Town & Country Planning Association.
99	Ball State University, Indiana, USA, 85, S.Talley.
100	The Prince of Wales's Institute of Architecture, London, UK, 97.
101	Oxpens Initiative, Oxford, UK, 97, Roger Evans Associates. Birmingham, UK, 94. Stockport, UK, 88, Community Technical Aid Centre Manchester. Forge Project, Cinderford, UK, 93.
102	Hackney, London, UK, 82, Hunt Thompson Associates. MUDStudio, Ball State University, Indiana, USA, 94, Anthony Costello (2).

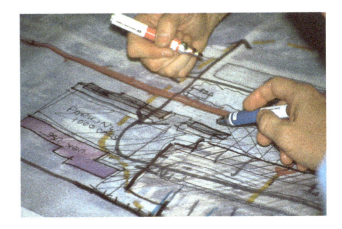

Dear Editor,

Your handbook is great. But in the next edition, please include:

1. A page on the .... method (info enclosed).

2. Scenario for .... based on our project here (details enclosed).

3. A really good book called .... (also enclosed)

Let me know when it comes out.

yours ever

PS. Check out www..................... if you haven't already. Some useful info there.

Editing workshop
Blown up photocopies of book pages pinned on the wall allow people to write in comments and amendments. Blank sheets stimulate people to think about additional material that could be included in the next edition.

Exhibition material
Display pages of *The Community Planning Handbook* are available from Nick Wates Associates, in colour or black and white, and at various sizes.

Editing workshop format

For helping make improvements to this handbook. Also useful for stimulating debate on community planning generally. Can be run as independent sessions or as part of a conference or other programme. Participants should ideally have had time to look through the book beforehand but this is not essential.

1 Setting up
Display some or all of the pages on a wall, preferably blown up to A3 size on a photocopier. Arrange in sections – 'Principles', 'Methods', 'Scenarios' etc – with large headings above. Insert blank pages in each section with headings 'Other principles', 'Other methods', etc. Have a supply of coloured felt-tips. (2 hours)

2 Introduction
Welcome participants. Explain purpose of event and structure of book display. (10 mins)

3 Participatory editing
Participants examine the display individually or in small groups and write comments directly on the pages or blank sheets. Informal discussion encouraged. (20–60 mins depending on whether people have looked through the book beforehand)

4 General discussion
On implications for local activity, initiatives needed etc. (20–40 mins)

5 Send in results
Mail or fax originals or copies of sheets plus any notes of the discussion to: Handbook Editor, c/o Nick Wates Associates, Creative Media Centre, 45 Robertson Street, Hastings TN34 1HL, UK
Fax: +44 (0)1424 205401
Email: info@nickwates.co.uk

Running time: 60–100mins
Ideal numbers: 5–20

Please complete and return the form below if you want to be notified of future editions or can offer any help or advice. Feel free to use additional sheets, enclose material or communicate in a different way altogether.

Name _____

Organisation (if any) _____

Contact details (address, tel, fax, email, web)
_____
_____

Comments on this edition (good and bad)
_____
_____
_____

Suggestions for a revised edition (suggestions adopted will be acknowledged)
_____
_____
_____

I/we can supply information/photos/drawings covering the following methods/case studies/publications/films etc. (all material used will be acknowledged)
_____
_____
_____
_____

Please let me/us know when the revised
English language edition is available ☐ yes ☐ no

I/we would be interested to have translations or adaptations in the following languages
_____

I/we could help with work on translations or adaptations ☐ yes ☐ no

I am happy for you to pass my details on
to other community planning networks ☐ yes ☐ no

Date _____

Return to: Handbook Editor,
c/o Nick Wates Associates, Creative Media Centre, 45 Robertson Street, Hastings TN34 1HL, UK
Fax: +44 (0)1424 205401 Email: info@nickwates.co.uk

Index

Page numbers in **bold** indicate main entries and in *italic* indicate terms in the glossary.

Note that only some of the Glossary items are indexed and that the Publications, Contacts and Websites sections are not indexed. You may find what you are looking for in these sections.

Nick Wates is a writer, and project consultant specialising in community planning and design.

Other books include *The Battle for Tolmers Square* (Routledge, 1976); *Squatting, the real story* (Bay Leaf Books, 1980); *Community Architecture*; (with Charles Knevitt, Penguin, 1987) and *The Community Planning Event Manual* (Earthscan, 2008).

He has written extensively for the architectural press, directed local regeneration projects and taken part in planning sagas in the areas where he has lived.

In 2011 he was invited to become a Fellow of the Royal Society of Arts based on his 'experience and expertise in urban planning and design' and his 'work to provide an accessible resource of best practice information in CommunityPlanning.net'.

He lives and works on the south coast of England in Hastings.

www.nickwates.co.uk

Jeremy Brook is a graphic designer specialising in the design of exhibition catalogues for art galleries.

He studied at the Royal College of Art and has taught part-time at the London College of Printing, Ravensbourne College of Design and Eastbourne and Hastings Colleges of Arts and Technology.

His previous and current clients include: Chris Beetles Gallery, London; De La Warr Pavilion, Bexhill; Hastings Museum and Art Gallery; Arts Council England; Surrey Institute of Art and Design; Towner Art Gallery, Eastbourne and Rye Art Gallery.

His previous books include *Erich Mendelsohn 1887–1953* (A3 Times, 1987) and *Hans Scharoun: the alternative tradition* (A3 Times, 1995).

He lives and works in Hastings.

www.graphicideas.co.uk